**Blood Rites**

Jimmy Lee Shreeve is a journalist who has written for the *Guardian*, the *Independent*, *The Financial Times*, *Midweek* and *The X Factor*, amongst others. He also hosts his own radio show – True Crime Hour – which has a dedicated following.

## Picture Credits

**Section One**

**Section Two**

# Jimmy Lee Shreeve

# Blood Rites

arrow books

First published in the United Kingdom by Arrow Books in 2006

1 3 5 7 9 10 8 6 4 2

First published in the United Kingdom in 2006 by Arrow

Arrow Books
The Random House Group Limited
20 Vauxhall Bridge Road, London, SW1V 2SA

Random House Australia (Pty) Limited
20 Alfred Street, Milsons Point, Sydney,
New South Wales 2061, Australia

Random House New Zealand Limited
18 Poland Road, Glenfield
Auckland 10, New Zealand

Random House (Pty) Limited
Isle of Houghton, Corner of Boundary Road & Carse O'Gowrie,
Houghton, 2198, South Africa

The Random House Group Limited Reg. No. 954009

www.randomhouse.co.uk

A CIP catalogue record for this book is available from the British Library

Papers used by Random House are natural, recyclable products made from
wood grown in sustainable forests. The manufacturing processes conform to
the environmental regulations of the country of origin

ISBN 9780099499541 (from Jan 2007)
ISBN 0 09 949954 1

Typeset by Palimpsest Book Production Limited, Stirlingshire
Printed and bound in Great Britain by Bookmarque Ltd, Croydon, Surrey

## Dedication

To my wife Nicky:
'Like a wildfire and the scent of the night . . .'


In memory of the writer William S. Burroughs
(1914–1997):
'Nothing is true, everything is permitted.'

# Contents

Heart full of Soul?
Why Sacrifice?

## Chapter 3: Professional Human Sacrificers

Mountain Slayer
Killing by the Book
Breaking the Rules
Wizard of the Four Winds
Thought Power
Is it Really Murder?
Devil Doctor of Lagos
A Hard-on for Hell
Was it Idi Amin?

## Chapter 4: Satan Loves You . . .

A Match Made in Hell
Belief in the Unseen
Dark Pact
Dead Love
Death at the Devil's Altar
Slain but not Forgotten
Turned on by Rotting Flesh
Rock 'n' Roll Can Never Die
Radio Satan
His Satanic Majesty's Request
Order out of Chaos

## Chapter 5: Death Dealers

Dead Babies
Hexing in High Places
Driving the Tractor on the Death Farm

Tantra: the Yoga of Killing?
Money for Nothing?
Sacrifice: The Art of Giving Something up
A Necromancer in the Family . . .

Boneyard Blues
Commercial Magick
Loose Talk
Cops Turn Sorcerers' Apprentices
Ain't Never Gonna Stop . . .
Death of a Palo Priest
'Dem Bones, Dem Bones Gonna Walk Aroun"
Shake, Rattle and Roll
Ancestor Power
Gimme Some Head . . .

A Strange Experience at the Metropole . . .
Bicameral Man
The Bicameral Mind and Ritual Slaying
Autonomy

# Introduction: First Rites

'He knows death to the bone – Man has created death.'

W. B. Yeats 1865–1939: *Death* (1933).

*London, England, 2001*: Headless and dismembered body of a 5–7-year-old African boy found in the Thames. Police believe the unidentified boy, who they nicknamed 'Adam', was sacrificed as part of a 'Juju' ritual.

*New York, USA, 2000*: Newborn baby girl, with umbilical clamp still attached, found floating in a jar of formaldehyde. Cops say she may have been sacrificed as part of a ritual by a 74-year-old Palo Mayombe sect 'witch'.

*Bochum, Germany, 2002*: Murderous young gothic woman, known as the 'Bride of Satan', tells German court how Satan ordered her and her husband to hack a friend to death and drink his blood – in a grisly human sacrifice.

*Lima, Peru, 2004*: Decapitated baby boy found on a hilltop surrounded by containers of blood. Investigators believe the killing was a ritual sacrifice to appease a pre-Columbian earth deity.

These and other equally macabre news stories had been jumping out at me since 2000. I'd been picking them up from the wires since doing an article on human sacrifice for a magazine I used to write for. It had become a kind of habit to collect stories of ritualistic killing, which, in my view, couldn't be described as murder – not strictly speaking, anyway. The motive didn't fit the usual models of jealousy, robbery or out-and-out craziness. Instead, it was about magick and sorcery. These killers weren't psychos. They were simply attempting to make their spells and magickal ceremonies more powerful – and this involved the offering of blood.

I'm not saying I didn't find these killings blood-curdling and abhorrent. I did. But it was more than that: I just couldn't believe what I was seeing. Like most people I thought human sacrifice went out with the Aztecs. Yet here it was going on today and uncomfortably close to home – in Britain, Europe and the US, as well as in more far-flung areas of the world.

Because I'm a freelance journalist, I knew that one day I would have to face these terrible cases head-on – dig deeper and uncover the reasoning behind them. While I found the crime aspect of the murders interesting, what really intrigued me were the beliefs that drove people to these extremes. I've had a certain amount of involvement with magick myself (which, I should state at the outset, is in no way as dark as it is sometimes painted) and the experience has left me with a curious combination of arch scepticism and belief in the magickal universe. My magickal heyday came during the 1980s when I used to hang out with a Voodoo doctor called Earl Marlowe (now passed into the great beyond). I used to play in a band with him in London. We played blues, reggae and calypso songs. We never made the big time. But we had a wild time playing around Britain's clubs and wine bars – even busking on pleasure boats from time to time.

Besides singing, Earl used to do spells and fortune telling for people – he had a hundred or so clients. He brought me in on this and used to call me his 'apprentice'. It was a fascinating experience and gave me a good grounding in practical magick, which has been described as 'the art of manipulating reality to your own ends'.

I was already familiar with magick and mysticism, having first got interested at the age of 16, while working in an antiquarian bookshop in Northampton. Someone sold the shop a full set of the works of the mystic Aleister Crowley (who at one time was unfairly dubbed the 'wickedest man in the world'). I duly nabbed the books at a good discount and began to experiment with his techniques of mind expansion.

Because of my personal experience of magick and Voodoo I felt I had the right credentials to look into the all-too-common cases of human sacrifice that have occurred over recent years. I wanted to get a grip on the motivations of *why* people were doing it. To me, the whole deal seemed crazy and nonsensical. For example, in one case, in Malaysia, a spirit medium brutally sacrificed an American woman to a fearsome Hindu goddess to gain winning lottery numbers. He duly bought a lottery ticket and lost. How could the woman's death have been more in vain? And then, after the 'Adam' torso-in-the-Thames story broke, a Voodoo priest in London admitted that gangsters, murderers and rapists had asked him to perform ritual murder on their behalf, in a bid to protect them from the law. Wouldn't it have been easier to have just stopped committing crimes?

When you look into human sacrifice you soon discover it's *not* about logic. It's about superstition and belief. When someone is sacrificed they are usually offered up to deities or spirits as gifts – the idea being that the ritual sacrificer, or the person who has hired his or her services, gets a gift in return, be it riches or power, or some other material want. It's practical magick with a homicidal twist. But those who do it don't necessarily think they are doing wrong; as far as they are concerned it is justified and it certainly ain't murder.

I began my investigations with the Adam case, which hit the headlines in September 2001. A little black kid had been hauled out of the Thames. He'd had his head and limbs cut off. Scotland Yard at first thought he was the victim of a sex killer and had been dismembered so the body couldn't be identified. But then a number of experts brought the cops to the shocking conclusion that the boy might have been sacrificed in a ceremony – possibly to protect criminals from the law – that had roots in the dark side of traditional African religion. It turned out Adam had been poisoned 48 hours before his death with the Calabar bean, a highly toxic vine from West Africa. This, said experts, would have left him paralysed but conscious while his throat was cut. At a memorial service for the boy, Commander Andy Baker, who headed the case, said: 'Just imagine your worst nightmare and that would be nowhere near.'

Shocking though the case was – and although I commend Scotland Yard's tenacity and dedication in trying to bring the killers to book – I had reservations about some of the conclusions they came to. A number of the experts they consulted, who insisted the boy's murder had been a witchcraft sacrifice, had been fundamentalist Christians, who seemed to see dark rites and 'Satan' in everything. They had an agenda, which arguably could have been to discredit traditional (non-Christian) African religion. If so, the Adam case provided a prime opportunity. The press, however, never once covered this aspect of the Adam case. I've made a point of covering it in full because I believe it should be brought to public attention.

You'll also read how I very nearly got arrested when I went to Scotland Yard to meet the leading detectives on the Adam case – and how a friend of mine, Canadian shaman Dr Crazywolf, did a ceremony on Hampstead Heath to set 'Adam's soul free'. After going into a shamanic trance and consulting with his guardian spirits, Crazywolf came to the conclusion that Adam had been sacrificed by evil witchdoctors in a ritual to make the boy's soul their slave in the spirit world.

After the Adam case, I look at a particularly macabre occupation – that of 'professional human sacrificers', who have been known to operate in South America and Africa. One such professional from Peru, Máximo Coa, once described how he would typically ply his victims (usually female) with alcohol and cocaine, before cutting off their heads and using their blood to make 'holy aspersions around the place'. It was said he raped his victims before dispatching them. There's also the story of the so-called Devil Doctor of Lagos, another pro, who operated in Nigeria during the 1960s and 1970s. He reputedly sacrificed a British soldier in a chilling ritual called the '200 Cuts'. This involved making 200 cuts with a scalpel in the victim, done with the precision of a master surgeon, so the victim stayed alive and conscious throughout the ordeal. The 201st cut was the killing cut. An African colonel allegedly commissioned the grisly ritual. He attended the ceremony, laughing with undisguised glee at the gut-wrenching agonies suffered by the victim. He was also clearly aroused by the torturous ceremony – an observer noticed a large bulge in the crotch of his trousers . . .

Satan plays a bigger part in this book than he did in the Bible. The 'Dark Lord' only has a minute mention in the holy book, yet a fair amount of blood has been spilt in his name. In one case, three youths in a small town in California, who were obsessed with Satan and death metal music, brutally killed a 15-year-old virgin, then allegedly had sex with her corpse. They killed the girl as an offering to Satan in the hope that he would make their own death metal band famous. The youths did get their 15 minutes of fame, only it was as depraved necrophiliacs. The boys demonstrated how, in the wrong hands, Satanism can push those who follow its path to extremely negative behaviour. Undoubtedly they represent a small minority and it would be wrong to tar all Satanists with the same brush. That's why I make a distinction between Satanists who kill or indulge in antisocial behaviour, and those that are members of the Church of Satan, which was founded by Anton LaVey, author of *The Satanic Bible*. These latter types of Satanists aren't generally credulous, out-and-out believers in anything; instead they tend to mix elements of humanism and rationalism with their occult interests, and are invariably honourable and upstanding citizens (contrary to popular belief).

Besides this, I cover a spate of grave robberies that occurred in New Jersey in recent years. Skulls and bones were allegedly stolen by members of the Palo Mayombe cult – which has roots in Africa and is similar to Voodoo – for use in magickal rites. The bones would be put in large cauldrons, along with the rotting remains of sacrificed animals. On raiding a Palo Mayombe temple, suspected of having illicit bones, one cop said it had 'an odour that you keep with you – like your first DOA'.

There are also very recent stories of human sacrifice, such as the ritual slaying in February 2006 of two men by members of the Naula tribe who live on the remote

Seram island in Indonesia. To this day, sacrifice is a central element of the tribe's culture. It's even required as part of the tribal marriage contract; the groom has the unenviable task of handing over a severed human head from another tribe to the bride's family.

My coverage is at times unconventional and outrageous – but, for me, this is the best way of getting to the heart of any story. To help bring insight into why it is people perform ritual sacrifice and to provide an overview of magickal thinking, I've included anecdotes from my own involvement in magick and the occult. I've also included talks with experts on crime and ritual killing, some transcribed from my occasional 'True Crime Hour' radio show.

At the end of the book, I outline a very strange experience I had which led to my finding a workable model to explain the motivations behind the practice of blood sacrifice. It enabled me to bring together a number of disciplines – from hypnotherapy and split-brain research to theories on the evolution of consciousness – and come up with possible answers not only to why it is people are driven to sacrifice, but also to why they believe in invisible entities that can offer them rewards in exchange for blood. Clearly, I'm a journalist and amateur antiquarian, not a scientific researcher. So the theories I put forward in this book are intended to stimulate debate, and are meant to be catalysts, not the last word.

That said, are you ready to hit the blood-soaked road to Hades? And find out what deadly craziness *Homo sapiens* can sink to?

Jimmy Lee Shreeve
Thursday, 1 May 2006
Norwich, Norfolk
www.jimmyleeshreeve.com

# Chapter 1: A Voodoo Orgy Of Madness

Torso in the Thames . . . Hunting The Juju Killers
. . . New Scotland Yard . . . Visions of Doubt . . .
God Squad . . . Fighting Victimisation . . . Last Rites
. . . Fear and Dread in Blighty . . .

'So many gods, so many creeds, so many paths that
wind and wind, while just the art of being kind is
all the sad world needs.'

Ella Wheeler Wilcox 1855–1919
*The World's Need.*

While I'm a newspaper journalist with a rational turn of
mind, I'm also an antiquarian with a long-time interest
in magick (the additional 'k' signifying the occult and
sorcery rather than conjuring). So when a little black boy
was found dismembered in the Thames in 2001, apparently murdered as part of a sacrificial rite with alleged
roots in West Africa, I knew I had to investigate the case.
The journalist inside me wanted to get to the truth of the
story, while the esoteric aspect of me wanted to find out
if the magickal arts had been defiled by some sinister group

practising ritual human sacrifice – which was what I feared.

So I set out on my quest, which would prove both a real-world journey and a visionary one. I was a cross between the fictional private consulting detective, Sherlock Holmes (who was of a strongly rational bent), and his creator Sir Arthur Conan Doyle (who had a strong spiritualist side). In other words, I was arch–sceptic and modern mystic rolled into one. For good or ill, this seemed like the best mindset for digging into the terrible killing of the nameless boy, dubbed 'Adam' by police, whose torso had been cast into the ebb and flow of the Thames as an offering to a pagan deity.

## Torso in the Thames

The story began on the afternoon of Friday, 21 September 2001. A slight chill hung in the early autumn air, like an impending curse. An IT consultant was walking briskly over Tower Bridge, on his way to a meeting, when a strange object bobbing around in the Thames below caught his attention. The object was brown and spherical, and was moving westward at some speed, caught by the river's strong seasonal tides. He thought it was probably a beer keg, thrown off one of the disco boats moored along the Thames. When he saw the object was wearing orange shorts, he concluded it must be a discarded tailor's dummy. But his interest had been caught, and he followed its progress. The next moment, as the current turned, the object shifted, revealing severed stumps of bone. He froze in horror. It was a human body. 'Jesus,' he breathed, as he rummaged frantically for his mobile phone and dialled 999.

A police launch recovered the remains from the river alongside the Globe Theatre in Southwark. In 20 minutes, the body had travelled just over one mile. Studies of tidal patterns suggested the body had been thrown into the river anywhere between Chiswick in the west and the Thames Barrier in the east. That gave police 30 miles of river to investigate, and experts were unable to say if the torso was thrown into the river from the south or north bank. What investigators did ascertain was that the torso had been in the water for up to ten days, that he was a black boy between 4 and 8 years old and that he had been murdered.

But there was a lot that baffled the forensics team. For one thing, bodies are usually dismembered either to hide the victim's identity or to easily transport and dispose of the corpse. Yet in this case no effort had been made to weigh down or conceal the torso once it had been dumped in the Thames. What's more, the orange shorts made the torso stand out like a beacon. Equally puzzling was the finding that the shorts had been placed on the torso *after* the boy was killed (the legs could not have been hacked off with them on). Answers to these questions became apparent as the investigation proceeded.

The forensics team mapped a profile of the boy's DNA, which would be used to identify his parents if they were ever found. They also covered the torso in tape in an attempt to lift off any hairs or fibres that could have belonged to the killer. This drew a blank. Swab tests found no evidence that any sexual assault had taken place – which ruled out the homicidal pervert theory. Initial toxicology tests found the boy had recently taken a cough suppressant called Pholcodine, which can be bought over the counter at any chemist's. Because of this the police speculated that the murderer or murderers had taken care of the boy before killing him. 'It wasn't obvious then, but looking back on it now, it shows some sort of duty of care to this child,' Ray Fysh, a scientist with Britain's Forensic Science Service and forensic co-ordinator on the case, later told the *Toronto Star*.[1] Further analysis would reveal a toxic substance in the boy's intestine that would have played a key part in making the boy's death horrific beyond imagination.

The way the boy's limbs were cut off had the precision of a master butcher. The killer either used a set of heavy, razor-sharp kitchen knives, or one that was sharpened regularly during the dismemberment (which was done after the boy's death). 'They cut the skin, peeled the muscle back, and then cut through the bone. They never went through a joint,' Fysh said. He added that the boy had died from violent blood loss caused by a knife wound to the neck, and that there was no blood in the lungs, which meant the boy probably died lying down or upside down. Another thing Fysh and his team discovered was that the first vertebra of the boy's neck was missing. They found this very odd and could come up with no explanation for it.

Scotland Yard detectives were equally baffled. They had no leads as to the identity of the boy, who they christened 'Adam'. They were also a long way from finding out who the killer or killers were and the motive for the murder. What sort of person would have committed such a crime – and why? It made no sense because it didn't fit the model of any conventional murder. Nothing seemed to add up. The only other case on their records that bore any similarity to this one occurred in 1969 in London, when police discovered the torso of a baby girl dismembered in much the same way as Adam. Though no one was ever arrested for the crime, many suspected the murder was part of an African ritual killing – a human sacrifice.

Could this have been the fate that befell Adam?

About six weeks after Adam's torso was found, this looked like a distinct possibility – a clue was uncovered that raised the prospect that the occult played some part in the boy's murder. Police searching for the rest of the body found seven half-burned candles wrapped inside a white cotton bedsheet, which had been washed up on the southern bank of the Thames. The name 'Adekoyejo Fola Adoye' (which has roots in the Yoruba tribe of West Africa) was written three times on the sheet, and cut into the candles. But this turned out to be a red herring. Police discovered that Adoye lived in New York, and that his London-based parents had held a perfectly innocuous thanksgiving on the banks of the Thames to celebrate the fact that he had survived the 9/11 terrorist attacks. Such riverside services with a simple offering are common among Christian Yoruba believers.

Despite this setback, police still suspected that Adam's killing had a witchcraft motive. So they turned to Dr Richard Hoskins,[2] a specialist in African religions at King's College, London, for advice. He confirmed their suspicions: 'The case of Adam is definitely a ritualistic killing. There is no doubt in my mind,' he said. 'The remarkable thing is that he was brought from Africa to the UK specifically for the purpose.' Shocking though Hoskins' statement is, it is no surprise when you consider just how common ritual sacrifice is in Africa. Official figures state that around 300 ritual slayings of humans are performed every year in South Africa (with police only managing to investigate 40 or 50 of these); about the same number are killed annually in Nigeria, where the victim's blood is offered to gods, spirits or ancestors. What's more, according to Europol estimates, there have been at least nine cases of ritual killing across Europe in the past fifteen years or so. Hoskins believes others are bound to happen as more African immigrants enter European countries.

Scotland Yard were now firmly on the trail of Juju[3] – a generic term for traditional African magick and religion – which they were certain was the motive for the killing of Adam.

Not long after the Adam case hit the headlines, I decided to find out for myself whether there was any truth to the possibility that this was a human sacrifice with roots in

Africa. From my experience of traditional African spirituality, I knew that Juju encompasses many different beliefs and practices, but is essentially pagan and involves the worship of many gods and spirits, as well as ancestors.

The well-known spiritual paths of Voodoo, Hoodoo, Santeria and Macumba grew out of Juju when slaves were transported from Africa to the Caribbean and to North and South America during the seventeenth and eighteenth centuries. Juju shamans and witchdoctors are highly skilled herbalists who treat the ailments of rural and city dwellers alike. Although they don't take the place of conventional doctors, they are often seen as the more powerful healers. But Juju practitioners don't just treat medical problems; they also help people with material and worldly issues, such as the need to gain more money, attract love, or wreak revenge on an enemy. This is done by casting spells and performing magickal rituals. Sometimes this involves the sacrifice of an animal, other times herbal concoctions are enough.

A small minority of practitioners, however, believe that the most powerful magick comes from the sacrifice of a human. The late Idi Amin of Uganda, for example, is believed to have extensively employed black magickians, working in the African sorcery tradition. One account claims that Amin abducted a British soldier, and then employed one of the most powerful sorcerers for hire in Africa, at the time, to slowly skin the abductee alive in a ritual to capture his soul, and make it a slave for Amin.[4]

Stories such as these, along with the figures quoted earlier, made it a distinct possibility that Scotland Yard were correct in thinking Britain had got its first definite case (in modern times, at least) of ritual human sacrifice. But I wanted to get the opinion of a practitioner of African magick and religion. Through some contacts who had known Earl Marlowe,[5] the Voodoo doctor I was associated with during the 1980s and early 1990s, I tracked down a 'root doctor'[6] in the Stoke Newington area of north London. His name was Edmond Labady and, while he wasn't in any way involved in nefarious practices, I was told he'd have a good idea of what was going on. At the time, Labady lived in a typical north London terraced house – Edwardian and spacious with solid, thick walls. Ivy and honeysuckle weaved around trellis works in the small front garden. At first glance nothing gave away the fact that Labady was a practitioner of magick in the African and Voodoo traditions. Closer scrutiny, however, revealed sections of angular symbols painted around the frame of the front door. I recognised them as being a mix of Voodoo veves (ideograms representing the various spirits and deities of Voodoo) and symbols from other magickal traditions, including ancient Egyptian inscriptions.

I rang the bell. A few seconds later Labady was ushering me into his lounge. He was in his sixties and his glossy and only slightly greying hair was slicked back from his forehead. His piercing eyes and neatly trimmed goatee beard gave the impression of regality, as if he were in control of his own little kingdom. After he'd made me a black coffee, into which he dropped a couple of capfuls of dark rum, I asked him if he thought Adam could have been the victim of a ritual human sacrifice.

'That's the way it looks to me,' he replied. 'Some bad work is going down. Evil people calling the spirits for very selfish ends.' He lit a cigar, mused for a moment, then said: 'It could well have African roots. I've travelled to West Africa on and off, in search of my roots and magickal knowledge and stuff like that, and I know that ritual killing is rife, 'specially in Nigeria. Yeah, lots of Nigerians get killed by headhunters,' he said. 'These people – they cut out the body parts and sell 'em to Juju priests, so they can use 'em in their potions.'

'What are these potions used for?' I asked.

'For all sorts of purposes,' he replied. 'For politicians to get elected or to attract riches, to protect people from sickness, accidents and spiritual attacks [curses]. Mostly body parts are used for moneymaking. People see it as a way of getting rich quick. Some think a ritual with human blood or body parts can bring 'em money and wealth. But it's not just in Nigeria, it goes on in Ghana, the Democratic Republic of Congo, Liberia and Uganda. That's the way it is.'

Labady added that there had been so many ritual killings in Lagos in 2001 that *The Punch*, a Nigerian national newspaper, ran a story with the headline 'Ritualists lay siege to Lagos'. As far as he was concerned, it would be no surprise if the murder of Adam turned out to have been a human sacrifice. With many Nigerians and other Africans making their homes in Britain, he said, it was inevitable that a few practitioners of the dark side of sorcery would have slipped in too – possibly looking for new clients and new territories.

After leaving Labady, I headed over to Alexandra Palace, the majestic Victorian exhibition centre which lies close to Wood Green in north London. It's somewhere I used to go to relax, partly because – being set in nearly 200 acres of parkland – it is one of north London's main green lungs, and also because it offers views right across the city. You can sit back and lose yourself in the sheer size of the metropolis and muse on what the millions of people are doing. Some will be successful and wealthy, others poor and needy, the majority somewhere in between. Some will be cruel and violent, others kind and considerate. And some will be killers who have never been caught. The human animal is very diverse and sometimes very dangerous. And all are represented in the urban sprawl of London. But I was on a mission to find out more about a new breed of killer in Britain – the ritual sacrificer. So I grabbed a large Plymouth gin from the Phoenix Bar and sat outside the Palace to think about what Labady had said.

The police were saying the Adam killing was the worst, most chilling murder they'd ever come across. There was no disputing that. But I couldn't help thinking that, in some sense, the killing of Adam was not murder. After all, the perpetrators probably believed they were offering the boy as a gift to the gods. They didn't necessarily see the killing as wrong. It was part of their spirituality. Macabre and grotesque it surely was, but a genuine belief system nonetheless. Most people would call it a terrible travesty of spirituality. Yet 2,000 years ago, in Britain, the ancient Celts piled sacrificial victims into huge wicker men and burnt them alive. A few hundred years later when the then pagan Anglo-Saxons colonised Britain, they regularly sacrificed animals and, on occasion, humans (but these were typically criminals or enemies they'd captured). The more I thought about it, the terrible, savage killing of Adam was beginning to bring to light a serious clash of cultures. Ancient shamanism was shaking a stick at the comfortable values of the West – making us feel decidedly edgy and bringing out the deep-rooted fear and dread many of us feel of Voodoo and sorcery. As I took a final sip of gin and got up to head home, I started to think that the cultural implications of this case could well have an underlying impact on our society for years to come.

As it was, the Adam case didn't shock the nation as much as it might have. The story got overshadowed by the terrorist attacks on the World Trade Center on 11 September 2001. People the world over were reeling at the sheer audacity and enormity of the attacks – not to mention the massive loss of life. And the media naturally ran the ins and outs of that fateful day for weeks to come. So the Adam story pretty much came and went – until early 2002 when, due to the efforts of the Scotland Yard press office, the media jumped on the story and began exploring it in detail. One revealing piece cropped up in the *Daily Mail*[7] in November 2002. Part of the article included an interview with a 72-year-old Voodoo priest called Malcolm Toussaint, who moved to England from Haiti in the 1950s. Echoing the comments made to me by Edmond Labady, he told the *Mail* that ritual killings are far more common than most people think. Toussaint then helped recreate the likely events that led to Adam's death. The boy's journey, he said, would have begun in Africa, where he probably lived in a small village in Nigeria. Toussaint went on to say that some people in very poor areas of Africa, of which there are many, sell their children to sacrifice hunters – wealthy individuals who seek out children to buy and sell on to witchdoctors and others wishing to perform ritual killings to improve their fortunes, place hexes or to protect themselves from the law.

The sum offered for the boy, said Toussaint, would have been around £2,000, at least four times the average annual income in Nigeria. He didn't think the sacrifice hunter would have spelt out to the boy's parents that the money was in exchange for their son's life. But they wouldn't have been under any illusions about why a rich stranger wanted to take their son to England, although they would probably have told themselves that he would be reincarnated into a better life. To get Adam to go with the rich stranger, they would have told him he would be well fed and would get a good education in England, which would help him to earn a lot of money. And that one day he'd return home to visit his family as a successful man.

Once in England, continued Toussaint, Adam would have been taken to a derelict house where he would have been given a sedative to keep him calm. His clothes would have been removed and, half an hour before the start of the ceremony, the boy would have been strangled by the Juju priest. Then, having summoned the spirit Elegua,

the spirit which grants access to the supernatural realm,
and asked for permission to perform the ritual, the priest
would have started the hour-long ceremony. First, using
a razor-sharp knife, the priest would have gouged out the
boy's brown eyes, a Juju symbol of independence. He
would then have sliced off the penis, which is believed to
represent eternal life. It would then have been preserved
in an alcoholic spirit like white rum and burned for good
luck at a later date. After that, the priest would have cut
open Adam's neck and would have sucked out a mouthful
of warm blood from the gaping gash to make sure it was
pure. The boy's head would then have been sliced off
because it symbolises intelligence and the arms and legs
would have been removed as they represent creativity and
mobility.

Chillingly, Toussaint concluded by saying the killing
of Adam wasn't the first of its kind in Britain. Human
and animal sacrifices, he claimed, have been going on regularly in London ever since he moved there more than 40
years ago. He even claimed that gangsters, murderers and
rapists had asked him to perform ritual sacrifice for them
– but he wouldn't do it.

## Hunting the Juju Killers

The Juju angle certainly took Scotland Yard by surprise.
They weren't used to the occult as a motive for murder
– money, jealousy and sheer viciousness made more sense.
This was why, six months after Adam's torso had been
discovered, detectives investigating the case had flown
7,000 miles from London to South Africa. One of the
locations they visited was a 'muti'[8] or medicine market in
downtown Johannesburg. The British press recorded how
Commander Andy Baker, a balding, middle-aged man with

a determined face, picked through the piles of monkey skulls, baboon hands and scaly lizard tails on the various stalls. He could well have been thinking that this was a hopeless case. After all, the FBI had said it couldn't be solved. And the truth was, the odds were against cracking it, what with the wall of silence and the unique motive that lay behind the macabre child killing.

It was now 22 April 2002. Baker was with his colleague Detective Inspector Will O'Reilly, who has the world-worn look of TV detective Columbo (and, when in Britain, even wears the classic beige raincoat). Despite the complexities of the case, neither was about to give up. They were determined to bring the perpetrators of this terrible killing to book. The two policemen mingled with regular muti customers, who happily sifted through decaying animal parts and jars of congealing fats. Baker and O'Reilly were accompanied by officers from the Pretoria-based Occult Related Crime Unit (ORCU) – originally set up by long-standing detective Colonel Kobus Jonker (now retired). The unit was the scourge of muti practitioners across South Africa. The stallholders were clearly uneasy. So when Baker asked one peddler of alternative medicines what was in his potions, he met with an evasive reply. 'It is powerful stuff, guaranteed to cure all ills,' was all the peddler would say.

As they walked around the muti market it became increasingly clear how significant traditional medicine and witchcraft are to sub-Saharan life. The items on sale – stomach-churning to most Western eyes – included weasels impaled on sticks, dried bats, the rotting carcass of an eagle wrapped in yellowing newspapers and the decomposing skull of a cheetah cub. All were intended for use in shamanistic rituals to cure health problems, attract love, sex and money, or to curse an enemy. In the soaring heat, the stench of the market must have been overpowering. The two London cops had entered a world ruled by spirits and sympathetic magick. A far cry from the logical and rationalistic world of policing. In this world, a run of bad luck, illnesses such as AIDS, poverty or a failing relationship would be put down to the wrath of a spirit. Such problems are often dealt with by conducting an occult ritual using herbs, potions and animal parts. Rituals typically involve the sacrifice of an animal – a chicken, goat or whatever is readily available. But most chillingly of all, the ritual sacrifice of humans – mainly children – is not uncommon. It is seen as a highly potent form of sorcery. Shamanism here is not of the variety touted by dewy-eyed new age enthusiasts in the West. More often than not it is bleak and loveless, with little regard for the sanctity of human life. Many Africans live in fear of witchcraft because of the ritual murders that can follow in its wake. As the police officers surveyed the muti market, Captain Lynne Evans of the occult unit reportedly took them to one side and quietly told them: 'You could probably get human body parts down here if you knew what to ask for and how to ask for it.'

Later that day, Baker and O'Reilly met former South African President, Nelson Mandela, who had agreed to make a pan-African appeal for information about the London child murder they were attempting to solve. Baker said after the meeting: 'Mr Mandela is a highly respected, valued and revered man by people across the world and in particular by the African community. Scotland Yard is deeply grateful he has agreed to help with the inquiry, and we hope that his valuable contribution will encourage those with information to come forward.'

Scotland Yard were describing the investigation as probably the most ambitious and unusual they had undertaken. 'This type of crime is entirely beyond our experience – it is unique in Britain,' O'Reilly said during the week-long visit to South Africa. 'We have come here not because we think Adam came from South Africa, but because this is where the experts are who can help us understand this culture and belief system.'

One of the first spiritual leaders Baker and O'Reilly consulted was Credo Mutwa, a leading South African 'sangoma' or traditional healer. His modest home, twenty miles outside Johannesburg, was filled with candles, medicinal plants and small statues. He sat at a large table with the two officers. Although normally amiable and of hearty temperament, his voice by all accounts became hoarse with anger as he studied the photographs of Adam's tiny torso. Dressed in floor-length robes and his head draped in cloth, Mutwa gave the detectives a shocking interpretation of the boy's killing. He said the killers would have drunk the boy's blood after his death, using a skullcap cut from the severed head. 'His finger joints would have been used as charms or ground into a paste for part of a ritual in order to give these criminals strength,' Mutwa said. 'I think this is a human sacrifice to some sort of water deity carried out by a gang of people strengthening themselves to do some very ugly crimes. They have made the sacrifice because they are filled with fear for what they have done or what they are about to do.'

Mutwa said the killers were followers of 'Obeah'[9] – a West African form of witchcraft – who practise 'the horriblest form of human sacrifice usually on a child who has not yet reached puberty'. He said the orange shorts that the child was dressed in after his death 'signified a resurrection' and concluded that a close member of the boy's family would have been involved in his sacrifice. Finally, he advised the policemen: 'I suggest you look in West Africa, from Nigeria onwards for where these people are from.'

*

Meanwhile, back in the UK, scientists were using ground-breaking scientific techniques to pinpoint Adam's home country. DNA analysis suggested the boy might have been West African, echoing Credo Mutwa's words. But the technique could not actually *prove* that Adam had lived there. So the forensics team sought assistance from Nick Branch, a pollen expert from the Royal Holloway, University of London. Branch looked at the pollen preserved in Adam's lungs and digestive tract to try to find out where Adam had been living – grains of pollen can provide a 'botanical fingerprint' of a specific region. Branch found no pollen in the lungs, but did find some spores in the intestines. The spores were found to be from various plants and trees of British and northwestern European origin. The pollen would have been swallowed and breathed in with food, which takes around 72 hours to pass through the body. The only conclusions to come from this were that Adam had been fed less than 72 hours before death, and that he'd been in Britain during that time.

Next the team called in Kenneth Pye, a professor of geology at the University of London, whose testing procedures hinge on the idea that what you eat will reveal where you have lived for up to the last decade. He homed in on the mineral strontium, which works its way through the food chain – from water to earth, plants to animals, and finally into the bones of people. We literally walk around with a strontium signature that matches the one in the environment where we live. What's more, if we move from one country to another, it takes six to ten years before the strontium signature in our bones changes to match the new location we have moved to. That being the case – and given his estimated age – the forensics team knew Adam's strontium signature would not only determine his place of birth, but also the place where he grew up. Again the trail pointed to West Africa: Adam's strontium signature matched one found in a zone of ancient, Precambrian rock which, in Africa, is mostly found in Nigeria.

'So I and Will O'Reilly went on a two-and-a-half-week reserach trip in Nigeria, picking up soil samples, animal bones from local markets, and also some human bones from two universities with pathology departments,' said forensics co-ordinator Ray Fysh. They analysed the samples for various isotopes, the main focus being on strontium, and compared signatures with traces from Adam's bones. 'We came down to a 50- to 100-mile stretch from Benin City to Ibadan, along which runs just one major road,' Fysh added.

Within days of making these findings the search for Adam's sacrificial killers moved to Nigeria. Somewhere in the scattered villages, buried deep in the jungle and linked by pot-holed roads, lived Adam's family. His parents, sisters, brothers, aunts and uncles. If they could be found, one or more of them may know something that could lead the police to his murderer.

Before heading out to Nigeria, Commander Andy Baker issued a statement:

All we know for sure is that Adam was the victim of a witchcraft-type ritual killing. He had not been in Britain very long because scientific analysis of his stomach contents shows that he had been eating British food only for a week or two. We are certain he spent the first few years of his life in Nigeria. In this country there is a tradition of human sacrifice and child abduction. We think Adam was taken from here but killed in London by a high priest of black magick or Voodoo. By analysing the chemical contents of his bones, scientists deduced he could only have come from one tiny corner of the world. The water he drank and the food he ate have left indelible signs in his bones and tissue. It gives you a narrow belt of territory between two Nigerian cities, Ibadan and Benin City. We have DNA samples from him and we can cross-match that against people who we think may be his relatives. When we know who he is, we have a good chance of finding out why he was killed and when we know that, we have an even better chance of discovering who did it.

Nigeria is a scary place. According to news reports, as the police convoy kicked up dust on a lonely dirt track, the Scotland Yard men saw a dead man lying by the roadside. He must have been there for a few days because the relentless African sun had flayed the skin from his naked back. Buzzards and black kites wheeled and swooped above, awaiting their chance. The armed column of jeeps and 4x4s ploughed on without slowing – the team travelled nowhere without at least six local officers armed with Kalashnikov assault rifles. Like South Africa, Nigeria is a land of Juju sorcery where invisible spirits rule and have a big hand in human affairs. But it is no fairy-tale world of magick and mystery. Millions of Nigerians live in fear of the curse of 'bad Juju', which can be invoked in many ways. You can use parts taken from jungle animals, monkeys, snakes, lizards and birds to brew foul concoctions to improve your life, or heap bad luck and misery on the lives of others.

During a break, O'Reilly told reporters: 'There is still a widespread belief in the supernatural and the power of evil spirits, especially in the country areas.' This was a far cry from his turf in south London, where the vast majority of people have a 'nuts and bolts' outlook on life and don't see the machinations of spirits and demons behind everyday events. 'The local police tell me,' he went on, 'that a common practice is for Voodoo priests to take body parts from people who have recently died, often by raiding cemeteries, and to sell them to gullible clients in the belief that they have been taken from human sacrifices.'

While naive people may be taken in by sham ingredients purloined from graveyards, serious practitioners of the dark side of Juju have to be sure that the body parts are from a genuine human sacrifice. Nigerian police officers have publicly admitted that many children and adults are abducted to die this way. Yet politicians in Nigeria are keen to play things down. Not surprising, considering that several people who disappeared during the 2003 elections in the region were believed to have been sacrificed to earn votes for candidates. They would either have been killed as part of a ritual to gain the blessings of the gods; or they would have been slain for their body parts, which would have been used to make up magickal talismans or fetishes to influence the 'higher powers' in the universe to bring given politicians more votes.

When the Scotland Yard men visited the country's most powerful tribal chief, Oba Ikanude, the Ooni of Ife, he was sceptical. At his cinder-block and corrugated iron palace in the town of Oshogbo, the elderly head of the Yoruba tribe, who sported a £20,000 diamond-inlaid Rolex watch and owned a £4-million house in London's Belgravia, said: 'It used to happen occasionally but that was all a long time ago.' Local police chief Alhaji Shehu Bayero, however, told the London cops a different story. 'A few months ago, I investigated the ritual murder of a young woman. The killer was impotent. He was told by a witchdoctor that if he killed a woman and ate part of her insides, he would be able to have sex. He saw a woman walking near his farm, stabbed her to death, cut out part of her intestines, cooked them and ate them. Now he is in jail. I think he was a crazy man, but he was a believer in the power of Juju.'

The British team learned that in Juju, parts of a victim's body have different powers. To eat the brains means you will be endowed with more knowledge. Eating an eye gives the power to see the future. The heart and blood give you strength and power. Devouring a woman's genitals or breasts guarantees you will raise many children. To take the eyelids or eyelashes gives a priest unassailable power to summon evil spirits. Nefarious Juju does not always involve cannibalism. A human hand buried outside a shop, for instance, is believed to 'beckon' more customers and boost business.

Another snippet of information the detectives unearthed was that in the town of Oshogbo, the Oshun river – which winds through a belt of tropical rainforest – is said to be a traditional site for sacrifices to the water god who bears the same name as the Oshun. Detective Constable Barry Costello, another member of the investigating team, was reported as saying that this had a large bearing on the case: 'We believe that Adam was killed to appease the water god Oshun. That is why his body was put into the Thames. His killers put a pair of orange shorts on his torso. It is traditional that in a sacrifice to Oshun, the victim's remains must be dressed in an orange garment before being committed to water.'

In the villages around Ibadan, the second largest city in Nigeria, Andy Baker and his colleagues got down to the kind of routine police work that brings results. First they distributed hundreds of posters in English and the local language asking for information about the boy. They then spent a month visiting schools and police stations, and conducting house-to-house inquiries in 1,000 Nigerian villages. Police also offered a reward of £2,500 (500,000 Nigerian naira) for any information leading them to Adam's relatives. On top of this, in both Nigeria and Britain, they put up £50,000 for information leading to the arrest and conviction of Adam's killers.

# New Scotland Yard

Currently the Adam case remains an international whodunnit without a resolution. But that could change at any time – as I found out when I visited New Scotland Yard, on 11 November 2005, to meet the two leading detectives on the case, the dogged Baker and O'Reilly (note that this was an informal interview and not in any way an endorsement of this book). Ironically, before meeting them, I came perilously close to being arrested myself. After taking the tube from Liverpool Street to Westminster, I walked down Victoria Street to Broadway, where New Scotland Yard is situated. Police with sub-machine guns stood guard outside the towering building that is home to one of the most famous police forces in the world – yet which architecturally is more akin to the 1960s brutalism of the Broadwater Farm estate than to the modest grandeur of the buildings that housed the force back in the days of its founder, Sir Robert Peel.

I walked into New Scotland Yard via the visitors' entrance. The young police officers manning the security checkpoint told me to empty my pockets of money and keys, and anything else metallic – all a part of the heightened security measures we've seen since the London bombings. I did as they asked. But, then, just as one officer was about to run a scan over me with his electronic baton, I recalled I did have another metallic item in my back pocket, which I'd forgotten about – my trusty Swiss army knife. I hastily pulled it out, saying: 'Just remembered my knife, carry it all the time – I expect you'll want me to hand it in?' This did not go down well. It turned out that my knife, being an older model, had a locking blade and, unbeknown to me, was now illegal. It was considered an offensive weapon. The situation got very tense. One of the officers glared at me in disgust and asked: 'What do you think you're doing coming into the headquarters of the Metropolitan Police with an illegal knife?' I could only tell him that I don't go anywhere without a pocketknife, which didn't help, and brought more looks of disdain. Eventually, I managed to convince them that I wrote for national newspapers and that I had legitimate (not murderous) business with the heads of homicide. After lengthy consultations with each other, they let me through – but not before confiscating my knife.

Clearly you could dismiss me as unprofessional for taking a knife into New Scotland Yard (of all places). But, looking back, I'd say the incident was born of a deep-rooted feeling that I didn't belong in one of the main heartlands of policing in the UK. It was like I'd wandered into the enemy's lair. I'd also say that, by taking the knife with me, I had unconsciously 'shot myself in the foot'. This could be because my background consisted of playing in rock bands and dabbling in the arts, and never involved college and career. It's essentially anti-establishment. And deep down I couldn't enter New Scotland Yard without somehow making this plain, even if it was in a stupid and risky fashion. It was obvious I should have left the knife behind. But even though I thought I was behaving myself – by preenting myself in a professional manner – my outlaw side came out.

When I finally got out of the security check-in area, I was met in the foyer by one of the New Scotland Yard press officers, who said she would take me up to Commander Baker's office. As we walked the seemingly endless corridors, I was struck by the sense that the very walls of the building literally oozed power and authority. When we got to Baker's office, it turned out he had been delayed in a meeting. So his PA made me a coffee and I sat down to wait. As I listened to the press officer and PA talking, I got the impression that they were slightly intimidated by Baker, not necessarily because he was unpleasant, but simply because of his status – after all, as chief of homicide at the Metropolitan Police, he is a very powerful figure. But I also sensed a certain rigidity, as if any display of informality would be out of place. I've had the same feeling on the occasions I've visited military bases; any level of casualness, such as wandering over to aircraft to look inside, results in a team of military police training sub-machine guns on you. Because they're edgy for a living, they expect you to be too.

Eventually, I found myself sitting around a table with Baker and O'Reilly, both of whom, I should say, came across very personably. They told me that the case wasn't closed and that they were still pursuing various leads. Neither could give me straight answers for fear of compromising any future court cases. But O'Reilly said the main motivation for ritual killings is simple: it's seen as a way of 'getting rich quick'. Because of the Adam case, O'Reilly has made a deep study of ritual human sacrifice cases and his knowledge has grown to the point where he is now consulted on the subject by police forces from around the world. It occured to me that his being so engrossed in the subject at both the theoretical and investigative levels has led to his incurring the wrath of numerous people involved in the unsavoury side of magick and witchcraft. In fact, it turned out he'd been cursed on a number of occasions; someone even sent a letter to him at New Scotland Yard, warning him off and informing him that they'd laid a hex on him. Did this bother him? I asked. 'No,' he said, directing his steely gaze on me. 'I have a rational mind and don't believe in that stuff.'

Practitioners of magick, however, often say that not believing in the efficacy of curses and hexes doesn't necessarily guarantee immunity. How much truth is in this? In his book, *Blue Roots*,[10] American writer Roger Pinckney relates how a white attorney from South Carolina once hired a Gullah (black American) housekeeper, but later dismissed her because he found her surly and unmotivated. The woman left the house in a huff, muttering about rooting and hexing her former employer. A new woman was hired, and on her first day on the job, she discovered three brand-new sewing needles tied together with black thread and stuck inside the couple's mattress. The maid recognised it as a 'suffering root', threw the needles into the stove, and urged the attorney's wife to seek immediate help from a Hoodoo doctor. The wife laughed the incident off – until the following morning when she awoke to find her skin covered with a scaly rash. She then sought help, not from a conjure man but from a medical specialist in Charleston. The diagnosis: a severe bout of chickenpox, the worst the doctor had ever seen. A day later, her infant son also came down with the pox.

A month later, they had both recovered, but then the attorney himself was stricken with severe abdominal pain. He was rushed to hospital for an emergency appendectomy. As it happened, an older son was already there for a long-scheduled removal of his tonsils. But during the operation, something went wrong. The boy stopped breathing and was revived only after much effort by the panicked nurses. Both father and son eventually went home, but their troubles were far from over.

The attorney suffered a long series of debilitating post-operative infections. Then, on a visit to his physician, he was struck by the similarity between the stitches holding together his infected incision and the needles tied with black thread found beneath his mattress. He immediately demanded the stitches be removed. The doctor protested. It was too early, especially considering infection had delayed the healing process. But the attorney persisted and the doctor complied. Two days later, he was completely healed. Neither he nor any member of his family suffered any further inexplicable and catastrophic ailments.

It should be strongly borne in mind that this story is anecdotal. I relate it simply because many practitioners of magick and the occult will have similar stories to tell. But if it is an accurate account of the facts, I would say that the attorney and his family all had a certain level of belief in (and fear of) the occult and that any apparently unnatural symptoms that manifested were essentially psychosomatic and came about as a direct result of their fears. The curse only worked because belief was there, even if the people in question denied it.

An acquaintance of mine, an occult bookseller and magickal supplies retailer, however, claims to have proven that you don't need to be a believer for a curse to work. When I spoke to him, he asked not to be named in this book. So I'll refer to him as 'Mike'. He also wanted me to make clear that he and his small staff are all Christians – somewhat unusual for a company that supplies books on magick and witchcraft paraphernalia, but refreshing in its eccentricity. Anyway, some years ago Mike was talking about Voodoo dolls and curses with one of his staff – who I'll call 'Phil' – who dismissed it as 'all rubbish'.

'We had some Voodoo dolls in stock, so I took one out and wrote Phil's name on the label and tied it around the doll's neck,' Mike told me. 'I then turned my back on Phil and stuck a pin in the doll and put it away in a drawer. I turned back to Phil and said, "Right, let's see what happens".'

At that point, Phil went upstairs to make tea for

everyone. When he came down he looked suspiciously at
Mike and told him that, while upstairs, he'd had a sudden,
excruciating pain in his left leg. He said it was so painful
he couldn't put his foot on the floor. Mike went over to
the drawer, pulled out the Voodoo doll and showed it to
Phil: the pin had been pushed through its left leg. Phil
was aghast – the curse had apparently worked. Voodoo
curses were no longer down to a psychosomatic reaction,
as he had previously believed.

Mike told me that there had been a 'consequence' for
his experimentation with cursing. 'I was ill for three days
afterwards,' he said. 'I was full of aches and pains. I think
that was the comeback. You see, I believe there is a karmic
balance; if you throw a stone in a pond you make a splash
and that is the magick. But there's a price to pay for
disturbing the balance. You can't control all the ripples –
the repercussions – of the stone hitting the water. And that's
the danger and is the reason why, as Christians, we say don't
do magick because you're interfering with the natural order.'

Presuming Phil's leg pain was not coincidental (and it
could well have been), then the curse would appear to
have worked, despite a lack of belief on Phil's part. But,
in reality, some degree of belief is likely to have been there
– after all, Phil was involved in selling occult books and
magickal supplies. At some level, Phil probably couldn't
control the nagging doubt that 'maybe there is some truth
in Voodoo?' He may also have felt edgy about the whole
thing and considered that they were 'playing with fire'.
This could easily have set off a psychosomatic reaction.

That said, even with a sceptical attitude, it is hard to
maintain an air of indifference when someone lays a curse
on you – as I know from experience, having been hexed
a few times as my alter-ego Doktor Snake. At some deep
level most of us fear the power of witchcraft to do us
harm. And yet what is it? It's simply a self-styled sorcerer

– who is really just a human being like you and me – petitioning gods or spirits to wreak harm on you, while mixing up a herbal potion and maybe fashioning a doll effigy of you out of clay or cloth. Dark and ugly it may be; but what is there to fear about it? This is a question I asked far-edge philosopher and SF writer, Robert Anton Wilson,[11] when I interviewed him for a magazine back in 1999. Although he experimented extensively with magick during the 1970s, he made clear that he didn't take 'spirits' literally (adding that he doesn't take anything literally). 'All of our perceptions derive from subconscious editing and orchestration of the billions of signals we receive from the universe every second,' he explained. 'We edit and orchestrate the signals to fit our current reality-tunnel or belief system.' In other words, we create our own realities. That said, Wilson theorised that people's fear of cursing could stem from primal memories of shamans performing sympathetic magick to make hunting expeditions more successful, along with hexing enemies and those who have displeased them in some way. This probably scared the hell out of people, which would have given shamans a strong power base of control over the general populace. According to Wilson, this ancient fear of the power of magick could still reside in the depths of our unconscious minds today. It would certainly explain why so many of us react with a slight start when a gypsy woman offers us a sprig of heather we don't want and we buy it anyway out of fear that, if we don't, she might hex us or give us the evil eye. If we were rational about it we would recognise that she had no more inherent power than a plumber or bank teller; but few of us are truly rational when faced with even the merest possibility of witchcraft being directed against us. Doubts creep in and bring our primal fears to the surface.

Does this mean that O'Reilly has cause to worry, despite

his declared rationalism? Is his professional scepticism enough to protect him and keep inherent fears at bay? In truth, it is probably more than adequate, especially since he hasn't suffered any ill effects from being cursed. But some investigators prefer not to leave things to chance. In his book *A Shadow in the City*, acclaimed US non-fiction author Charles 'Chuck' Bowden[12] paints a vivid, almost film-noir picture of the life of jaded narcotics officer Joey O'Shay (an alias), who orchestrates an enormous heroin bust in an unidentified American city. An undercover investigator for over twenty years, O'Shay lives in an underworld of violence, misery, superstition and creeping uncertainty – and naturally deals with some very dangerous people. To counteract this, he sets up a Voodoo altar, complete with figurines and other objects of symbolic significance. As Bowden said to me a month or two after his book's release: '[In] my current book, you will find a Voodoo-type altar as a centrepiece. The narc in the book used it as protection from all the black magick being hurled at him in his work, and he does stumble on what he believed was ritual sacrifice.'

O'Shay got very deep into his undercover work and in many ways ended up living on the edge. He was no longer sheltered by a nine-to-five job and comfortable home. Order and certainty were no longer a part of his life. This possibly made him revert to a more ancient mindset, one in which a magickal universe was an everyday reality. This is not to be scoffed at: put in a dangerous, on-the-edge situation, even hardened sceptics could find themselves making Voodoo dolls and muttering incantations to protect themselves. They would vehemently deny it, of course. But none of us know what we would do given desperate circumstances. If we were involved in the world of drugs and magick, as O'Shay was, there would even be a good case for setting up spiritual protection; if nothing else it would persuade and reassure the unconscious aspects of our mind (the side of us that can cause psychosomatic symptoms) that we are invulnerable to psychic attack. It's very much like the way hypnotherapists might use positive affirmations to make someone feel more confident and relaxed in certain situations.

## Visions of Doubt

After I left Scotland Yard, the sun was beginning to sink low in the sky. Dusk being a time of day I enjoy, I decided not to take the tube back to Liverpool Street station; instead I walked over to Covent Garden and holed up in a bar to think about the case. I ordered a large dark rum with one block of ice and sat at a table in a corner. The great thing about central London pubs – in common with those in most large cities around the world – is they have an air of anonymity, which always makes me feel completely comfortable and at ease. Their impersonal nature offers a kind of safety away from the herd. Cult writer William S. Burroughs[13] used the term 'interzone' to describe such places (the 'interzone' was also a parallel universe in his book *The Naked Lunch*). You can lose yourself and no one pays you any attention. Around me were middle-aged men having a quick pint after work, young guys watching sport on the TV, a couple of girls awaiting their boyfriends and a family of tourists from Korea, who asked me to take their picture. When I said yes, they gave me a camera and stood around the table, smiling with their arms around each other. Once I'd taken a couple of shots, I gave them the camera back and they thanked me profusely. It was no problem. I was happy and content in the knowledge that they would forget me within minutes. I was just another face in the interzone – nothing but a speck of dust in the cosmos. And that's how it should be.

After ordering another rum, I got to thinking about Burroughs and his sharp, pithy social commentary which, in many respects, shocked and outraged the world. What would he have made of the Adam case? Although he had lived in America I was sure he would have been aware of the story and very likely would have been unable to resist bringing it into his literary mythos. As I sat there musing in an almost meditative state, these thoughts started to take on a life of their own. Maybe I had dozed off. Or maybe I had slipped into an altered state of reality. Whatever the case, just at that moment, two men walked in the door of the pub. One was a raw-boned figure, wearing a hat and raincoat, looking like he'd walked off the set of a 1940s crime noir movie; the other had a greying beard and thick-lensed glasses, and had the look of a New York intellectual. It was Burroughs and his long-time friend, the poet, Allen Ginsberg.[14] The fact that both had died in the late 1990s didn't seem to faze me. Burroughs waved in my direction, just the trace of a smile cracking his aged face. 'Another?' he asked, pointing to my empty glass. 'Yes, I don't mind if I do,' I replied.

Once the two had got drinks, they came and sat at my table. Putting on a slightly camp drawl, Ginsberg said: 'I just lurve these London bars . . . they used to be so full of the most delectable boys . . .'

'Enough, Allen,' Burroughs cut in. 'Boys can come later.' He then looked me directly in the eyes and said: 'We're here for a reason, Jimmy Lee. We've been reading your reports on the killing of Adam on the Internet and we believe you are missing the implications of the case.'

'It looks like a witch-hunt, literally and metaphorically,' Ginsberg interjected, straightening his red and black tie, which he wore with a deep blue, button-down collar shirt.

'Think about it,' continued Burroughs in his dry mono-tone, which retained just a hint of his St Louis roots.

'When you kill someone you need to slice off the head and limbs to make the corpse impossible to identify. It's far more professional that way and improves the odds of not getting caught. Even a low-rent sex killer knows that.'

'What Bill is saying,' Ginsberg said, 'is that the kid's murder might not have been a ritual sacrifice, whatever the police are saying. The killer might have been a psychopath or pervert, but no one is exploring that possibility. It's been dismissed out of hand.'

Burroughs took a long, slow sip from his vodka and Coke, then added: 'Somewhere in all this is an agenda, and we think that agenda can be traced back to organised Jesus freaks trying to discredit magickians and witchdoctors, who they consider agents of Satan.' As far as Burroughs was concerned, the 'control system' was taking the opportunity to lay the blame for Adam's killing firmly at the door of occultists. 'Even the press swallowed the ritual sacrifice notion hook, line and sinker,' he continued. 'Why? Because the sacrifice story panders to the deep-rooted fears our culture has about blacks and Voodoo.'

Burroughs went on to say we are preoccupied with certain phantoms. One is that Voodoo or Devil worship is taking place out in the woods; the other is Satanic child abuse and abduction. He cited how, in the US during the 1980s and early 1990s, there were vastly overblown stories of child abuse, Satanic rites and the wholesale slaughtering of people. It was commonplace at that time for 'experts' to claim that 50,000 children were missing, an absolute absurdity given real FBI numbers. But it led to photos of children on milk cartons as the urban legend grew. 'There was no truth in it,' said Burroughs. 'In fact, the Feds did a big investigation and couldn't find a grain of evidence to support any of the claims. So you have to watch out for this in the Adam case. The sceptical voices aren't being heard and that's not good for anybody.'

Just then the bartender called, 'Last orders!', making me jump. I got up to grab a final shot of rum, turned to Burroughs and Ginsberg to see if they wanted one for the road, but they were gone. Disappeared into the mists of the ether. It was as if I'd seen two ghosts or fallen into an alternate universe. Looking at it rationally, though, I recognised that my unconscious or deep mind was trying to tell me something – something important. Quite possibly because of my visit to New Scotland Yard and the fact that I'd felt like a fish out of water. But it was more than that. I'd been sensing something was wrong with the Adam case for some time. And it looked as if my unconscious was doing its level best to bring it to the surface; hence my 'waking dream'.

The way I see it is my unconscious mind threw up a symbol that was going to grab my attention. That's why it stuck the legendary William S. Burroughs – one of my early literary heroes – in front of me to comment on the Adam case and make me start thinking a bit deeper about it. I could easily have stuck to straight journalism in this book and conveniently written out my 'inner life', but I feel strongly that if you are to get across anything resembling the truth in a book, you have to bring in the way your internal mental world interacts and responds to the 'reality' outside. In fact, there are no 'inside and outside'; the inner world blends with the outer world. They are essentially one and the same, blurring in a psycho–geography of living consciousness.

When you look over the Adam case there are many persuasive elements that suggest Adam's murder must have been ritual sacrifice. Take the orange shorts the boy was wearing when his torso was found in the Thames. Forensics said they had been put on the boy after he was killed, and experts on African religion, who advised Scotland Yard, said the colour of the shorts had ritual significance. South African shaman, Credo Mutwa, told detectives that the orange colour of the shorts signified a 'resurrection'. They were also told that, in a sacrifice to the god Oshun, the victim's remains must be dressed in orange before being committed to water – which, certainly on the surface, looks like what could have happened to Adam.

## God Squad

But was all this just too convenient? A few days after getting back to Norwich from my visit to New Scotland Yard, I started to dig around to see what I could find out. Using a few Boolean searches on the Internet, I came across an article called 'Clueless', which mercilessly debunked the Adam investigation. It was by Adam Kuper,[15] a professor of anthropology at Brunel University, who grew up in South Africa. Amongst the many aspects of the case he questioned was the claim that the orange shorts had ritualistic signifi-cance. 'The police claimed, quite wrongly, that a Yoruba river god, Oshun, is associated with the colour orange, and that human sacrifices are made to him . . . no sacrifices of this kind have been documented for more than a century.'

Earlier, at a multiculturalism conference in November 2002, Kuper accused Scotland Yard of indulging in the worst sort of cultural imperialism:

> Some policemen walking along the Thames came across a Yoruba ritual which was a celebration of the fact that a child that had been travelling from the United States had escaped the 11th of September bombing. They said well, of course, once we'd inves-tigated this we found out that there was nothing sinister going on – but it shows that these kinds of rituals are about. This is, ladies and gentleman, a classic blood libel. This is a classic libel associated

with a minority group by the authorities of a country, which reflects the collective fears and hatreds, which feed on stereotyped group differences and the notion of unification. Why has nobody stood up in the press to denounce this? Why has it seemed plausible to the journalists and intellectuals who write about this? I have here an article from *The Observer*, which carries a series of 19th-century stereotypes at which Kipling would have blushed. And it ends with a statement that Scotland Yard believe the death of this child may be linked with an extreme element of the Yoruba people, a tribe with Voodoo-like rituals. Is this how we think about life in London today? Is this the discourse which we're entering into? It is . . . What we must do is break down this kind of stereotyped thinking, this attribution of group identities. Break down this easy association of culture and race.

Are Kuper's criticisms of the police investigation valid?

One area of the investigation that could be brought into question is the impartiality of some of the experts consulted by Scotland Yard. One of them – Colonel Kobus Jonker, the now retired head of the South African Police Service's Occult Related Crime Unit (ORCU) – is a fundamentalist Christian, who had a tendency to see the baleful influence of 'Satan' in many of the crimes he investigated. This may have been why he was so adamant that Adam's killing was a ritual sacrifice.

Kobus Jonker joined the South African police in 1969. As time went by he became a well-respected senior detective, investigating drug trafficking, diamond and gold smuggling, robberies and murders – the usual fare for an investigator. But in 1981 he became a born-again Christian. Not a problem in itself. But in Jonker's case it seemed to change everything. A few months after his conversion, he investigated the case of a woman who was killed when she walked under a car late one night. The dead woman had 'Jesus' tattooed on the sole of one foot, 'Christ' on the other and '666' on her arm. Jonker's interpretation was that the woman was a witch symbolically 'trampling' Jesus into the ground with every step. He also claimed that she killed herself as a gift to Satan. Jonker had become utterly convinced that Satan was real and at work in the world. So he stopped investigating murders and robberies and began to devote himself to fighting Satanism full time. With his neatly trimmed beard and hearty smile, Jonker was often depicted in media articles holding a skull (something I'm equally guilty of) and declaring that his strongest character trait was his 'position in Jesus Christ'.

In an interview with *The Financial Times*,[16] he told reporter Sarah Duguid how he had seen a pentagram inexplicably appear in the blood on a suspect's arm. He also described how he thwarted a female assassin who turned up at his office with a pistol inside her handbag. She left still clutching the weapon, apparently unable to take it out of the bag. Jonker claimed her hand had been paralysed by his prayers. So convinced was he by the threat of Satanism that he asked his superiors if he could set up a specialist police unit to investigate occult crime. They were sceptical at first. But when Jonker raided a house in 1991 and found a Bible bound in chains, the walls smeared with blood and a Chinese woman's head in a cupboard, they changed their minds and gave him the go-ahead to form the Occult Related Crime Unit, with Jonker at the helm.

The unit was not open to all police officers, however – candidates had to be devout Christians. 'The ordinary guy cannot investigate occult crimes,' Jonker told *The Financial Times*. 'There are things you see and experiences you have as a result of the supernatural. You must be strong in faith to be in the occult unit,' he said. Jonker's occult unit had given a whole new meaning to the term 'God squad'. But by 2001, after a heart attack, Jonker retired from the police force, although he remains available for 'professional help and assistance and advice at occult-related scenes'.

It could be argued that Jonker's strong religious convictions didn't influence his police work. Yes, he put a Satanic slant on many of the cases he investigated – but why should that matter if he was bringing bona fide criminals to justice? Clearly, it shouldn't matter; after all, people the world over have many varied, and sometimes fanciful, beliefs while maintaining impartiality and professionalism in the workplace. There are those, however, who claim that, besides catching real criminals, Jonker had a tendency to target those who follow alternative lifestyles and hold occult beliefs. On the Internet forum *Dark Light*,[17] which discusses gothic music, a contributor called James from South Africa says of Jonker:

> I have had the loathing displeasure of meeting old Jonker, and he's far from open-minded, throwing everything including Wicca under the Satanic category. [A] few years ago he raided a close friend of mine's house, seizing computer HDD's, occult material, etc, because someone in our 'upstanding' community saw him as the antichrist. Jonker didn't [hesitate to act].

Another contributor called Olivier, also from South Africa, says:

> I have the displesure [sic] of my uncle taking over from Jonker in the West Rand, 'sob', his name is Kaptein Jannie kombrink, He gave me lots of shit, but also asked me for advice several time . . .

Nowadays he just leaves me alone. We have a mutual understanding in that regard. They seem to follow a recept [sic], or a check list, and when they investigate, they start from the top working the check list to the bottum [sic]. ex.

- Wears black clothing – check
- Wears Make up – check
- Listens to Goth and Alternative – check
- His room is a Satanic Shrine – check
- and so the list continues . . .

Similar complaints and criticisms of Jonker and the South African Police Service's occult unit can be found elsewhere on the Internet. While they could arguably be the usual unsubstantiated ravings you find on the web, they do show that at least some young people in South Africa, who follow alternative lifestyles and/or spiritualties, believe they have become the victims of a witch-hunt by the police. Even though Jonker has now retired, the South African Police Service (SAPS) still maintains an occult-related crimes page as part of its website.[18] It makes interesting, if somewhat worrying, reading. For example, this is how the SAPS defines occult-related crime:

> Occult-related crime means any human conduct that constitutes any legally recognised crime, the modus operandi of which relates to or emanates primarily from any belief or seeming belief in the occult, witch-craft, satanism, mysticism, magick, esotericism and the like. Included in the scope of occult-related crime are ritual muti/medicine murders, witch purging, witchcraft-related violence and sect-related practices that pose a threat to the safety and security of the Republic of South Africa and/or its inhabitants.

This sounds reasonable on the surface, especially when you consider that muti/medicine murders reportedly involve killing people, usually children, for their body parts. Likewise, upholding the safety of South African citizens is a laudable aim. The worrying aspect of this statement, however, is the way it targets the occult, witch-craft, Satanism, mysticism, magick and esotericism, all of which are simply alternative ways of looking at the world and only very rarely have criminal acts associated with them. You could also ask yourself why Christianity and Islam aren't included in the list, as historically these creeds have both had their far share of atrocities committed in their name.

The site then goes on to offer a set of guidelines to help parents recognise when their children may have been 'sucked' into the occult or Satanism. These include:

* Phone calls from persons requesting to speak with someone other than your child's name. Callers may be inquiring for your child and using his/her Satanic/demonic name.
* Changes to the appearance of the child's bedroom. Some bedrooms have pentagrams or other symbols that are taped, burned or painted on the floor under the carpet or bed or on the back of paintings or pictures and the walls are painted a dark colour. Candles and occult objects will be hidden away.
* Child views a disproportionate number of video-tapes/DVDs of horror movies/heavy metal music.
* Child is engaged in illegal drug use and/or sexual activity.
* Child has an interest in computer. (History settings on the Internet browser will probably be cancelled to wipe evidence of visited sites. There

will also be passwords on the computer and down-
load folders.)
* Birthdays might be filled with anxiety. (Birthdays
  are important days for Satanists.)
* Child is curious about drugs, specifically hallu-
  cinogens.
* Depression.
* Child starts to wear pale make-up and or dyes hair
  black.
* Draping hair across the left eye.

The cause for concern about these guidelines is they could
apply to a good many teenagers in nearly every part of
the Westernised world. The fact is, teenagers into gothic
and heavy metal music will often decorate their rooms
with pentagrams, mainly because many bands working in
those genres put such symbols on their CD covers. It's a
way for teenagers to identify with their favourite bands.
As for hiding candles and occult objects away, it should
be borne in mind that candles are regularly used in church
services too. And teenagers the world over tend to be
interested in sexual activity; many also experiment with
drugs, more often than not with no ill effects. As to being
involved in Satanism, even that may be no bad thing –
certainly when you look at the variety propounded by
Anton LaVey, author of *The Satanic Bible*,[19] which,
contrary to popular belief, encourages an ethical and
honourable way of living one's life.[20]

Canadian police officer Kerr Cuhulain,[21] who is also a
practising Wiccan, has spoken out against the SAPS Occult
Related Crimes programme. He says: 'As a police professional I'm appalled to see such misinformation and religious dogma in police practice ... There is nothing
professional, objective or impartial about ... the Occult
Related Crime Unit. It is amazing that the SAPS should

allow such an abuse of their system. Police departments should be the defenders of the rights and freedoms of citizens. Freedom of religious association is one of those freedoms.' Commenting on one of the publications that came out of the Occult Related Crimes programme, *The Servamus Special Edition*, which put forward similar misinformation to what is found on the SAPS website, Cuhulain adds: '[This] is obviously an attempt to indoctrinate police and the public into religious intolerance. It is full of misinformation and borders on the classification of hate literature.'

Clearly, being a Wiccan (neo-pagan), Cuhulain has a vested interest in condemning the attitudes of the South African Police Service. He is naturally moved to defend the rights and freedoms of fellow pagans everywhere. But even if you don't have any connection with the occult or paganism, it is clear that the SAPS have little understanding of alternative belief systems involving the occult. The question is: did Scotland Yard take this into account when detectives went to South Africa to consult the SAPS's Occult Related Crimes Unit about the Adam case? And could the stance of the SAPS have influenced them into accepting that Adam's killing was ritual sacrifice, when according to the academic Adam Kuper it might not have been?

## Fighting Victimisation

In a bid to get answers to these questions I turned to Tony Rhodes, director of the Subculture Alternatives Freedom Foundation, or SAFF,[22] a UK-based, not-for-profit organisation founded in 1988 to protect minority religions from victimisation and suppression. When I asked about the Scotland Yard line that the murder of Adam was a ritual sacrifice, he rejected the notion outright, saying: 'The SAFF stance on the claims of ritual killing is simply that the claims are false.' He then went on to explain that in cases like the murder of Adam it is vitally important to separate the motive from the method. 'To be a true ritual sacrifice, both the method and the motive must be present and are complimentary to the deed,' he said. To illustrate his point Rhodes outlined how murders fall into one of four categories. These are:

SPONTANEOUS MURDER: The first category of murder is unplanned and occurs spontaneously as a result of situations (e.g. the bank guard who is shot by bank robbers when trying to be a hero; the passer-by who is stabbed after going to the aid of a woman being mugged; the drunk driver who kills a child; the crime of passion where a husband finds his wife and her lover in flagrante delicto, and so on).

PECUNIARY ADVANTAGE: The second category of murder involves criminals planning and executing a slaying to gain some advantage (e.g. extortion, kidnapping, gangland killings, insurance claims, and so on).

LUNATICS: The third category of murder is perpetrated by people who are mentally ill. They either do not see reality properly and do not realise the gravity and repercussions of their actions; or they conjure any excuse from their sick minds in order to overcome their moral misgivings and justify killing another (e.g. religious nuts, care-in-the-community, people pushed into nervous break-downs, and so on).

ASSASSINATIONS: The fourth category of murder is committed by lone individuals who justify taking the life of another because of a belief in a cult, patriotism, principle, race, nationalism or religion (e.g. special agents, mafia killers, assassins, terrorists, cult killers, and so on). It also includes mass murder, where, on behalf of a nation, tribe, race or religion, an appointed authority (priests, dictators, presidents, politicians, judges or generals) changes the rules in an ugly and terrifying way. They might start wars, order soldiers or police to kill, or sentence criminals to public execution – all to confirm their religious or sociological tenets, on the justification of protecting the interests of society.

Looking over Rhodes' list, it was clear that each classification was exclusive; they can't be 'mixed and matched'. As Rhodes explained: 'Spontaneous murder cannot be pre-planned. Pre-planned murder cannot be accidental. Lunatics are not motivated by pecuniary advantage, and so on. Likewise, in the case of assassination – soldiers working behind enemy lines, the warder pulling the lever on the electric chair and cases of ritual sacrifice – only Class 4 is involved.'

He went on to stress that motive is everything in a murder case. Yet a murderer can easily claim, in hindsight, that a demon made him do it, in a bid to lessen his sentence or save his skin. 'Our files are full of hundreds of instances where criminals have "turned to God" in custody and been given preferential treatment by the courts. But just because it was in the long-term interests of the prisoner to say a killing was a ritual sacrifice, doesn't mean it was one. Any case that has any components relating to categories 1, 2 and 3 cannot be termed a ritual sacrifice.'

Rhodes said that SAFF has investigated thousands of cases of alleged ritual sacrifice and none, in the organisation's view, turned out to be legitimate in that it fitted the

1, 2 and 3 murder categories, but not 4. 'Often, Christian fundamentalist groups will hijack particularly horrifying murder cases, and inject a ritualistic element, to promote their claims that the Devil is alive and well and active on planet Earth,' he said. 'When these doctored tales get media coverage it leads to social strife, racial tensions and a propensity for the plebs to take the law into their own hands – as was seen when the *News of the World* ran its misguided "hunt down your local paedophile" campaign.'

We all know that sensationalism sells newspapers, books and TV documentaries, presumably because that's what we, as members of the general public, want. But Rhodes believes that highlighting sensationalist subjects like ritual sacrifice, particularly when the evidence is tenuous, is nothing short of irresponsible. 'It not only primes the minds of susceptibles to use the idea of ritual sacrifice as an excuse for their deeds, but also sensitises the mass mind to accept such acts. It also offers corrupt police forces a very useful method of pursuing prosecutions which would otherwise, due to scarcity of proper forensic evidence, fall flat and not get to court. Our files are full of cases where the prosecution successfully relied on shock-horror claims of occult involvement to sway a jury, when based on the actual evidence a prosecution probably would not have been obtained.'

Rhodes considers this a crucial point because, if the police have solid forensic evidence, they would not need to use what he calls the 'ritual sacrifice device' in order to gain a successful prosecution. 'Ergo the only reason for the police/prosecution to involve such claims – which to an intelligent observer degenerates their case – is as a last resort, which underlines the basic failure of their detective work,' he said.

Rhodes believes this is what has happened in the Adam case: 'Because Scotland Yard has no real evidence they have resorted to ritual sacrifice speculations, and this makes up the entire case. Those people who see ritual sacrifice under every stone [such as the South African Police Service's ORCU] are very quick to ascribe it to any case which appears to have sacrifice components and this often happens when the police investigation has stalled. If in doubt, blame the occult.'

Rhodes and his colleagues at SAFF don't profess to know who killed Adam; but they do strongly allege that some key players who prompted the police to think along the lines of ritual killing were previously involved in promoting the now discredited Satanic Ritual Abuse Myth, or SRAM, that took hold through the 1980s and early 1990s. The Satanic Ritual Abuse Myth was originally created by Christian fundamentalists in the US in the mid-1970s in a bid to regain influence over more moderate Christians. It worked so well that it turned into a full-blown panic that seized the nation. Evangelical networks then spread it to Britain and throughout most of Europe and even to South and West Africa. In every country except Britain the notion of Satanic ritual abuse gained legal credence – self-proclaimed experts in the subject (who were really fundamentalist Christians) toured the US giving lectures to law enforcement groups on how to recognise and deal with the threat to children from Satanists. In the end, the FBI investigated the allegations and couldn't find even one scrap of evidence to substantiate the claims. In the UK, the scare didn't gain the legal foothold it did in the US because it was debunked by SAFF and a handful of reasoned academics and reporters who could see through the fundamentalists' propaganda.

Now, according to Rhodes, such dangerous propaganda could be resurfacing in the Adam case:

The original Satanic Ritual Abuse Myth was not about black people, foreigners, tribal ceremonies, muti, Juju or Voodoo – or anything like that. It was purely a re-popularisation of the white Catholic/Protestant myths about demonology, which the Christian church developed in the middle ages and used repeatedly to justify the killing, torture and suppression of dissenters all over the world. But because the Satanic Ritual Abuse Myth was totally discredited, fundamentalist agitators found themselves sowing their misinformation on fallow ground – until the Adam case came along.

Cult cops like Colonel Kobus Jonker, who had been arguing the Satanic Ritual Abuse Myth for nearly two decades, appear to have simply modified the original scare to fit the details of the case and injected a black context, then fed it back to the British police. In fact on the very weekend that the Thames Torso was discovered [21 September 2001] Jonkers had travelled to Britain to speak at one of those Satan Seminars still held by RAIN [Ritual Abuse Information Network]. RAIN was originally set up in 1989 by a cadre of first-level Satan-hunters in social work, who promoted the SRA myth in all the failed cases which caught the headlines during the 1990s, including the Rochdale and Orkney tragedies. The government should have completely banned this lot, but daren't say boo to a goose where social workers are involved, it would seem.

There is therefore a direct link with the original Satan hunters in social work (who had previously denied that they trafficked with fundamentalists over the scare) and Jonkers, an out-and-out fundamentalist Christian cult cop, who immediately stepped in to give expert evidence to the Metropolitan police about the so-called Voodoo killing of Adam based on nothing more than his religious fundamentalist

ideas about magick in South Africa. I repeat, in case
the nuances escape the reader: Jonkers was already
working with the discredited band of Satan hunters
in Britain to establish the idea of Satanic Ritual
Abuse in Africa BEFORE Adam's body was found
in the Thames.

Rhodes also believes that Scotland Yard was caught in a
catch-22 situation over the Stephen Lawrence case, in
which a black teenager was stabbed to death in 1993 by
white racist thugs who were never brought to book due
to a catalogue of errors by police. An inquiry carried out
by Sir William McPherson even ruled that the police were
'institutionally racist'. According to Rhodes the police
investigating the Adam killing may have been over-sensi-
tive to further accusations of institutional racism. He said:
'This may have led to them accepting any utterances from
the most voluble coterie of people in the black community. Some of these were black Christian church leaders
with a vested interest in undermining traditional African
herbal medicine and religion.' He believes some took the
opportunity not only to rubbish non-Christian aspects of
African culture, but also to 'take the moral high ground
and use the case as yet another example of the work of
the Devil, in order to galvanise their own congregations
into informing on African shamans who were by and large
simply helping people with the old ways.'

Rhodes went on to highlight one of the major ironies
of the case: 'While Scotland Yard were busy chasing their
tails, trying to find links to the ritual killing scenario, a
little African girl called Victoria Climbié,[23] who was being
looked after by fundamentalist Christian relatives, was
progressively beaten to death to drive the Devil out of
her. Who is to say whether the prominence given to the
idea of pagan ritual murder caused Climbié's black social

workers to accept the situation – which should have been noticed and terminated before the child was killed – because her relatives attended a black Baptist church, and thus were seen as above reproach?'

Rhodes finished by asking why it was that Scotland Yard were investigating ritual sacrifice by Voodoo or muti practitioners (of which, SAFF research shows, there have been no cases over the past two decades) to the exclusion of Christian fundamentalists (of which, he says, there are lots of instances of child murder and cruelty)?[24]

Whether Rhodes is correct in believing ritual sacrifice wasn't involved in the killing of Adam is difficult to say. It's a convincing argument. But it is important to recognise that the members of SAFF, the organisation Rhodes heads, are involved in magick and the occult themselves and therefore have a personal interest in protecting such practices from slander and misinformation. This is not to say they don't have a point. On the contrary, the SAFF position on the Adam case is, in my view, very reasoned. And even if it does turn out that SAFF is wrong in its reading of the killing of Adam, the organisation is still a voice that needs to be listened to.

## Last Rites

Sadly, Adam's identity has still not been established. His family may not even know what happened to him. Or maybe they do. Perhaps they did sell him to a people trafficker, convincing themselves that the boy was destined for a better life in Europe. None of this is out of the question: human life is cheap in many countries in the developing world. It could well be the same here if we didn't have the economic stability we've got. Whatever the case, the boy's family in death became the team investigating his murder.

In September 2002, a year after Adam was killed, 30 police officers, scientists, pathologists and other experts involved in the case attended a service for the boy at City Hall in London. O'Reilly gave a reading from the Bible and the leader of the investigation, Commander Andy Baker, gave the address. Canon Barry Wright, senior chaplain of the Metropolitan Police Service, finished the service with a short silence to celebrate Adam's life. After the ceremony O'Reilly and John Azah, from an independent advisory group, laid a wreath from a boat at Tower Bridge, near to where the body was found. During the ceremony, Baker summed up the case by saying: 'Just imagine your worst nightmare and that would be nowhere near.'

Tests conducted by scientists at the Royal Botanical Gardens at Kew in October 2003 revealed just how chillingly true this was. Not long after Adam's body was found, the forensics team discovered a strange plant material in the boy's gut, which they couldn't identify. They also found a sand-like mineral and a substance resembling clay pellets, along with particles of gold. The scientists at Kew found a close match to the plant material – the Calabar bean, a highly toxic climbing vine from West Africa. Police issued a statement saying Adam had been poisoned 48 hours before his death with the Calabar bean, which would have left him paralysed but conscious while his throat was cut.

Wade Davis, author of *The Serpent & the Rainbow*, which argues that an extract from the puffer fish was the poison used by Voodoo sorcerers in Haiti to create zombies (although some experts are highly sceptical of his findings), told the National Geographic Channel that the Calabar bean is 'a very toxic plant, because the poison acts in such a way as to bring on total paralysis and an insanely painful death'. Dr Richard Hoskins – the expert on African religion and adviser to Scotland Yard – added that the Calabar bean, along with the other ingredients found in

Adam's gut, all pointed to Nigeria, and that witchdoctors in the region were known to use such ingredients in magick. 'The [beans are] ground down and then burnt in a pot. Taken together this is the final clinching point that proves as near as certain that this was a sacrifice,' he said.

According to Nigerian folklore, the Calabar bean is believed to possess the power to reveal and destroy witches. If the bean is given to an accused person to eat and they vomit within half an hour, they are considered innocent; but if they die, they are guilty. However, the Calabar plant isn't all bad news. Nowadays, an extract of the Calabar plant, called Physostigmine, is used in the treatment of glaucoma and to enhance memory in patients with Alzheimer's disease.

It's undoubted that Adam died a terrible death. If it really was a ritual sacrifice, the question is why was it done – and what did the killers gain from doing it? Before I had a chance to look into finding answers to these questions I got a call from an old friend of mine, Dr Crazywolf,[25] an indigenous shaman from Canada. It was early January 2006, and he wanted to fly over on a visit – which put me in a quandary. I really wanted him to come, but I was on a fevered deadline for this book and couldn't see how I could find the time to show him around or even talk to him. But then it occurred to me that we could mix pleasure with the business in hand. The truth was I couldn't think of a better qualified person to talk to about the reasons why Adam might have been sacrificed. So I said, 'Yeah, come on over, fix up a flight, and I'll pick you up at the airport.' Within a couple of weeks Crazywolf was holed up with me here in Norwich.

I'd originally got to know Crazywolf back in 2000. He'd read my 'Doktor Snake' book on Voodoo and magick, and had enjoyed it, which is what prompted him to track me down on the Internet and send me an e-mail. We hit it off right away and have been in touch ever since. But this was our first meeting in person, one which we both agreed was way overdue.

On his mother's side, Crazywolf's roots are in the Ojibwa tribe, which has some 50,000 members living on reservations in Ontario, Manitoba and Saskatchewan in Canada. In the US there are around 30,000 Ojibwa living on reservations in Michigan, Montana, North Dakota and Wisconsin. Although I referred to him above as a shaman, Crazywolf dismisses the term as a myth dreamed up by anthropologists. 'It's more accurate to call me a spirit doctor,' he told me as we walked alongside the River Wensum, which winds around the city of Norwich, not far from the historic cathedral. 'People on the reservations still go to the spirit doctor to help them solve problems in their lives. I use what's called a spirit pot, or "pot de tête" [this reveals a Voodoo influence in his magick]. In it I put chicken bones, feathers and herbs and burn them. From the smoke I can divine the way the whirlings of fate are impacting a person. I can then travel into the spirit world and try to influence the glimmering strands of destiny in their favour.'

Crazywolf is a muscular guy of 40, who stands well over six foot tall and has a long mane of black hair that falls in swathes over his shoulders. Strangely his steel blue eyes change colour to green or hazel, mirroring his moods. He drives a black 1997 Cadillac STS Deville around his home town and on the reservation where many of his family members live. He makes a good living doing magickal and fortune telling work, both for tribal people and for everyday Canadians looking to inject a slice of authentic spirituality into their lives. Over the last five years or so, since going on the Internet, he has picked up clients from around the world, some of whom he visits in person, all expenses paid. As we walked along the winding river, he told me how the Ojibwa are one of the most superstitious of all the tribes in North America. 'They take things like omens very seriously,' he said. 'And that's why they come to me for divination ceremonies, they want to know what their dreams mean and what the significance is of the various signs they see, like a crow landing in their path, that kind of thing.'

Over a coffee in the cathedral café, I ran him through the Adam case. The various blood-curdling details I related got us some odd looks. But I couldn't worry about that. I was trying to get a final take on why it was Adam had to die, presuming he really had met his end at the hands of deviant magickians. When I'd related the whole story, Crazywolf said he was sure it was a witchcraft murder. 'As you know, I have some experience of African and Voodoo sorcery and I would say it is undoubted that the boy was killed as part of a rite,' he said. 'It could have been criminals soliciting the spirits to protect their evil endeavours from the eyes of the law – maybe a big drug deal was going down. Or it might have been about people trafficking – you said that played a role in the case. Either that or they could have sacrificed Adam to make him a spirit slave in the shadow world. These things happen. Not often. But they're always done by sorcerers of the dark path. Unimaginably evil people who will stop at nothing to further their own ends.'

He then looked me in the eyes with a sudden, fierce stare: 'Has this boy had his soul set free?'

'Er . . . No, not that I know of – what do you mean?'

'Well, you said the police held a service for the boy. But that was a Christian service. It didn't fit with the boy's native spirituality. He probably wouldn't have been a Christian, not if he came from West Africa,' Crazywolf said.

He had a point – one that hadn't occurred to me. But thinking about it, the police held their service at St Paul's, which would have been very heartfelt but probably didn't fit with what Adam would have known. If Adam came from Benin, for example, which was one of the areas suggested by police forensics, Voodoo has been an official religion there since 1996, and more than 60 per cent of its people are said to believe in it. So Adam could well have been among them.

Crazywolf went on to say that a ceremony needed to be done that would free the boy's soul from captivity – and that ceremony had to fit in with the boy's religion. 'A Christian service is all well and good, but it wouldn't do anything to pull the boy's soul out of the clutches of the black magickians,' he said. 'It's down to us, Jimmy Lee. We're going to have to do a ritual to get that boy out of limbo and send him to the otherworld, where he can be at peace.'

Although I had some scepticism about Crazywolf's analysis of what had happened to Adam, I wasn't going to shoot down his idea. He believed in the literal reality of spirits and the spirit world, as do millions of others around the world. Who was I to argue with such a body of opinion? And besides, the idea was wild and I *never* turn down a chance to hit the ethereal highway and crank up the action.

Crazywolf felt that the most appropriate place to do the ritual would be in London, ideally near the spot where Adam's torso had been found. I wasn't too sure. For one thing it was a very public place and likely to draw unwelcome attention. Not just from passers-by, but possibly from the cops too – particularly as I was planning on flying a Confederate flag on a stake while wielding a World War I bayonet. This, I should add, was not insanity on my part. Both items had been given to me years ago by a leading member of a Hell's Angels chapter (also a follower of Aleister Crowley's philosophies), whom I'd got to know quite well, and were the closest things I had to 'sacred items', which Crazywolf insisted I would need if I were to play a useful part in the ritual he had planned. In the end, though, I managed to persuade him that we should do the ritual in a quiet part of Hampstead Heath, having first unobtrusively visited the area along the Thames where Adam's body had turned up.

Thankfully he was happy with that. So, having first collected the ritual items he needed, such as candles, herbs, chicken bones and a large pot, we set off for London on the 1 p.m. train. We got into Liverpool Street just under two hours later. I grabbed a couple of bottles of rum and a pack of King Edward cigars in an off-licence and we took a tube to London Bridge and walked along the Thames, roughly following the direction Adam's body floated in after it was spotted from Tower Bridge. We stopped now and then for Crazywolf to go into quiet reflection, or 'spirit trance', as he called it. He muttered and nodded, as he stared down at the choppy waters of the Thames, then said: 'Adam, the dear child, was used in a drug deal or slavery ring. The heinous few who did the deed, I shall cast symbolic revenge upon – for nothing is as precious as a child's life. No gods, however ancient or dark, want something so sacred. For as the gods embody and envy life, so too do they value it. A ritual animal sacrifice is understandable, but what these evil ones did went far beyond that and those who cast off Adam's life were drug-running heathens who followed Voodoo in an extremist way. They were not experienced fetish-wearing doctors. And they know well they crossed the line so far that there is no mercy for them!'

By the time we reached the Globe Theatre, Crazywolf had come out of his trance-like state, and we decided it was time to head up to Hampstead Heath to perform our ritual. So we crossed Blackfriars Bridge and picked up a

Northern Line tube from Embankment to Archway. We then walked the backstreets past Highgate Cemetery to Hampstead Heath. Crazywolf loved it all, especially the historic buildings that make up much of Hampstead and Highgate – 'Oh, it's *soooo* British . . .' he said in wonder. And although I'd previously lived in London for many years, I felt just the same. As Dr Johnson said: 'When a man is tired of London, he is tired of life'. He was right.

Crazywolf and I walked all the way across Parliament Hill, past the sports ground, until we reached the west side of the Heath, which is generally less populated. It was now around 4.45 p.m. and getting dusk. Despite it being a freezing January day, neither of us was cold, having been warmed up by the long walk. We eventually found a secluded area, shrouded by trees and undergrowth. Crazywolf then took the various ritual items he needed out of his rucksack and took the large pot out of the sports bag he was carrying. He placed herbs and twigs in each of the four quarters – north, south, east and west – of the ceremonial area, and placed the pot in the centre. In the meantime, I found a stick, sharpened one end with my Swiss army knife (the new one I bought after Scotland Yard confiscated my last one) and thrust it into the ground. I then flew the Confederate flag on it. Not exactly a conventional sacred item, but Crazywolf seemed happy. I then stood there holding my World War I bayonet, while Crazywolf filled his makeshift spirit pot with herbs, powders and chicken bones, all the time intoning incantations and petitions to the spirits. Finally, he pulled a petrol lighter out of his pocket and set alight the concoction. Soon wafts of heady smoke filled the area. Within seconds I was feeling light-headed and felt myself sinking into a visionary state. Crazywolf assured me there weren't any drugs in the pot, not illegal ones anyway, but admitted that some of the herbs he'd included were used by spirit doctors to induce trance states and were about five times more powerful than street cannabis. I decided a few swigs of rum would help me keep a clear head, so I pulled out one of the bottles and gulped back a sizeable medicinal dose. Crazywolf looked round: 'Go easy on the booze, man,' he said, 'that's meant to be your offering to the spirits when we're done.'

'These invisible guys like their drink, then?'

Crazywolf smiled: 'It's all about showing respect to them, offering a gift, a libation of alcohol goes down real well with them. But one bottle will do them – you can get down to sinking the other one, so long as you save some for me.'

With that, Crazywolf started chanting to the spirits of his tribe. 'I call to you spirits!' he cried. 'Come to me, Bearwalker, medicine man of the Midewiwin.'[26] Eventually he slid into a trance, muttering, grunting and shaking. From what he'd told me I knew that some of his tribal spirits were animal and some were human-like. I also knew that Crazywolf's 'power animal', or familiar spirit, was a wolf, and that this wolf was to lead Crazywolf to Adam, who was apparently trapped in some kind of limbo – the spirit slave of evil witchdoctors. Crazywolf would negotiate with whatever entities were guarding Adam. If they refused to go along with his requests, Crazywolf planned on pulling Adam out by force. If it meant a 'spiritual war', he was ready for it, he'd told me earlier.

Around twenty minutes after the ceremony had begun, it looked like war had broken out. Crazywolf let out three fiercesome howls, and danced frenziedly around the ritual area, screaming and shouting. I hoped to Christ it wouldn't attract the cops. I really didn't fancy spending a night in the cells trying to explain what we were doing on Hampstead Heath – somehow I didn't think doing a seance to free a murdered boy's soul would prove acceptable. But, then, Crazywolf threw himself on the ground and shouted, 'Smash the pot, Jimmy Lee! Smash the fucker to pieces!'

I raised my bayonet high in the air and brought it down on the pot, trashing it completely. Sparks flew and burning embers shot everywhere. I quickly stamped them out, then went over to Crazywolf, who was still lying on the ground. 'You okay, old chap?' I asked, offering him a swig of rum, which seemed to revive him. He pulled himself up and said: 'The job is done. The boy's soul is free. I had to wrestle him away from some very bad, ugly and brutish entities, created by the evil magickians. But he can now rest in peace. Our work is done.' With that we poured libations of rum as gifts to Crazywolf's spirits and left most of the pack of King Edward cigars for them too. Crazywolf said they love a cigar. 'Can't blame them,' I said, lighting one up for myself, while Crazywolf gulped back some seriously medicinal quantities of rum.

We then tidied up the ceremonial area as best we could before walking back to Archway, where we caught the tube to Liverpool Street. We jumped on the train for Norwich, and got in around midnight.

It had been a wild and unpredictable adventure. To this day I'm not sure what to make of it. Because I don't take anything literally and uphold the notion, 'Nothing is true, everything is permitted', reputedly coined by Islamic assassin and mystic Hassan i Sabbah (circa 1034–1124), I don't necessarily accept that spirits and other invisible entities have an existence beyond the vast depths of our unconscious minds (by that token, of course, I might be quite wrong). That said, I couldn't help but feel that some level of 'healing' had gone on. Maybe it had. Who knows? One thing was for sure, I was glad I'd been involved with the ceremony; it kind of reminded me of some of the things Voodoo man Earl Marlowe did. The world is a better place for such people. They don't worry about fitting into the staid rules of behaviour and convention. And nor do I.

# Fear and Dread in Blighty

> 'The British nation is unique in this respect.
> They are the only people who like to be told
> how bad things are, who like to be told the
> worst.'
> Winston Churchill 1874–1965: speech in the
> House of Commons, 10 June 1941.

Since the Adam case hit the headlines police and various experts in witchcraft-related violence have expressed fears that we could see more sacrificial killings on these shores – that Adam's murder could be just the beginning. Three months after Adam's body was found, for example, Scotland Yard's Andy Baker said in a statement: 'There is some suggestion of [African witchcraft] ceremonies taking place in the UK and strong rumours that body parts are used. They could be brought in or taken from murdered bodies. Our fear is that it is the first of many . . . the rumours are it is opening up.' He went on to say that with the movement of people around the world, the spread of African witchcraft practices is bound to come to Britain because we have a high African population.

It is certainly true that traditional African healers, or witchdoctors, both good and bad, can now be found in many of Britain's major cities – from London to Birmingham and Manchester to Glasgow. It isn't just the credulous or gullible who consult them either. As Dr Richard Hoskins points out, traditional healers, known as 'sangomas', are consulted by people from all walks of life. 'For hundreds of years, sub-Saharan Africans have turned to traditional healers to cure their ailments,' he says. 'Even here in the UK you will find that well-educated, professional people will go to such men to solve problems or cure diseases.' In London alone, hundreds of witchdoctors ply their trade across the city – from Brixton and Peckham to Whitechapel, Stoke Newington and Barking. They advertise on flyers or in the classifieds of *New Nation* and the *Voice* newspapers. The only downside is that some are less than ethical.

The London *Evening Standard* newspaper visited three natural healers while doing a special report on muti in Britain. One healer in Wood Green claimed to be able to cure cancer. Another, calling himself a 'professor', in Dalston, demanded £550 for a cure for impotence. Another, who described himself as a 'sheikh', in east London, confirmed he could put a curse on a business partner who the reporters said had ripped them off. The *Evening Standard*'s inquiries were hampered because the Africans they interviewed were too afraid to talk openly. According to Hoskins, fear of sorcery runs deep in the psyche of many Africans, and this could explain their reticence. 'There is an extreme fear and a belief in black magick through every stratum of African society. And rather than diminishing, I would say it is increasing in Britain,' he was quoted as saying. At the same time, Hoskins went on to stress that the knowledge traditional healers have gained over the centuries should not be dismissed. 'They have identified which plants are good for which diseases and Western medicine is now learning much from them,' he said. '[But] the problems arise with the use of human body parts to cure ailments. I interviewed a muti [medicine] man in his home in Durban, South Africa. It was pretty scary. We were surrounded by jars full of human body parts. A good muti man will have a contact in the local mortuary. But in many cases, people are killed for their body parts.'

Hoskins expressed concern that social factors could lead to the practice becoming more common in Britain.

'The problem in London [and other major cities in the UK] is that communities are dislocated. In small communities in Africa, a delinquent muti man could not get away with wrongdoing. Here, bad elements can slip in and out of areas anonymously, making unfounded claims and peddling spurious cures to desperate and gullible people. We know [muti practitioners] are carrying out animal sacrifices, mostly chickens, rabbits and goats. My concern is that without the usual community checks and balances, it isn't a huge step for them to begin seeking human body parts.'

Dr Yunes Teinaz, health adviser to the director general of the Islamic Cultural Centre and the London Central Mosque, said he has increasingly heard reports of attempts by unscrupulous practitioners to acquire human parts. Sections of the Christian and Muslim communities in Africa practise Voodoo in contravention of their religions. In Britain, the Muslim community is particularly active in trying to stamp it out. Dr Teinaz, who is also an environmental health officer, added: 'There is a concern that human body parts are being used. We know that much of the bush meat trade (wild game imported from Africa) is used in potions and ointments for black magick treatments and we know that other animals are sacrificed for Voodoo purposes in the African community. But we have deep concern over human body parts. We think they could be coming in with the bush meat.'

With the growing numbers of African witchdoctors operating in the UK it looks more and more feasible that Adam was a victim of human sacrifice – certainly on the surface. Indeed, as police have argued, it stands to reason that practitioners of the dark side of African witchcraft would have come into the country alongside the good ones, and could well be practising the macabre arts of ritual killing. As mentioned earlier, Scotland Yard detectives suspect that Adam was not the first Juju slaying in Britain. They believe a murder committed in 1969 – in which a black baby girl was found hidden in the bushes in Epping Forest, Essex – may have been a sacrifice. The girl's torso was discovered by a party of school children out walking near Connaught Water, a beauty spot on the edge of the forest. The head was later found close by. The girl's body was thought to have been in the forest for around two weeks. The girl's father – believed to be from northwest Africa – was the main suspect, but he fled the country before he could be arrested for what was dubbed the 'babe in the wood' slaying. Detectives thought he cut off his daughter's head, legs and arms during a ritual to bring him good luck.

On this evidence, you could certainly be forgiven for wondering if the Adam and the 'babe in the wood' killings were not the only ritual murders in this country; it could be that bodies have not been unearthed or that some murders have not been recognised as ritual sacrifices. That's certainly been implied by some press reports. But the Subculture Alternatives Freedom Foundation would dispute there is any solid evidence to support this – or even that Adam was killed in a ritual sacrifice.

Another sceptical voice about the conclusions the police came to on the Adam case, and other so-called ritualistic crimes, comes from my friend Ian Henshall, author of *9.11 Revealed*,[27] a controversial exposé of the events surrounding the terrorist attacks on the World Trade Center. I spoke to Ian to get his take on why it was police seemed to seize on one hypothesis (that of ritual sacrifice) to the exclusion of all other possibilities. 'We found looking at the 9/11 issue that the facts are dependent on investigators' pre-existing belief systems,' he said. 'Clearly some murders are particularly horrific, so if you happen to be of a religious disposition you might start to feel that there has to be some underlying motive for the crimes, something dark and Satanic even. This might not be a reasonable assumption. But the fact is, reason is a secondary thing to the human animal. We are primarily ruled by emotions and self-interest, and it's very hard to transcend that.' He went on to explain that, in the Adam case, police publicly put forward a hypothesis which meant there was immediately a strong incentive to keep control of the evidence – otherwise that hypothesis could be disputed, making it look as if the police had got it wrong. 'Arguably,' he concluded, 'there might have been a strong institutional bias against anybody threatening that hypothesis too, which may explain why there were no sceptical reports in the press. I'm not saying there was a conspiracy. On the contrary, I'd say the flushing out of contradictory evidence is an unconscious process, at least in the majority of investigators.'

While this may be a fair point when it comes to some investigations, having met the detectives on the Adam case, I feel that they had a hell of a difficult job and did their level best to be as open-minded as possible. But whatever the eventual outcome of the case, one thing should never be forgotten: DI O'Reilly has given his all to solving the case and bringing the killers of Adam to book. It is his personal mission and one day, due to his sheer determination, he will win out against the odds and the Adam case will finally be closed.

When I got to the end of my investigation into the Adam case I felt none the wiser as to the truth of it all. Many more questions had been thrown up than answers. But maybe that was a good thing. After all, as a journalist I believe it was my duty to unearth every possible angle to the Adam case to encourage debate and other investigations. A piece of the puzzle had been missing throughout the media coverage of the case, and that was the side that questioned whether the police were on the right track in thinking Adam had been the victim of a sacrificial rite.

Only time will tell whether Adam met his end through a dark rite or conventional murder. But if it was sacrifice, it brought home to me that practical or 'causal' magick – that is, the art of attempting to manipulate your lot through spells or petitioning the gods for favours – has the potential to take a shockingly dark turn, depending on your culture and the belief system you follow. But this realisation did not shake my view that magick, at its highest level, is a system of self-development and mind expansion that has led to many great works of art and literature (and even breakthroughs in science). The Irish poet W.B. Yeats (1865–1939), for instance, was at one time a member of the Golden Dawn, an influential magickal society that operated from the late nineteenth to the early twentieth century and had many illustrious members including fantasy author Arthur Machen and occultist, writer and mountaineer Aleister Crowley.

But in the end, the only thing that matters is that a young boy is dead. He died in macabre and agonising circumstances and, if nothing else, this first chapter of *Blood Rites* should serve as a tribute to him. My friend Dr Crazywolf, who did the ritual to 'free the boy's soul', is firmly convinced that Adam is now a 'free spirit, roaming the cosmos'. Before he went home to Canada, Crazywolf and I raised a glass to the boy, with the toast: 'In the evening when the white dust falls, may Adam's soul join the glimmersparks shining in the heavens . . .' What else could we do? It was the only way to exorcise the fear, dread and horror that surrounded the boy's last days on earth.

I'll be posting any updates that might arise on the Adam case on my website. Visit: www.jimmyleeshreeve.com.

# Chapter 2: Hearts of Darkness

Blood on the Tracks in Eire ... Fake Sacrifice ...
Mugged for Body Parts ... Land of Magick and
Sorcery ... Fidelity Charm ... Flying Wizards and
Shapeshifters ... The Political Beast ... Money
Magick in Theory and Practice ... Killer Children?
... Early Reports of Ritual Killing ... Leopard Men
... Berserkers ... Cannibal Soldiers ... Heart Full
of Soul? ... Why Sacrifice?

'Those who have crossed with direct eyes, to death's
other kingdom remember us – if at all – not as lost
violent souls, but only as the hollow men, the stuffed
men.'

T.S. Eliot (1888–1965)
*The Hollow Men* 1925.

I'd been monitoring the newswires for stories of ritual
sacrifice from around the world since 2000, so I was well
aware that the Adam case was not exceptional. Similar deadly
scenarios had cropped up everywhere from India and
Malaysia to Trinidad and South America. In sub-Saharan

Africa the practice appeared to be rife. In Nigeria, rogue sorcerers were sacrificing people – sometimes even newborn babies – in the hope of getting rich quick. And in South Africa, children had been literally mugged for body parts, which were sold for use in macabre potions and talismans.

Due to my long-time interest in magick and shamanism I knew that ritual sacrifice has a long history in Africa (as it does here and in most other parts of the world). A few hundred years ago it was officially sanctioned as part of tribal life. Now it is underground and is mainly practised by small pockets of disreputable shamans who have little regard for the sanctity of human life. But I still found it hard to fathom why the practice is still around today. Is it because of the political disarray, famine and general oppression that is so common in many parts of Africa? Is the practice so rooted in traditional African culture and belief that some find it difficult to stop? Or is there some other reason?

Before I could begin to explore these questions my attention was briefly diverted back to Europe . . .

## Blood on the Tracks in Eire

In an unexpected twist, nearly four years after Adam's torso was discovered, the ritual killing deal moved across to rural Southern Ireland. The first I heard about it was when I got a call from a friend of mine, Sam Johnson, a blues singer and guitarist who went to live over there about six years ago, after getting a small legacy. He and his wife and two children moved out of an inner-city area of London in search of a better life in rural Ireland. They got it and are very happy. But when he called me, he was frantic: 'We moved out here to escape the madness of inner-city life. But, fuck, man, we've got blood sacrifice on our doorsteps now. It's unbelievable. The news is saying the daughter of Malawi's justice minister has been stiffed in some sort of ritual. Thought I'd better let you know right away – as it's your territory . . .'

I put the phone down. More blood. More craziness. I fired up the online news engines to check out the story. Sam had been right. The dismembered body of Paiche Onyemaechi (age 25) – the daughter of the Malawi chief justice minister – had been discovered on 23 July 2004. Two sisters out walking had seen her remains poking out of undergrowth. Her head had been cut off and, according to some reports, there were strange marks on her body. Her remains had been left in a bin bag beside a stream in Piltown, a small picturesque village in County Kilkenny. The Irish police, the Garda, had suspicions that her murder might have been a ritual killing, and consulted the team at Scotland Yard investigating the Adam murder. They believed there were similarities between the two cases. Like Adam, Paiche had been decapitated, and her body found close to water. Also there were ties to Nigeria – Paiche's husband, Chika Onyemaechi (age 31), was originally from the country. The link sounded tenuous to me; but the press wires were making the most of the connection with headlines like: 'Irish fear Voodoo ritual in woman's death'.

Paiche came to Europe in the late 1990s and studied business administration in London, which was where she met Chika. The two left the capital in 2001 and made their home in Waterford, Southern Ireland, where they felt settled enough to start a family. Paiche worked as a lap dancer in nightclubs in Limerick and Dublin, which led police to look at a possible prostitution link to her death – they wondered if she had been murdered by her pimp, a man close to her who had forced her on to the game. Chika reported Paiche missing on 8 July. But he then went missing himself after her body was discovered. He left their two sons, Andrew (age 3) and Anthony (18 months), with a neighbour and hasn't been seen since. Maybe he was killed or maybe he had something to do with his wife's death? The cops ran forensic checks on the couple's house in Waterford City's upmarket St Herbalain Park district, and analysed their blue Fiat car for traces of blood, hair or fibres. Chika has not been named as a suspect.

While Chika didn't make Paiche's funeral, her family from Malawi did fly over to attend the service at St Patrick's United Methodist Church in Piltown. Her brother Leon said: 'We last spoke to Paiche in June and she was full of life and joyful. Everyone is deeply, deeply saddened about the news of our lovely sister. Her boys are doing fine but are asking where their Mam is.' He added that he was baffled as to why anyone would want to kill a woman described as highly popular with her neighbours. After the service, Leon, his sister Lucy and their father, Leonard Unyolo, chief justice minister of Malawi, returned to Africa – taking Paiche and Chika's two boys with them.

Before he left, however, Unyolo had a 30-minute meeting with his counterpart, Irish justice minister Michael McDowell, who pledged his country's commitment to bringing Paiche's killer to account. Superintendent Michael Devine, leading the investigation, added that: 'No stone will be left unturned in the hunt for the killer.'

Devine later confirmed that Paiche's head had still not been found, despite police searches of large areas of land around Piltown. But detectives believe she was most likely murdered in or near her home in Waterford. Curiously, local people reported a strange smell coming from waste ground near where she lived. Perhaps it was Paiche's decomposing head or even another corpse? Or perhaps locals were getting over-imaginative, what with the ritual murder speculations? What is certain is Devine rubbished reports in tabloid newspaper, *Ireland on Sunday*, which claimed cattle had been ritually killed close to where Paiche Onyemaechi's body was found. 'Nothing like this has been reported to our investigation team. I'd be surprised if anyone believed what they read in that newspaper. It's news to me,' he said.

## Fake Sacrifice

Just as the story started to die down, another gruesome killing occurred, this time in Dublin. The remains of Farah Swaleh Noor (age 38), who hailed from Somalia, but had lived in Ireland for nine years, were found in the Royal Canal, near Croke Park, on 30 March 2005. He had been stabbed repeatedly in the chest, before being chopped up with an axe, and decapitated. After the frenzied attack, flesh-eating acid had been poured over his body. It is believed Noor had been dead for more than a week before his extremely decomposed torso was discovered, wrapped in a black bin bag, by a man out walking his dog. Noor's arms and legs were found nearby but his head has still not been recovered. Detective Inspector Christy Mangan – who crops up regularly on Irish news broadcasts – said Noor's family in Mogadishu were anxious to have all his remains. 'They are very traumatised by what has happened and [by] the fact he was dismembered and killed in a violent way,' he said. It was also revealed that Noor was a serial womaniser; he'd had at least two children with different women in Ireland and was conducting relationships with countless others when he died.

Because of the similarities to the killing of Paiche Onyemaechi, the tabloids had a field day, with headlines screaming: 'Voodoo killer stalks Ireland'. It wasn't just hype, though. Acting on information from ritual killing experts in Nigeria, the Irish cops were investigating the possibility that the victim had been sacrificed in a money-making ritual. A senior police source told the *Daily Mirror* on 3 April that: 'The whole area of ritual killing is something that we've had to familiarise ourselves with in the past number of years. Generally, ritual killing is common practice in Nigeria. And every year hundreds of Nigerians lose their lives to ritual murderers, also known as head-hunters. These headhunters go in search of human parts – heads, breasts, tongues and sexual organs – often at the behest of witchdoctors and traditional medicine men who require them for sacrifices or for the preparation of assorted magickal potions.' The previous day, the Irish Refugee Council confirmed to *The Daily Mirror* that many Nigerians seeking asylum in Ireland cite the threat of ritual killing as their reason for fleeing the country.

But by summer Irish detectives had ruled out ritual sacrifice as a motive and had come to believe the murder was the result of a domestic dispute. They did, however, suspect that Noor's head had been removed to *suggest* he had met his end in a ritual slaying – one reminiscent of what may have happened to Paiche Onyemaechi. Later in the year two individuals were pulled in and accused of killing Noor. Neither had anything to say. And, at the time of writing, neither has yet come to trial.

Red herrings, like this, may become more common as murderers attempt to foist blame on ethnic communities, particularly Nigerians, who are currently associated in the popular mind with ritualistic killing. But is this association with human sacrifice justified? According to Leo Igwe, of the Nigerian Humanist Movement, the practice is all too common in his country. He told reporters: 'Recently there have been several reported cases of individuals who have been kidnapped, killed or had their bodies mutilated by rituals in Nigeria. In December [2004] in the Ibadan province, police arrested a taxi driver who used his 14-month-old baby for rituals. He killed his child in order to secure a human head, which was one of the materials listed for him by a local witchdoctor for a moneymaking ritual.' Igwe added that, while it is difficult for Europeans to understand this kind of behaviour, such rituals have a long history in West African culture.

By saying this, however, Igwe does his people a disservice. He probably doesn't mean to, but he makes them sound uncivilised – as if they were 'savages'. But as I mentioned earlier, sacrifice – both of the human and animal variety – also has a long history here in Britain. For the ancient Celts, who believed their gods manifested in streams, wells, mountains, rivers and forests, the practice formed the cornerstone of their spirituality. So central was it that one of the ways disobedient or rebellious tribes were punished was by barring them from attending religious ceremonies, all of which would have included sacrificial rites. Ceremonies were presided over by the Druids, an elite caste who held enormous power in Celtic society and acted as lawyers, judges, doctors and advisers to Celtic kings – as well as being religious leaders and prophets. Sacrifices were conducted in sacred oak groves, which were believed to possess terrifying and all-pervading supernatural power – making even the Celts themselves wary of venturing into such places. In his *Pharsalia*, the Roman poet Lucan described a Celtic sacred grove in southern France:

A grove there was untouched by men's hands from ancient times, whose interlacing boughs enclosed a space of darkness and cold shade, and banished the sunlight from above . . . Gods were worshipped there with savage rites, the altars were heaped with hideous offerings and every tree was sprinkled with human gore . . . The people never resorted thither to worship at close quarters, but left the place to the gods for, when the sun is in mid-heaven or dark night fills the sky, the priest himself dreads their approach and fears to surprise the lord of the grove.

Along with sacrificing animals, such as sheep, goats and bulls – and presuming the ancient Greek and Roman accounts were not merely propaganda designed to discredit the northern 'barbarians' – the altars of the Celts regularly ran crimson with the blood of humans. Writing in the first century BC, in his *Histories*, Greek historian, geographer and philosopher Strabo described how humans were killed for divination:

They devote to death a human being and stab him with a dagger in the region of the diaphragm and when he has fallen, they foretell the future from his fall and from the convulsions of his limbs and moreover, from the spurting of the blood, placing their trust in some ancient and long continued observation of these practices.

Strabo also described other methods used by the Celts to dispatch victims to the great beyond – along with how they would incinerate people and animals in a huge wicker man:

They used to strike a human being . . . in the back with a sword . . . They would shoot victims to death with arrows or impale them in the temples or having devised a colossus of straw and wood, thrown into the colossus cattle and wild animals of all sorts and humans, and then make a burnt offering of the whole thing.

If, like me, you enjoy exploring ancient sites or so-called 'places of power', you'll find many have sacrificial connections. However 'spiritual' and peaceful they may seem on the surface, a lot of stone circles, man-made mounds and other 'geo-spiritual' structures ran with blood, as ritual killing was a central aspect of religious devotion in ancient times. Archaeological excavations at the Celtic hill fort at Danebury in Hampshire, for example, uncovered the wholesale burial of human and animal sacrifices in the pits where grain was stored. Once empty, these pits were filled with corpses and body parts, along with heads (a key aspect of Celtic worship and magickal practice). Also interred were sheep, cattle, pigs, horses, dogs and ravens, along with various parts of animals. Besides the bloody remains were tools, bridles, saddles, grain and quern stones (on which grain and cereals were ground).

Several of those buried in the Danebury pits showed signs of extensive injury – almost as if excessive violence, or 'overkill', formed a necessary part of the sacrificial ritual. One man had sustained a severe blow to his right eye from a blunt instrument, seriously damaging it, or even destroying it altogether. The pelvis of another victim had been butchered with a thick sword-like blade; the pelvic girdle and femur heads were cut from the torso and legs while the flesh was still intact. Whether this occurred during the killing process or after death can't be determined. But it does go to show that we in Britain indulged in ritual killing rites similar to those that may have happened to Adam some 3,000–4,000 years later. Other bodies in the silos met equally vicious ends; some were crushed with blocks of flint or chalk, while others were stoned to death. The victims were mainly young men, but women and children have also been unearthed from the gruesome silo.

According to Barry Cunliffe, professor of European archaeology at Oxford University, the 'pit tradition' at Danebury probably lasted from 700–100 BC. He estimated that the burials took place on average once every six years or so, making the practice an exceptional rite rather than a common procedure. In *The Ancient Celts* (1997) Cunliffe says that the contents of the Danebury pits are generally interpreted in two ways: (1) as thanks offerings to the underground spirits or guardians for preserving the grain stored in the silos; or (2) as appeasements to the gods to better ensure a good harvest.

Less is known of the practices of the Irish Celts, but a twelfth-century source states that the ancient Irish used to offer firstborn children to their great stone idol, Mag Slocht. According to legend, Ireland was first peopled by the Formorians, a greedy group of gods who made their worshippers give up two-thirds of the children born each year for sacrifice at the fair of Taillte.

Even the Christians seemed partial to the occasional blood sacrifice. One Irish saint was buried alive as a foundation sacrifice. The legend forms part of the story of the founding of the monastery of Iona. Saint Columba said to his monks: 'It is good for us that our roots should go under the earth here; it is permitted that one of you should go under the clay of this island to hallow it.' A monk called Oran volunteered for the assignment, and the church was built over him. The reward? He would go straight to heaven (or, at least, that's what Saint Columba told him would happen).

The Norse, Saxon and other Northern European peoples, whose blood runs through most people of English descent, were also partial to ritual killing (you can't help but wonder who wasn't into it). Nine was the Norse gods' sacred number and every nine years a spring festival was held in Uppsala in Sweden in honour of the god Frey. Nine human victims, along with nine horses and nine dogs, were hanged as part of the celebrations. At a similar ceremony, held in winter in Denmark, nine humans and an equal number of horses, dogs and cocks were sacrificed. Legend has it that when King Auun of Uppsala was growing old, he sacrificed nine of his sons to Odin (chief of the Norse gods) in order to prolong his life. After Auun had offered up his seventh son, he lived on but became senile, and after killing his eighth son he spent a further nine years lying in his bed. On sacrificing his ninth son, he pushed on yet another nine years, but had to drink out of a horn, like a baby at a bottle. At that point he wanted to kill his last remaining child, but the Swedish people wouldn't let him do it (they probably realised what a drooling psychopath he was) – and so he finally died.

Both the Norsemen and the Germanic tribes regularly sacrificed war prisoners to their gods – Roman captives, for example, were hanged on trees. The object of such rites was more to give strength than to exact vengeance. The German epic, the *Niebelungenlied*, tells how, in 437 AD, the Burgundians drank the blood of their fallen foes after their victory against the Huns, in order to take on, or consume, their valour. The Germanic tribes also used the widespread custom of foundation sacrifice and would regularly enclose a living person within the masonry of a new building. Children's bodies were inserted in coastal dykes in the belief that this would preserve a settlement from the waves. An account from the city of Odenburg, which may be exaggerated, states that children were still sacrificed for this purpose up until the seventeenth century. When setting out on overseas raids, the Vikings frequently sacrificed humans to the sea god. More offerings were made if bad weather delayed the departure of an expedition. If victims were in short supply, a member of the crew was chosen by casting lots. The Vikings also tied victims to the rollers over which a new ship slipped into the sea – reddening its keel with human blood.

This is our heritage. It might be one we would rather forget. But it happened all the same. In the interests of fairness, I thought it should be pointed out before we move on to look at human sacrifice in Africa, where, as we have seen, many allege it is commonplace even today. Sometimes people, usually children, are killed during rituals; at other times they are killed to harvest body parts – as the next story reveals.

## Mugged for Body Parts

On 30 July 2004, 10-year-old Sello Chokoe stood on a lonely hill overlooking the vast grass and shrub veld. His village, Moletjie, in South Africa's northern Limpopo province, lay a couple of miles away. He lived there with his mother and two siblings. A neighbour he knew vaguely had asked him to come up to this desolate spot to look for his donkeys. Sello sighed. The donkeys were nowhere to be seen. The place was deserted. But he was sure he'd come to the right spot. Then he heard something – a movement behind some rocks. Maybe it was the donkeys? The next thing he knew, three men sprang out at him. One of them smashed him hard over the head. As Sello staggered to the ground he felt blood trickle down his face. The men dragged him to the rocks and wedged him between the two biggest ones. They sprinkled herbs and liquids over Sello, and began a macabre ceremony, involving the calling up of ancient spirits. After the prayers and incantations were complete, one of the men pulled out a razor-sharp knife and sliced off the boy's penis, right hand and right ear. He then gouged a hole in the boy's skull to take slivers of his brain.

When his attackers fled the scene, Sello, half-conscious, shaking and bleeding, dragged himself from the rocks where he had been abandoned. A boy out collecting firewood with his mother found him and the alarm was raised. Sello was airlifted to hospital, but died of his injuries ten days later and was buried in his, now fear-wracked, village.

Disturbingly, Sello's attackers weren't vicious, hate-filled psychos. They were simply conducting business – earning extra money by harvesting body parts for the dark and murderous side of muti, the traditional medicine of South Africa. Muti murders, especially of children, are disturbingly common in South Africa. Police investigate an average of one a month. Recently six men were arrested in Free State Province for trying to sell a human head, a pair of hands and feet, a heart, genitals and intestines. Not long afterwards twenty picnickers found the head of a 5-year-old floating by a dam near Johannesburg. The list goes on.

The majority of South Africans are revolted by muti killings, and police say they diligently pursue each one. But reaction to such cases is often strangely muted. This could be because they are common and have lost their shock value, and because South Africa notches up around 22,000 murders in general each year. Some experts give another reason: they say muti killings highlight an aspect of ancient culture that modern South Africans would prefer to leave unexamined. 'It tends to get swept under the carpet,' says Anthony Minnaar, a senior researcher with the Institute of Human Rights and Criminal Justice in Johannesburg. 'It points to a belief in witchcraft and spirit worship – things people don't want to acknowledge.'

South Africa's medical system boasts modern hospitals and pharmacies, but it coexists with healers whose prescriptions can include the grisliest of curatives. Faith in them is more widespread than the nation's modern veneer suggests.

The beliefs that lead to muti killings tend to follow a similar pattern. A troubled client approaches a healer, who commissions a third person to collect body parts. Muti folklore states that a hand buried in a shop's doorway will attract customers; genitals will enhance virility and fertility; and fat from a stomach will bring a good harvest. Parts severed from live victims are said to be the most powerful because their screams awaken supernatural powers; parts from children are considered particularly potent.

The South African police say most muti killings occur in rural areas, where tribal structures and superstitions are strongest. But urban areas are not exempt. Not long ago, a man was arrested in Krugersdorp, just west of Johannesburg, after offering to sell a human head for $1,300. Around the same time a journalist, posing as a buyer at a traditional medicine market, located under a flyover in Johannesburg, was offered a human brain, an eye and kneecaps for $230.

In 1995, the South African government set out to combat muti killings by investigating witchcraft-related violence. It also proposed regulation of traditional healers and an education campaign to 'liberate people mentally'. A spokesperson from the security ministry, however, said privately that the education campaign never got going at all. Takalane Mathiba, the head of a private association that registered 80,000 traditional healers, said his group was doing all it could to help police, but it couldn't control the shady operators trading in human organs and bones. Some police officials, however, saw a sign that the tide was turning: public outrage was gradually replacing fear of shady healers' supposed powers. In a case in the Free State, for example, the arraignment of six suspected ritual killers drew 200 protesters demanding their execution.

Despite such protests, fear still reigns supreme in most districts. At Sello Chokoe's homestead, even the elders were too afraid to point any fingers directly at a neighbour, a traditional healer called Peter Kagbi, even though many villagers suspected him of Sello's murder, behind closed doors. Kagbi, in his late 60s, was the neighbour who had, reportedly, sent Sello to fetch his donkeys, without Sello's mother's permission. He was questioned for four days by police over Sello's murder before being released pending further investigations. Kagbi admitted to sending Sello to fetch the donkeys, but denied involvement in the murder. He said he saw nothing wrong in sending Sello without his mother's permission as he had sent the boy on similar errands before. Sello's family hotly disputed this.

Kagbi said he had been threatened by the community and had been told they planned to burn him alive because he was a wizard. 'Some are accusing me of killing Sello but I did not,' he insisted. 'I have not fled my home despite the threats because, if I do, the community will regard that as an admission of guilt.'

Even if Sello's killers are eventually captured and convicted, it will be little consolation for his anguished single mother Salome (age 39). 'Anything that does not bring back my son is hardly of any importance to me now. No mother wants to lose a child this way,' she says. Her distraught state would not be helped if she discovered that Sello's body parts were likely to have been sold for no more than £200 each, the price normally charged for a child's body parts in the muti industry.

Another case was featured in a BBC 2 documentary called *Nobody's Child*, which was broadcast in 2002 and covered the Adam case and muti murders in South Africa. Helen Madide, from the Thohoyandou area of South Africa, told how she was forced to kill her young child, Fulufhuwani, as part of a muti ritual. She said she was recently separated from her husband, Naledzani Mabuda, a traditional healer known as a 'sangoma' (very much like a shaman), and that while they tried to sort out their differences she had returned to her parents' village. But the child, Fulufhuwani, regularly went to stay with his father and grandmother. Around this time Helen said her husband started to tell her disturbing stories. '[He told me] his ancestors said that he must kill me and the child so that he can be rich,' she said. 'He showed me the path and forced me to go along that path. He was pushing me and demanding me to go whether I like it or not. He said he was going to kill the baby first while I see the baby, then secondly he will kill me.' Helen said she had tried to get away from Mabuda, but he had caught her and forced her to hold Fulufhuwani's legs while he cut the child's throat. 'When the child was dead, he started to cut all those pieces, the hands, the legs and even the sex organs,' she said. Mabuda then locked Helen up with the child's body. But his relatives, fearing for his wife and child, called the police. Although Mubuda was sentenced to life in prison, Helen was acquitted – but this didn't cut much ice locally, as she is now shunned.

A similar incident occurred in autumn 2003 in a squatters' camp, south of Johannesburg, where a traditional healer lived. Neighbours said they'd never seen anyone come out of his shack proclaiming 'Hallelujah! I'm cured!' But the word was, his medicine was good. Business, however, came to an abrupt halt when 3-year-old Thabang Malakoane disappeared while his mother dozed in their shack next door. When the boy's body was found in a rubbish bag under a thin layer of soil, the left hand and genitals had been cut off. The brain, heart and other vital organs were gone too. People in the large camp, made up of litter-strewn yards and chicken-wire fences, pointed the finger at the healer and a second man involved with him. They accused them of committing muti murder and harvesting the boy's body parts for potions and talismans. The police took the men into custody, but couldn't gather enough evidence to charge them. No witnesses had been forthcoming – police said people were too afraid to speak out. Gladys Mbanzi (age 34), however, who lived nearby, said: 'If they come back here, the community is going to kill them.' She added that if her two boys were ever to disappear, it would 'burn down their shacks. The community has found them guilty.'

Maybe the two men were guilty. Maybe they weren't. Either way, it looked like a witch-hunt was going down. But that is no surprise: witch-hunts are commonplace in Africa. In some parts of the country, being suspected of being a witch can prove deadly. In Bangui, in the Central African Republic, for example, hundreds of men, women and children are charged every year for practising witch-craft – a crime punishable by execution or imprisonment. The Bangui Police Department even has a specialist team that investigates sorcery-related crimes. Worryingly, their methods aren't a big improvement on those used in medieval Europe during the seventeenth century, when the guilt of witches was decided using trial by ordeal – if a person was innocent it was believed they wouldn't float when thrown into water and that they wouldn't be injured when touched with a red-hot metal bar. Lucy Jones, a writer for the *Washington Times*, reported in 2002 on how Martin Nagoagoumi, a 'witchcraft detective' with the Bangui Police Department, kept a selection of sticks for beating confessions out of suspected witches; long, thin sticks were reserved for children, while a wooden beam punched through with nails was kept for adults who refused to admit to practising sorcery.

Lucy Jones spoke to a woman called Ermine Qualigon (age 70), who had the unenviable fate of being locked up in a cell at the Bangui police station, having been accused of witchcraft. Ermine admitted burying a piece of her daughter-in-law's miscarried baby, as part of a spell intended to make the woman infertile. 'My son's wife never gave me any food,' she complained. 'When my son and her had meat, they only gave me soup.' Ermine's son, who worked as a telephone technician, described to the police how his wife became mysteriously thin, and told them his mother had 'eaten' her flesh. Such is the belief in the power of magick that no one took into consideration the effect his wife's miscarriage may have had; it might have led to depression, which could have affected her appetite, or it may simply have undermined her physically, leading to weight loss.

Thirteen-year-old Blaise Damagoa had also been locked up on suspicion of witchcraft. He told Lucy Jones how a neighbour had given him a cake, and that after he'd eaten it she'd told him it contained a human heart. The neighbour said that the cake would enable him to make people sick just by touching them. 'I changed,' he said. 'I refused to go to school. I told my brother what had happened. He beat me up, then reported me to the police.'

Shockingly, children accused of witchcraft are forced to share cells with adults, and food and medical care are not provided (prisoners rely on the help of relatives). Teenage girls, whether found guilty of witchcraft or not, usually come out of custody pregnant – having been repeatedly raped by male inmates. When a case goes to court, the odds are invariably stacked against the accused. In courts, 'truth' herbs are used to make suspects confess. And because spells often involve burying pieces of clothing, bits of fabric are dangled in front of juries as evidence.

The Bangui 'sorcery cops' are themselves a superstitious bunch, and don't take any chances when it comes to being hit with negative sorcery. They routinely get witchdoctors to 'vaccinate' them with herbal concoctions designed to give them immunity against spells. They consider this necessary because they believe the number of people who practise witchcraft is on the rise. Heads of state in the region are also firm believers in magick. Incoming leaders often abandon the palatial homes of former leaders – fearing the power of resident spirits – and have new dwellings built.

A tiny minority of sceptical voices in Bangui, however, say that jealousy and rivalry lie at the core of most witchcraft cases. People accuse those who have slighted them of being witches, whether it is true or not, because they know it is likely to land the person in prison. It's a sure-fire method of wreaking revenge.

## Land of Magick and Sorcery

'Up the airy mountain, down the rushy glen, we daren't go a-hunting, for fear of little men.'

William Allingham 1824–1889:
*The Fairies* (1850).

Many in the West say it is a lack of education that keeps Africans believing in the power of witchcraft and the supernatural. This is probably true; once they've had science and evolution drummed into them, most tribal peoples begin to doubt the efficacy of causal magick and the existence of spirits. But the assumption that we know best in the West smacks of intellectual imperialism. I'm not saying that education would not be a very good thing, particularly for the poorest people in Africa. It would enable them to make money on the world stage – use of computers and the Internet, for example, would allow people to create and sell items online (this is happening in some areas). But, maybe, the best education that could be offered to Africans who still maintain a belief in sorcery would be one in which the teachers offered their knowledge, but also, in turn, learned the ancient traditional beliefs. This would make education more of a fair exchange of ideas, rather than a one-sided bulldozing of science and logic which, after all, are only our current belief systems: with future knowledge, the scientific truisms of today might be proved wrong tomorrow. Whereas the magickal myths and stories of tribal peoples could well offer an enduring truth. Many believe they do.

To illustrate the gulf in thinking between the West and the developing world, let's look at some of the stories of sorcery that have come out of various African states in recent decades.

## Fidelity Charm

In 1998, Edzai Rushambwa, a 30-year-old woman living in Mount Darwin, northern Zimbabwe, was complaining that she had failed to successfully remarry after her first husband died four years previously. She believed she was the victim of 'Runyoka', a traditional African Juju charm common among certain ethnic groups in Zimbabwe, which is used to prevent a spouse from committing infidelity. The enchantment was supposedly placed on Rushambwa by her late husband, who had died without removing it. At her rural village home, Rushambwa recounted how powerful the charm used on her had been. After the death of her first husband, she had married three times and each time the man died soon afterwards. She said she had consulted several traditional healers, desperately hoping to be rid of the enchantment, but had had no luck. Asked what caused the deaths of the three men, Rushambwa said it was because of some sickness, but she could not be drawn to specify what sickness. 'I have sought help but have had no success. I will keep on trying,' she said.

The Mount Darwin secretary for the Zimbabwe National Traditional Healers' Association, Benson Kaseke, said that although Runyoka is not approved by traditional healers, it is widespread in the Mukumbura area of Mount Darwin, on the border of Mozambique. Runyoka is typically used by people who suspect their spouses of playing away from home, he explained. 'No one wants to live with an unfaithful partner, hence the need for Runyoka.' He went on to say Rushambwa consulted him over her problem and that it was consistent with Runyoka. He admits there are some traditional healers in Zimbabwe who specialise in such sorcery.

One of the most common methods of administering Runyoka is to secretly spike a partner's food, but there are more blatant methods. One in particular is known in the local Shona vernacular as 'Rwebanga,' or knife. A husband buys a new knife, sprinkles it with some traditional herbs, puts the open knife at the doorstep of his bedroom and then summons his wife into the room. The wife walks in and strides over the open knife and thereafter the husband asks her to pick it up and snap it shut before handing it back to him. The husband then hides the knife in a place where it is unlikely to be found by anyone else. This is supposed to prevent the wife from indulging in extramarital sex. But if she does dare to have an affair, the adulterous pair risk the humiliation of being caught in the act by the husband, as they supposedly would be unable to uncouple themselves because of the power of the magick charm. 'They can only be freed when the husband opens the knife,' says Benson Kaseke.

Married women of the Tavara tribe, in the Mukumbura area of Mount Darwin, who have been enchanted in this way do not shake hands with men they are introduced to, for fear that the medicine would affect them. If a man does shake an enchanted woman's hand, he is said to feel numb and weak and only regain his strength after the hand is withdrawn. Kaseke says in some cases daughters are given Runyoka by their parents so they cannot engage in premarital sex. To undo the enchantment, the girl is requested to take her boyfriend to her parents' home where he is given the same medicine so he is not affected by it when they have sex.

## Flying Wizards and Shapeshifters

Stories of strange events abound in Africa. And not all can be easily dismissed as being anecdotal due to the fact that there are often multiple witnesses to the events (mass hysteria could, of course, offer an explanation). Take the following story, which was reported in the Zambian press in spring 1997. Angus Ngulube died on 7 April of that year. But at around 2.00 a.m., on the night after his funeral, his widow, Joyce Mbewe, and members of her family, were woken by a howling gale and the dull thud of something hitting the thatched roof of their house in Barlastone Park, Lusaka. Whatever it was then rolled off the roof and hit the ground. As the wind died down, the family heard the voice of a man asking the 'mother of Banda' to let him in. The widow's sister plucked up the courage to answer the door and allegedly found a 'small humanoid creature whose features varied from a cat to an owl'. The creature's left foot was injured and dripped with blood. As the family watched, the creature grew and took the form of a man. He claimed to have been travelling on an aircraft and said that he had come to eat the flesh of his grandfather. The police were summoned and took him away – suspecting that he was a wizard. He said his name was Kalasa Nswiba and that he was 70 years old. He had crash-landed because relatives of the man who had died in the area (Angus Ngulube) had fortified the place with strong Juju. As good Christians, Mr Ngulube's family denied this, putting it down to the superior power of God.

The testimony of Nswiba (if that was his name) varied. He told the *Times of Zambia* that he had been 'flying' with six other people in a 'magick aircraft' across Zambia. But he told the police the aerial trip had been in the Democratic Republic of the Congo. He said he got the blood-caked wounds on his left ear and right foot from falling into a ditch. The government started an investigation to see if the man really was in his village, as he said, the day before he allegedly crashed. The Traditional Health Practitioners' Association of Zambia said the man's story could be true and called on the government to legalise witch-hunting. Police spokesman Beenwell Chimfwembe, a fair-minded chief superintendent who has served on three United Nations peacekeeping operations, said an inquiry had been opened and the suspect would soon appear in court for professing knowledge of witchcraft, which was an offence under the Witchcraft Act. In the end nothing proved conclusive and Nswiba – who had been pictured in the local papers in a loincloth – was taken to a mental hospital for psychiatric evaluation. He probably would have been better advised to have claimed he'd been on a drinking binge and had no idea what had happened – such a fantastic tale was bound to lead the authorities to question his sanity.

Also common in Africa are stories of shapeshifting. One recorded instance was presented to the South African law courts in 1987. It came about when a young man, Naletzane Netshiavha, was roused during the night by a strange scratching noise at his front door. He went to the door and called out, 'Who's there?' But when there was no response he became frightened. To protect himself, Naletzane picked up an axe and then opened the door. To his horror, he saw what looked to be a large bat hanging from the rafters of his roof. He struck the beast with the axe, making it fall to the ground, and then fled in a blind panic. When he mustered the courage to return with reinforcements, witnesses saw the creature dragging its tattered body towards a fence in the yard. Naletzane struck it again and again until it lay still. A large group of people who had been watching from afar finally felt confident enough to approach for a better view.

Every one of the witnesses later described seeing a completely different creature when they spoke in court. To some it was a small donkey; to others it was a winged animal. But all agreed that, as it lay dying, the creature's form changed. The testimonies also concurred that it took on the body of a child with the head of an adult, before slowly developing a complete adult body. The body was later identified as that of Jim Nephalama, an elderly man, who was reputedly a wizard. Rumour had it that Jim often boasted that he had the power to 'do what he wished' with people. When the matter eventually went before the Supreme Court, the white judge concluded that Naletzane should have recognised that the creature was a man. He was found guilty of behaving in an irresponsible and violent manner and sentenced to ten years' imprisonment for culpable homicide.

# The Political Beast

Even politics in Africa is beset with reports of ritualistic murders. In August 2002, in the run-up to Swaziland's elections, the mutilated bodies of three children were found burned in isolated areas of the country. Numbers of others came to light too, including a 16-year-old girl. All were believed to have been killed as part of traditional rituals to bring luck to election candidates. Elections in Swaziland are held every five years and the next one was due the following year. As the jostling for votes intensified, candidates were increasingly turning to witchdoctors, some of whom were cashing in on the demand for luck potions prepared with herbs and human body parts. In June 2003 – four months away from the elections – King Mswati III urged Swaziland's politicians not to engage in ritual killings to boost their chances of winning. 'During election times, we tend to lose our grandmothers, grandfathers and young children,' he said in a televised address. 'They just disappear. But I want to warn you all that you should not resort to ritual murder.' A BBC report in the country's capital, Mbabane, confirmed that the number of ritual murders increases at election times.

In Liberia, in June 2005, the leader of the transitional government, Gyude Bryant, went further. He promised to use the death penalty against anyone found guilty of sacrificial killings: 'We'll find you, we'll arrest you, we'll prosecute you and let me say again to everybody, if the judge passes down a ruling to say you must die by hanging, I will hang you. I will sign the death warrant without batting my eye,' Bryant said. 'If you killed because you want to make a sacrifice to be president or senator, you fool yourself. Stop ritualistic killings, it will not pay you anything, it will not make you rich, it will not give you jobs.'

Bryant's comments followed a spate of reports in the Liberian press of sacrificial killings across the country, from Montserrado County, where the capital Monrovia is located, to the River Gee in the southeast. In one shocking case, newspapers reported that the body of a small boy had been discovered in a rubber plantation in Grand Bassa County, east of Monrovia. The boy's genitals were missing and his chest had been hacked open. Bryant was also responding to public outcry about ritual slayings. In January 2005, in Maryland County, in the southeast of the country, where Bryant hailed from, a violent backlash broke out against the practice. A crowd of angry youths armed with sticks and iron bars broke into the police station in the port town of Harper and beat up a group of suspected ritual killers who had been detained there. A dawn-to-dusk curfew was imposed and the UN Mission in Liberia (UNMIL) quickly dispatched extra peacekeepers to the town.

Bryant was, by no means, the first Liberian president to impose the death penalty against those found guilty of ritual killings. In the late 1970s, the then president, William Tolbert, signed the death warrant of several government officials accused of procuring human body parts for Gboyo (a local term for the practice of killing people for their body parts and using them in rituals).

Bryant's call for a stop to ritual killing, however, was a desperate plea which, arguably, wouldn't have cut much ice – so commonplace is the practice in the country. During Liberia's fourteen-year civil war (1989–2003), for example, there were so many cases of gunmen – some of them child soldiers – eating their victims' hearts and other body parts, that the Catholic Church issued a formal denunciation of these practices. In his book, *The Mask of Anarchy* (1999), Africa scholar and historian Stephen Ellis[1] said the practice could be traced all the way to the top of the ladder:

Nor was it just teenage fighters who held the idea that they could have access to spiritual power through the consumption of human flesh, or at least by a ritual use of human body parts . . . Most interesting is the allegation concerning [President] Charles Taylor himself made by his former defence minister, Tom Woewiyu . . . 'We saw a lot,' said Woewiyu, describing his time as Taylor's right-hand man, 'including the formation of a group of cannibals called Top 20. Taylor is a member of this group. Human sacrifices, under the direction of his uncle Jensen Taylor, take place in Taylor's house.' A group of sixteen NPFL [Taylor's army] generals and fourteen Special Force commandos made similar allegations concerning Taylor. They issued a formal statement affirming that 'we . . . stand in readiness to testify Taylor's ritualistic killings of our peers . . .' True or not, such claims are widely believed.

Unsurprisingly, Ellis' accusations didn't go down well with Charles Taylor. After *The Times* newspaper repeated the allegations in its review of *The Mask of Anarchy*, Taylor launched a libel case against Ellis, but withdrew it in early 2001, allegedly because of the high cost of pursuing the case in London.

The more you look into Africa, the more you see the sheer dread and horror its citizens live under. Bob Geldof and U2 singer Bono continue to highlight one side – the terrible starvation, famine and poverty that result from political corruption. But they never refer to the other side – the killing fields that are born of religious and magickal beliefs. Yet this could be an issue that both Africa and the West will be forced to address when the continent eventually becomes more politically stable and the immediate concerns of starvation and poverty are reduced.

But what is the extent of the problem? How many people lose their lives in the ritual killing fields? To find out, I spoke to a friend of mine, Fred van der Kraaij,[2] an inspector at the Ministry of Foreign Affairs in the Netherlands, who is an expert on the politics and culture of Liberia, having spent over sixteen years in the country at one stage in his career. He told me: 'I don't think it will ever be known how many victims die at the hands of ritual killers in sub-Saharan Africa. Nor will it ever be known how many perpetrators got away with their crimes. The truth is, many people continue to believe that human sacrifices are needed, and are even justified, to protect or further the interests of the tribal community. Or they see the hideous practice as necessary to improve social prestige or to gain material wealth, even to gain access to public office, in the case of politicians.'

On his website, www.liberiapastandpresent.org, Kraaij presents the following personal recollection, which suggests that just as many cases of ritual killing are covered up as are reported:

In 1976 I spoke to a medical doctor who worked in the same hospital where forty years earlier Dr Werner Junge [author of *African Jungle Doctor*] had worked, in Robertsport, regional capital of Grand Cape Mount County. I was told that some months earlier he had to perform an autopsy on a young girl with several parts missing. A typical case of ritual killing. A man and a woman had been arrested in connection with this crime. They had confessed to having committed the murder and admitted that they had acted on request of a member of the House of Parliament representing

Cape Mount County. Subsequently, by government order, the two accused had been transferred to Monrovia. Since then nobody had ever again heard of the case. Apparently, the affair had effectively been covered up.

Ritual killings are equally common in Nigeria – both in the Muslim north and Christian south. Back in March 2005, a Nigerian man murdered his friend in Central Plateau state to sell his body parts for use in rituals. Jacob Wakfan, age 35, confessed to luring his victim into the bush, stabbing him, and then removing his penis and tongue. 'The convict's desire to make quick money led him to commit this heinous and treacherous act,' concluded Judge Felicia Dusu, who then sentenced Wakfan to death by hanging.

## Money Magick in Theory and Practice

Minus the gruesome aspects, rituals that use body parts are not very different to non-nefarious rituals found in practical magick in the West or in Voodoo or Hoodoo folk magick. The basic logic is the same. In the classic annals of anthropology such rituals are known as sympathetic or homoeopathic magick. You basically enact in ritual or dramatic form that which you desire. Earl Marlowe, the Voodoo man I used to play in a band with during the 1980s and early 1990s, taught me many spells designed to attract love, money, sex and other worldly wants. One money spell he showed me involved using a Voodoo doll. Apart from the lack of body parts and other macabre items, the magickal working would be very similar in principle to the type of causal sorcery used by shamans and witchdoctors in Africa to improve fortunes. It is worth noting here as an illustration of how spells are performed. This is what you do:

> Either buy or make a Voodoo doll. Making one is easy: you just cut out a couple of pieces of cloth in the shape of a person, sew them together, and stuff them with material or cotton wool. But remember not to sew the doll up completely, as you will be stuffing ritual items inside it.
>
> Once you've got a doll, you set up your spiritual altar. For purists this can be quite complex. But all you really need do is mark out an area where you won't be disturbed and consecrate it with a cleansing incense. I used to use 'John the Conqueror' incense sticks, just because the John the Conqueror root is mentioned in a lot of old blues songs (and, besides, I'm not exactly a purist). You can also clap your hands to each of the four compass directions, and above and below, saying something like, 'May the mighty angels of light protect this area'. Once your sacred area is set up, you burn some Money Drawing Incense and pass the Voodoo doll through the smoke to consecrate it.
>
> Anoint a green candle with Money Oil and place it on a white saucer and light it. Using Dragon's Blood or Dove's Blood Ink, write out your request for money on a piece of parchment paper (your request could read along the lines of, 'Spirits, bring me money to meet my needs').
>
> Now put some coins inside the doll, along with a whole John the Conqueror root. Then sprinkle the doll with Money Drawing Powder and anoint it with Bayberry Oil. As you do this, recite the following incantation (or something similar):

> 'Money doll, money doll,
> Bring me riches, bring me gold,
> Money doll, money doll,
> Stuff my bank full of cash.'

Once the spell is cast, put the doll where you can always see it, and don't let anyone touch it. Every seven days, place one or two coins in front of the doll to feed it and rekindle its taste for money.

I used to do spells like this regularly back in the late 1980s and early 1990s. I was playing in bands. The lifestyle was precarious and money was in short supply. Such spells didn't make me a fortune, but money did seem to appear when I most needed it. So do spells work? Well, yes, I think they do, but not in some sort of Harry Potter way. Instead, I'd say they work in a similar way to self-hypnosis. For example, in the case of money spells you are essentially 're-programming' your unconscious mind to become more 'cash conscious'. This then flows through to your everyday life and eventually you begin to take actions in life that are more likely to bring you financial gain (you do have to be prepared to work on a material level too). The only real difference between spells and self-hypnosis is that spells are bolder, they attempt to achieve slightly more fantastical aims (like winning the lottery or attracting a desired member of the opposite sex), whereas self-hypnosis stays more down to earth by aiming to improve confidence or stop you smoking.

The fact that spells do sometimes seem to work, even if the real reason for this may be due to self-hypnosis rather than to supernatural power, is probably the reason why faith in magick remains so common in Africa. It is also possibly why those of a dark – and possibly desperate – turn will up the ante and use human body parts in their spells.

# Killer Children?

In August 2003 the African news wires reported the alarming plight of a group of women in northern Nigeria, who spent three days in fasting and prayer to protect themselves from being murdered at the hands of their own children. Both Muslim and Christian women took part in the prayers. Yusuf Israel, a spokesperson for the northern state of Taraba, said the women had been spooked by a spate of killings by children who had been 'lured into black magick cults' and convinced they should kill their parents. 'The women, under the leadership of the wife of the state governor, Priscilla Nyame, have begun three days of fasting and prayers for divine intervention against the new trend of ritual killings,' he said in an interview. 'What is more disturbing is the fact that the victims of these children are invariably their parents, whom they are ordered to kill by the cult they belong to.' Israel went on to say that: 'These children are initiated into ritual societies through gifts, usually edible things. Once they eat, they become initiated.'

To Western ears, these allegations of killer child cults and the subsequent mass hysteria smack of paranoid ravings. But bearing in mind the reports of child soldiers in Liberia eating the hearts and body parts of enemies, perhaps we shouldn't be too quick to dismiss such claims.

Habila Audu, a father of two initiated children, had good reason to believe such cults existed. He told the prayer gathering how he had been laid low in bed for six weeks by his two daughters who had cast a spell on him. He claimed he only escaped death when one of his daughters rebelled against the cult she was in.

Yusuf Israel said: 'Habila owes his life to the disagreement between the daughters. While one wanted to ritually drain his blood, the other insisted he shouldn't be killed. The trend is becoming rampant and the women felt it is only God who can counter this diabolical development because rituals can best be fought with prayers.'

How many in the country would have taken his advice is open to question. The vast majority of Nigeria's 126 million population publicly profess to follow Christianity or Islam, but many still retain traditional beliefs in witchcraft and will consult Juju priests to help solve their problems when all else fails.

What's more, in May 2005, in southwestern Nigeria, the cops pulled in a pastor and two others over their apparent involvement in the ritual killing of a 7-year-old boy. It seemed that even Christian ministers were not above the use of the sacrificial knife. Bashir Azeez, the commissioner of police in Ekiti state, said the suspects had confessed to killing the boy, whose headless body was exhumed from a pit in the home of one of the arrested men. Azeez said the suspect, from whose home the victim's body had been recovered, led a police team to a church, where the boy's head was recovered from the pastor. Apparently, the pastor had directed the other two to bring the head of a child for a moneymaking ritual.

## Early Reports of Ritual Killing

Europeans first began exploring the west coast of Africa in the fifteenth century. But it was some time before stories of human sacrifice began to filter through. One famous account came from French sea captain, J. E. Landolphe. In 1750 he visited Dahomey, a now-defunct kingdom situated in what is now southern Benin. He described seeing a routine sacrifice performed in honour of a new trading agreement signed with France. In front of the Oba (ruling king), two executioners, masked and dressed in long grey robes, clubbed a man unconscious and cut off his head. Before his death, the man was told to go to Olokun, god of fertility and the sea. On another occasion, Landolphe witnessed three men sacrificed as part of a yearly great yam festival.

Earlier, in 1727, the British Captain Snelgrave visited Agbomey, the capital of Dahomey. He reported that victory celebrations after a successful campaign claimed many sacrificial victims. But by far the most blood was spilt, he said, on two major occasions: the Grand Custom, which marked the death of a Dahomey ruler; and the Annual Custom which, through sacrifice, provided the late king with a ghostly retinue of servants on the anniversary of his death. Snelgrave witnessed a Grand Custom ceremony. He and a Dutch companion were led by priests to a place about a quarter of a mile from the settlement, where four small stages had been set up. The two were adamant they saw 400 victims dispatched by ritual sacrifice. But they only described the death of the first – an old man. The Juju priest placed his hand on the man's head and intoned words of consecration. The executioner then severed his head with one blow of the ceremonial sword. Women and children were apparently also sacrificed and, unsurprisingly, given the circumstances, uttered 'piteous cries'. Snelgrave maintained that some victims were killed by boys of around 7 or 8 years old and suffered prolonged agonies because the children barely had the strength to lift the ceremonial sword.

The Annual Custom was also observed and described in lurid detail by the great English traveller and explorer Sir Richard Burton – better known for his exploits in the Near East. He saw the ceremony at the beginning of 1863 and describes it in his book *A Mission to Gelele, King of Dahome* (1864). The proceedings were held in a 'victim shed', just outside one of the gates of the town. Burton says the shed wasn't dissimilar to an English parish church with its 'barn and turret'; the only difference being the roof was covered by a blood red, tattered cloth. Inside the building were twenty sacrificial victims waiting to be slain. (These were usually criminals or prisoners of war.) All were seated on stools and were tightly lashed to the interior posts that held the building up. Each had an attendant squatting behind them to keep the flies off. They were fed four times a day and their bonds were loosened at night so they could sleep – since the king wanted them to be in good humour when the killing began. Their outfits struck Burton as odd; they were dressed in long white nightcaps and calico shirts with a crimson patch on the left breast, along with European-style shorts.

When the time came for them to meet their ends the victims were trussed up in large baskets and hurled, along with a cat and a crocodile, from a raised platform. Their heads were then sliced off and their bodies brutally mutilated and left for birds of prey to eat. Burton also records the presence of armed warriors squatting beside King Gelele, with gun barrels trained upwards.

The most gruesome part of Burton's account, however, concerns the disposal of the victims after sacrifice: 'The approach to the Palace was not pleasant . . . Four corpses, attired in their criminals' shirts and nightcaps, were sitting in pairs upon Gold Coast stools, supported by a double-storied scaffold . . . At a little distance from these, on a similar erection, but made for half the number, were two victims, one above the other . . .' He goes on to describe a gallows, equally strewn with corpses: 'We then passed the south-eastern gate . . . [and in] front of sundry little black dolls, stuck in the ground at both sides of the entrance, lay a dozen heads. These were two batches of six each; their faces were downwards, and the cleanly severed necks caught the observer's eye. Around each heap was raised a rim of white ashes.'

In all, Burton counted 23 bodies, put on show as a result of what he called 'Gelele's evil night'. Burton states that the king paid his warriors for victims months before the ceremony and suggests that in an average year, when the Annual Custom took place, the total number of people sacrificed was about 500. That figure rose to 1,000 in years when a Grand Custom was held. Because he was well travelled, Burton was able to take a detached view of the sacrificial rites, maintaining that human sacrifice in Dahomey and its neighbouring kingdoms had been greatly misunderstood by the press, though he acknowledged that the death toll was heavy. He even went as far as describing the Dahoman rites as 'a touching instance of the king's filial piety, deplorably mistaken but perfectly sincere', and insisted that the offerings were not rooted in a lust for blood or a perverted delight in torture. On the contrary, the king was simply doing his duty in accordance with his ancestors and the religion of his people – it was expected. In fact, Burton was often more ready to condone than to condemn the mass sacrifices of West Africa. He said that to abolish human sacrifice would be to abolish Dahomey, and predicted that European pressure to end the practice would only lead to a rise in the number of victims. As a final justification of the practice, he cited how, in 1864, four murderers were hung on the same gibbet in Liverpool in front of 100,000 baying onlookers.

## Leopard Men

One of the earliest underground killing cults to be documented became known as the Human Leopard Society of Sierra Leone, on the west coast of Africa. The cult focused on the creation of medicines made out of human entrails. As long ago as 1607, a visitor to the region wrote of fierce, man-eating tribes who lived in the interior of the country and dressed as leopards. In 1807, coastal Sierra Leone became a British colony, but the leopard societies were so secretive that the authorities didn't get wind of them until 1891. A bill was quickly drafted outlawing the Society. It stated: 'Many murders have been committed by men so dressed to resemble leopards and armed with a three-pronged knife commonly known as a leopard knife.' The bill made it a crime to possess a leopard skin shaped to resemble a leopard, a three-pronged knife and an unusual native medicine known as 'Borfima'. The police were given powers to search for such items without a warrant. The chiefs of the inland tribes were subject to harsh penalties if they failed to report Leopard Society activities. But the human leopards were not intimidated by the might of Britain. In fact it turned out they'd got allies: in 1902 a Human Alligator Society was uncovered, which worked in parallel with the leopards. An extra prohibition was duly added to the bill, outlawing the wearing of alligator skins shaped to resemble the reptiles.

By 1903 it became clear that many chiefs in the region were involved in the cults. In the resulting crackdown, 400 tribal people were arrested, some highly placed, but few were brought to trial due to lack of evidence. As a result, more legislation and prohibitions were brought in. A special court of three European judges was also put in place to try offenders. Armed with these extra measures the government succeeded in bringing the activities of the leopard societies to a virtual halt within a few years. By 1912, seventeen cases had come before the court: 187 people were charged with murder, of whom 87 were given the death sentence.

But why did the human leopards kill? Well, the answer lay partly in Borfima. The ingredients needed to make this native medicine, which was typically kept in a tight leather pouch, included the white of an egg, the blood of a cock and a few grains of rice. But the key elements were human fat and blood – which could only be obtained by murderous ritual. Borfima was considered very powerful medicine; it could bring power and riches, but could also be used as a protective charm for anyone unlucky enough to be hauled before the British court, with its alien notions of justice.

Leopard societies were selective about who they killed to extract the fat and blood needed for making Borfima. The victim had to be a freeborn girl (not a slave or captive) and over 14 years old. Ideally the girl would be the eldest child of the family who provided her. In later years, a man or boy was considered acceptable, but a girl was still the preferred choice. Making the native medicine also took centre stage during the long and complicated initiation into the Human Leopard Society. Chillingly, the would-be initiate had to produce a sacrificial victim from his own or his wife's family.

Once a victim had been chosen, the human leopards hit the forest and marauded throughout the night, imitating the roar of their totem beast. At a specified time, the victim was made to walk along a special forest track. Leopard men kept watch on both sides of the track for the girl's approach, hiding behind the dense walls of creepers that thrive in the humid jungles of Sierra Leone. After the victim passed the watching leopard men, the silence would suddenly be shattered by a deep-throated growl. Then the leopard man who had been designated executioner would leap out of the undergrowth and – with a lightning strike – would tear out the girl's throat. His companions would then carry the girl off into the depths of the undergrowth, where her head would be hacked off and the liver, heart and entrails torn out. Once the leopard men had carefully examined the liver for signs that the body would make an effective Borfima, the corpse was divided into four quarters. These were then carved up and wrapped in banana leaves and handed out to each of the leopard men. Lastly, the girl's face would be cut away so that her remains would not be recognised.

This was the most common form of the ritual. But it differed from area to area. In one particularly grisly ceremony, the girl was not killed straight away, but forced to sit under a tree. The tribal chief who led the sacrifice, which was intended to bring good fortune to the tribe, would then sit astride her shoulders. Those present all laid a hand on the chief or the victim to make a psychic connection. After this the chief prayed that good medicine should come from the offering and slashed the victim's throat. Her body was then cut open and the other participants tore out the intestines. Victims sometimes survived the ordeal, but alive or dead, she would be taken to a platform outside the chief's hut and left there tied to a post. The following morning the body would be taken back to the jungle to be cut up. The chief received the hands and feet, and a small portion of the flesh was given to the mother and father of the victim.

## Berserkers

Ugly and terrible though these practices were, it is important to remember that they were religious acts. The British authorities, of course, saw them as murder, and were not interested in the tenets of tribal spirituality. But taking on the form of a beast goes back to the practices of ancient shamanism, and has a universal religious meaning. Through ritual and sometimes the use of hallucinogenic plants, initiates would become possessed by the spirit of their totem animal; they would become more than human, and take on the divine qualities of the beast. In pre-Christian Scandinavia, for example, there was a band of warriors called Berserkers ('bear shirts'), who seemed to have been members of a cult connected to the god Odin, and whose roots probably lay in ancient bear cults. In the *Ynglinga Saga* (1225), Snorri Sturluson describes them this way:

> His [Odin's] men went to battle without armour and acted like mad dogs and wolves. They bit into their shields and were as strong as bears or bulls. They killed men, but neither fire nor iron harmed them. This madness is called Berserker fury.

When the Berserker rage was upon a warrior he was thought of as a 'were-bear' (or werewolf), part man, part beast, who was neither fully human nor fully animal. The Berserkers could be seen as an elite fighting force, much like the modern SAS or Delta Force, but with a shamanic element inherent to their fighting technique. One thing is certain: the Berserkers scared the hell out of their enemies.

Like the Berserkers, the leopard men of Sierra Leone were also 'were-beasts', charged up on the power of their totem animal. They were literally possessed by the spirit of the leopard. Getting into this mind state – which could be compared to the trance states found in hypnosis – would have been down to wearing leopard skins and prowling and roaring around the dense forests. Like a Method actor today, they would have got so into 'character' that they actually became that character – which happened to be a beast of the jungle. Psychotropic plants or fungi may also have come into the equation. The upshot of it was bloody and unacceptable to modern tastes, but it was born of a belief that blood sacrifices to the gods and spirits leads to divine favours. Most often such practices were seen as doing good for the tribe. If that were part of our own cultural and religious consensus today, we would have little choice other than to wield the ceremonial sword and slice off the head of a chosen victim. As they say in the movies, it would be a case of: 'Shit happens, get used to it . . .'

## Cannibal Soldiers

That sentiment could certainly be applied today in the Democratic Republic of the Congo – such are the hellish events that have occurred there. Formerly known as Zaire, the country was ravaged by 30 years of misrule under the dictator Mobutu Sese Seko. After that it endured five years of anarchy and civil war, in which around three million people died. Most were civilians, and most died as a result of the ensuing starvation and disease. It was the worst calamity since World War Two. But that wasn't the end of the horror. One of the rebel groups vying for power was the Movement for the Liberation of Congo (MLC). In late 2002 – partly under the leadership of a commander dubbed 'King of the Imbeciles' – the group launched a truly vicious offensive in the Ituri forest, in the wilds of the eastern Congo, which is home to tribes of Pygmies. Towns were looted. Women and girls were raped. Villagers were executed. And, it was said, Pygmies were eaten. Mbuti Pygmy Amuzati Nzoli was widely quoted by the international press claiming that rebels attacked his jungle camp, cut up his family and grilled them over a campfire. They 'even sprinkled salt on the flesh as they ate', he said.

Sudi Alimasi, an official of the pro-government group Rally for Congolese Democracy-ML, echoed these allegations: 'We hear reports of [enemy] commanders feeding on sexual organs of Pygmies, apparently believing this would give them strength,' he said. 'We also have reports of Pygmies being forced to feed on the cooked remains of their colleagues.'

A human rights worker with the 16,000-strong United Nations peacekeeping force in Congo told *National Geographic*[3] magazine that: 'Cannibalism here is both an ancient tribal practise and a modern instrument of terror. But the attacks singling out Pygmies are new. The prevailing theory holds that soldiers ate them to absorb their unique forest powers – good vision, tracking skills, whatever.'

In the same issue, *National Geographic* also spoke to Major Edison Mungilima of the Mayi-Mayi, a loose grouping of Congolese tribal militias who have fought almost every other faction in eastern Congo, including the MLC. He said that fetishism (talismanic magick) had been part of warfare in Congo from the very beginning – but that it could be good or bad depending on the 'purity of the individual soldier'. He added that he personally was a 'liquid fighter', a warrior who could turn himself into water so that bullets pass harmlessly through him. Eating Pygmies, however, as the MLC were alleged to have done, was not on his menu. He considered such practices 'offensive' and said the Mayi-Mayi, at worst, might cut off an enemy's head 'to parade around a village as a flag of victory'. He was being economical with the truth. On an assignment in eastern Congo a correspondent for the *Guardian* newspaper saw many Mayi-Mayi fighters wearing parts of the bodies of their Rwandan enemies, in the belief that this would make them invincible.

## Heart Full Of Soul?

It would be easy to dismiss sub-Saharan Africa as hell on earth and strike it off your 'must visit' list. Indeed many journalists, including me, invoke Joseph Conrad's bleak fable, *Heart of Darkness*, every time they need a headline for a piece on Congo. It's all too easy to fall into stereotypes to kick-start a story. Take muti, the Zulu word for traditional medicine, for example. In Britain, because Adam was initially thought to have been a victim of muti 'killing', the term has become almost synonymous with ritual murder. Yet traditional healers in Africa are beginning to gain the respect and interest of those working in conventional medicine. One small Ugandan initiative, for example, placed a traditional healer next to a modern doctor to provide consultations for patients with HIV or AIDS.[4] There is still a good deal of scepticism about traditional African medicine, but according to Dr Sekagya Yahaya Hills, who is both a qualified dentist and a traditional healer, there are signs that some of the plant-based remedies may be both effective and low-cost. Speaking at the International Symposium on Biodiversity and Health, held in Ottawa in October 2003, he outlined the work being done by Prometra,[5] an international organisation for the preservation and restoration of the ancient arts of traditional medicine. He said long-term studies using a combination of African herbal medicines have shown positive results, and that Prometra has already filed five patent applications for the use of medicinal plants in the treatment of AIDS.

HIV and AIDS, however, are by no means the only ailments treated by traditional healers in sub-Saharan Africa. According to one estimate, 85 per cent of Africans use the services of traditional healers as their primary source of health care. François Gasengayire, a Nairobi-based specialist in biodiversity and traditional medicine with the International Development Research Centre (IDRC), says there is one healer for every 200 people in southern Africa – a far higher doctor-to-patient ratio than is found in North America or Europe.

Recognising that traditional medicine is 'the most affordable and accessible system of healthcare for the majority of the African rural population', the African Union[6] declared 2001–2010 to be the 'Decade for African Traditional Medicine'. The organisation's goal is to bring together all the stakeholders in an effort to make 'safe, efficacious, quality, and affordable traditional medicines available to the vast majority of our people'. The aim is supported by the World Health Organisation and the IDRC.

In South Africa, a bill to regulate the country's 200,000 traditional healers was finally adopted in 2004. Healers now have to be licensed before being allowed to work. Breaking these rules is punishable by a fine or a prison sentence of up to twelve months. 'This practice has suffered degradation during years of colonialisation in Africa, but traditional medicine has sustained many families for centuries in this continent,' said health minister Manto Tshabalala-Msimang. 'This is an equally important bill for national health care. It will create a framework for cooperation between mainstream health practice and traditional healing.'

## Why Sacrifice?

'What we call the beginning is often the end and to make an end is to make a beginning.'

T.S. Eliot (1888–1965)
*Four Quartets*, 1942

In common with the esoteric systems of the West, traditional African paganism (along with the healing practices associated with it) has a sophisticated body of lore concerning the nature of the cosmos and the soul of man. An aspect of this body of knowledge holds one explanation as to why sacrifice (both in its legal and illegal forms) remains so central to African spiritual practice. Credo Mutwa,[7] the larger-than-life Zulu shaman (or 'sangoma') who was consulted by Scotland Yard detectives working on the Adam case, is one of the most eloquent exponents of indigenous African mysticism around today. He says that human beings have two 'souls' – the ena and the moya. 'The moya we depict as a globe or sphere of perfect transparency,' he says. 'Inside each sphere are two worm-like creatures . . . one is blue in colour and the other red. We say that these . . . creatures represent the good and evil inside a person.' Mutwa believes it is essential for human beings to have an equal balance of good and evil. If either gains the upperhand – making the person either too good or too evil – the soul would meet a 'premature demise'. According to Mutwa, when we die, the moya goes on into other incarnations and can be reborn as a human or an animal.

The ena, also known as 'the self', however, has the shape of a person, but is made out of a 'spirit substance' – and it is not something we possess from birth. 'This soul develops as the person develops, out of memories and experiences,' explains Mutwa. 'If you were to see your ena you might imagine that you saw a ghost of transparent mist that resembles you.' In fact, he says that enas often live on for a time after death and this explains sightings of apparitions and ghosts. 'In the after-death state,' he says, 'an ena, like a physical person, needs nourishment – and this is derived from the prayers and sacrifices of the living. A sacrificed animal's ena goes to feed the ena [of the dead person] in whose honour the sacrifice has been conducted.'

Mutwa goes on to explain that people who practise ancestor worship go to great efforts to feed the enas of the dead they honour. By performing regular rituals and animal sacrifices they ensure the continued existence of that ena.

The ena is fed and sustained by blood. The enas of ancestors can be of valuable assistance to the living; they can be consulted for advice in times of trouble or they can serve as intermediaries by communicating with the gods on behalf of the people. But if the ancestors are forgotten about and are not fed, their 'enas eventually pass into non-existence, and a valuable communication with the gods is lost'.

Clearly, this aspect of sacrifice – the ritual slaying of animals – is fully legal and forms a common part of African religious and magickal practice. But the basic principle and reasoning behind it applies to illegal practice too. As one-time Juju man and sorcerer Isaiah Oke (discussed in the next chapter) points out: '[Disreputable shamans] reason that if the ritual works with an animal, it should be even more powerful with a human victim.' Such offerings, of course, would probably only be made to a deceased person who was less than savoury when alive – possibly a sorcerer who had worked on the dark side.

There are many reasons behind the practice of blood sacrifice. But essentially it boils down to the offering of blood to either feed the ancestors or vitalise gods. Yet even this is a simplistic way of looking at the practice because blood is not seen in its literal, physical sense. Rather it is seen as carrying the life force, or 'élan vital', of a living entity, be it human or animal. This is what the ancestors and gods are believed to feast on. It is their nourishment and what they crave; hence they will provide favours to the living in return.

Such ideas may sound alien and strange to us in the West. But it all depends what reality tunnel you subscribe to. My experience of life has brought me to the conclusion that we choose our own realities. The sceptical scientist opts for a non-supernatural worldview in which evolution and natural selection rule. The Catholic opts for the Holy Trinity. The Voodoo practitioner opts for a world of spirits and communion with the dead – as did the pagan Anglo-Saxons and Norse peoples. None of it is necessarily real – after all, we create our world via the input of our senses, which, in turn, is pulled into organised and understandable shape by our brains. It is a reality agreed by the various societies and cultures that make up our world. But it is not necessarily what is really 'out there'.

While researching human sacrifice in Africa it would have been easy for me to recoil in horror at the vicious scenarios I uncovered. People were murdering fellow humans – even children – in the most cold-blooded manner either as a sacrifice to the gods or to use their body parts for magickal talismans. It was terrifying. Yet I had to accept that the individuals committing such crimes are not necessarily evil incarnate (although they might seem so on the surface). In many ways they are victims themselves – victims of a belief system that revolves around feeding gods and spirits with blood in exchange for their favours. If such a notion is central to the way you view the world, I reasoned, then couldn't any one of us, given desperate circumstances, consider ritually slaying another human being? If our plight were bad enough – terrible poverty or illness, for example – we could be tempted to try anything. It's easy for us in the West to say we would never even consider such actions. But we are cushioned by our welfare system and National Health Service, which generally protect us from desperate circumstances. Plus, of course, we no longer believe in pagan gods and goddesses who require blood to sustain them, as we did some 1,500 years ago. If it wasn't for these things, it could well be a different story . . . Who are we to judge?

# Chapter 3: Professional Human Sacrificers

Mountain Slayer ... Killing by the Book ... Breaking the Rules ... Wizard of the Four Winds ... Thought Power ... Is it Really Murder? ... Devil Doctor of Lagos ... A Hard On for Hell ... Was it Idi Amin?

'Murder considered as one of the fine arts' (essay title)

Thomas De Quincey 1785–1859
*Blackwoods Magazine* February 1827

Some years back I came across a website with the full text of a book that had not only been banned but of which all existing copies had been destroyed. A group with anarchic inclinations, however, had posted it on the Internet. The book is called *Hitman: A Technical Manual for Independent Contractors* by Rex Feral, supposedly a one-time professional killer. I have to say I was intrigued. In cold, calculated terms the book detailed how you go about assassinating someone, along with how you set yourself up in the deadly trade. It was a 'how to' cookbook, with a macabre twist. I printed the book out and it became my bedtime reading for a week.

As I was short of money at the time, it looked like a reasonable business to be in. You just needed to study firearms and poisons, and maybe a spot of garrotting, and you were set to go. It was then a question of securing a contract, planning the hit and executing it. After that you could take it easy for a week or two. I was pretty certain that after the first few hits you'd get used to the trade and it would seem no more gruesome than running a butcher's shop or slaughterhouse. It's just that you'd never be seen as reputable or get any acclaim for your abilities. You certainly wouldn't get a CBE or MBE. So that ruled out the profession for me as I've got my sights set firmly on a knighthood.

Anyway, after looking at cases of human sacrifice in Africa, I got to thinking that killing people is quite a skill – the *Hitman* book describes it as an 'art'. If you don't know what you're doing when you kill someone, I reasoned, it's going to be very messy and you're far more likely to be caught. So logically, if you ritually kill people every so often you're going to need to be professional about it; otherwise you're going to end up in jail. Clearly, some people who have committed human sacrifice are amateurs and have been quickly banged to rights. But there must be some who are very skilled at the practice – professionals who know how to dispatch their victims into the great beyond in a clean and capable manner. I soon discovered that this is indeed the case. Professional human sacrificers are available for hire – if you know where to look, or who to ask. But do they consider themselves to be like hit men or assassins? Or do they see themselves as continuing a legitimate religious tradition, with roots in the ancient past?

The first case I came across that looked like it had the hand of a professional behind it occurred in Peru, some two decades ago. Curiously, after death, the victim went on to become a demi god to the local people, some of whom prayed to him for favours. Although people were horrified at the killing, they found a way to incorporate it into their spirituality and mythologies . . .

## Mountain Slayer

It all began on the morning of 17 February 1986. Police lieutenant Alfredo Gonzalez looked out of his window and it was still raining. For the last month torrential rains had hit the Lake Titicaca area of Peru, causing terrible flooding. Crops had been devastated and thousands of peasants found themselves homeless. So when pretty Indian woman Leucaria Limachi entered his office in tears, it came as little surprise – until, that is, she told him that the body of her husband Clemente had been found horrifically mutilated the night before. Not only had he been decapitated, but his facial skin had been meticulously scalpeled off then pushed up over his head, where it hung like a ghoulish mask. Both the severed head and torso had then been stuffed inside a hollowed-out rock in the foothills of nearby Mount Santa Barbara. Press reports, based on persistent local rumour, claimed that Clemente's death had something to do with ancient Indian mountain -top rituals, involving blood sacrifice (known as 'paying the earth'), which had been revived in a bid to halt the destruction wrought by the terrible flooding. The widowed Leucaria, however, believed that this was only half the story. 'The pagans killed him to pay the earth,' she agreed. But she also insisted 'the narcotraffickers did it so they could make more money.'

The belief was that drug dealers were using sorcery to protect themselves from arrest and capture, and to help make their businesses more lucrative. In some ways this could seem absurd because it suggests that money and protection can be gained by supernatural means – that sorcery actually works. If it didn't you would imagine that drug dealers would quickly discard the practice. In reality it is more complicated than this. For one thing, magick is not cut and dried. It isn't logical in the sense that you perform a money spell and a week later a cheque for £250 appears out of the blue (although it might). Causal magick is an art; you endeavour to manipulate the turn of fate in your favour, which may or may not bring you what you want. If nothing else, it's a way of stacking the odds in your favour.

At its best magick is a pathway to spiritual development; at its worst it is about attempting to use the supernatural for material gain. Both routes often lead to strange or uncanny events happening or to odd coincidences. High initiates see such experiences as being illusory, at best; sirens to lead you astray from the path of enlightenment. For the drug dealers in Peru, however, such experiences could well validate the practice of causal magick. It could make them certain of its effectiveness. But it should also be remembered that their being involved with sorcery would undoubtedly add to the fear and terror inspired by drug dealers – even more so if ritual killing were involved. No one would dare shop them to the law or do anything to oppose them. Even rival gangs would be wary. Clearly, it is in their interests to be associated with the dark side of magick.

Being reluctant to believe that ritual sacrifice still existed, the police made little headway on the Clemente Limachi case and eventually it was shelved. So the job of finding out the truth fell to an American writer called Patrick

Tierney. He'd gone to Peru in 1983 on a magazine assignment to investigate an autopsy that had been performed on an extremely well-preserved mummy – the 500-year-old remains of an Incan boy, discovered 30 years earlier on a remote peak in the Andes. The palaeopathology team concluded that the cause of death was neither disease nor illness: the boy had been the victim of a ritual human sacrifice. The discovery, confirmed by sixteenth-century Spanish accounts of the Incas' religious practices, prompted Tierney to mount his own investigation, which led to the even more startling revelation that human sacrifice was – and is – still being practised in remote areas of Chile and the Peruvian Andes. In his book *The Highest Altar* (1989), Tierney described how he followed the leads he had uncovered, tracking down specific incidents and trying to understand the complex social and political motives of the shamans who allegedly still practise human sacrifice.

After extensive inquiries into the events surrounding the killing of Clemente Limachi, Tierney collected a good deal of persuasive anecdotal evidence to back up his widow's assertions. It appeared that a group of shamans (known locally as 'yatiris') had selected Clemente to be the victim of a ritual killing. The shamans believed that the torrential rains, that were causing such destruction, had been unleashed by the gods of the mountains and a deity known as the 'Earth Mother', to punish local people for rejecting the old religion in favour of Christianity. Tierney also discovered that the shamans were working for a local cocaine trafficker who every so often commissioned blood rituals to help him gain greater wealth.

Despite the dubious motives behind the sacrifice, Clemente, in death, achieved cult status. Local people regularly visited his grave and prayed to him as if he were a saint, while shamans insisted that Clemente's spirit always helped them with their magick and rituals. Tierney asked a local shaman how he could be so sure it was Clemente – could he actually see him? 'Of course,' replied the shaman, gesturing into apparently thin air. 'Clemente is with us now – can't you see him?'

Tierney never conclusively discovered the identity of the people behind the killing of Clemente. But one name that kept cropping up was that of Máximo Coa,[1] a shaman who reportedly specialised in human sacrifices. One informant told Tierney that Coa had once lived in a community called Queñuani, but that the people had thrown him out because of his reputation for human sacrifices. 'Now Máximo just goes around at night on his donkey – you have to catch him in the mountains,' the informant said. Another person told Tierney that: 'Máximo is the only yatiri who knows how to perform the misa (ceremony) to get riches. [He] is the only one who works with Ñanqha, the Devil.'

A friend of Tierney's – Francisco Paca, a respected journalist for *La República* – had contacts throughout the region. He asked the president of Coa's former community, Queñuani, if there was a shaman in the area who really knew what he was doing. 'Yes,' he said. 'The best yatari for sacrificing llamas is a man named Máximo Coa. Every December he used to perform that ceremony for the crops. But the man got carried away several times, and sacrificed some people – women especially. He was even in Puno jail because of sacrificing people. The police let him loose, but he went back to his old ways. In fact, he even wanted to sacrifice his own wife. Finally, the community got angry, sacked his house, and kicked Coa out.'

Rumour also had it that Coa had a penchant for sacrificing 15-year-old virgins and was currently said to be living with a young girl next to a cemetery (presumably an ideal combination for someone in his profession). Through his contacts, Tierney managed to track down Coa's 'sworn enemy', a retired army officer called Anastasio Rivera – whose testimony added even more weight to the reports that Coa was a serial human sacrificer. '[Coa] once tried to kill my wife,' he told Tierney. 'But she escaped ... She'd left me because we weren't getting on well. She went to Coa to bewitch me ... to get Coa's help in some rite. It's to people like that, poor and needy, that he always promises things, solutions.' Rivera's wife's suspicions were aroused when she looked under the bed and found a pan smeared with blood, along with two knives. 'My wife was the chosen one,' said Rivera. 'And after [Coa] killed her, no doubt he would have accused me of doing it.'

Rivera went on to say that 23 years previously Coa had been convicted of killing a young woman called Herminia Alave and her baby daughter and had spent six years in prison for the crime. Rivera then took Patrick Tierney to a spot on the shore of Lake Titicaca where he said Coa had deposited the remains of the young mother and her daughter. '[Coa] had a special room in his house for sacrificing people,' he revealed. 'That's where he quartered their bodies, chopped them up into pieces. He carried the pieces of Herminia Alave and her young child down to the shore in two bags on top of two burros [donkeys], and buried them in a little mound by the water.'

According to Rivera, no one knew what had happened to the mother and child for a long time. They had simply disappeared. But then a dog dug up the head of one of the victims, causing an outcry in the local community. At first no one suspected Coa. He took flowers to the funeral and put on a great show of grief. 'He took off his hat and cried,' recalled Rivera, and even went as far as asking who could have committed such a terrible crime. Eventually, though, Coa was linked to the murders. Apparently, the two victims had been seen in his house. The young mother was separated from her husband and was thought to have gone to Coa to ask him to perform some love magick, which was another of his specialities. Unbeknown to her, Coa had been commissioned to do a human sacrifice and she and her daughter happened to be in the wrong place at the wrong time.

'Coa confessed to the whole thing very cynically, without any remorse,' said Rivera. 'He said he had done these things to pay the devil and get rich. But he never revealed the names of his clients. You should have seen how they rewarded him – he lived like a king in jail. The rich people . . . made sure he had everything he wanted.'

Rivera claimed that Coa worked for the local mafia who, he said, ritually killed people in order to perform 'get rich quick' pacts with the Devil. Coa himself later admitted that he'd performed ritual killings for three of the richest and most successful smugglers in the city of Yunguyo. Clearly, Rivera was prejudiced against Coa due to his wife going to the shaman for his help. But it is known that drug traffickers in the region use ancient magickal practices, including ritual killing, in a bid to improve their finances and keep the law off their backs. And this comes as no surprise. Such people are outsiders who live on the edge; behind every corner lies danger from rival gangs and the threat of arrest. So – just as their ancient forebears did – they put their faith in the raw, unseen power of nature, which in their cosmologies takes the form of gods and spirits. But there are also other elements involved. Letting it be known that you are under the protection of terrifying, powerful deities, for example, is a good way of exerting control over fellow humans, especially if they are credulous enough. You wouldn't even have to send henchmen round to keep them in line; you'd just have to threaten to curse them. There's no doubt about it, magick is great for gangsters. And not just in the developing world. Even in the sprawling metropolises of the West, the occult can still hold power. During the 1960s, London gangster Ronnie Kray declared that he was psychic and that he could read people's motives from their auras. Also, at that time, Ronnie consulted a clairvoyant from Walthamstow who told him he was under the protection of a powerful spirit guide that instructed him through his inner voice. All he had to do was listen. The idea that Ronnie could read minds made it very difficult for anyone weaker to lie to him, and the general air of the occult only served to add to the Kray twins' violent mystique. And it would have been the same for the drug traffickers Coa allegedly worked with.

When Tierney finally caught up with Coa, he learned more about his background and got some insight into how he got into the gruesome trade of sacrificing people. Unsurprisingly, his biographical details are sketchy and prone to exaggeration. But Coa told Tierney that he had been born near the city of Yunguyo in southeastern Peru, and later crossed the border to Bolivia to work in the mines. He made good money, but eventually got sick. His search for a cure took him to Charazani in Bolivia, where he consulted the Callawaya travelling healers, who were known throughout the five Andean countries. The healer who dealt with Coa told him he was sick but assured him that everything would be fine. He said: '[You can] be at peace about your life and future because from now on you can prepare misas, you can do payments to the earth, you can do everything [that a shaman does] . . . with that you'll earn your living. You'll make progress.'

In short, Coa, supposedly, had undergone the typical sickness phase shamans go through when they receive their calling from the spirits. This shamanic illness,[2] which is also called an initiatory crisis, is part of a magickal rite of passage. It often involves the shamanic candidate singing or dancing in a disturbing or unconventional manner – as if they are possessed. But to us in the West they'd probably appear mentally ill. We wouldn't be able to deal with them. We'd shoot them full of drugs and lock them up in a psychiatric institution. But to people in indigenous cultures, the strange behaviour of a shamanic initiate is seen as a sign of their vocation, and is dealt with in a respectful manner.

Máximo Coa received his shamanic vocation in 1956 at the age of 41. By 1962, he was beginning to build up a clientele and make a little money from his talents as a healer and magick worker. Come the 1970s he was in big demand: 'Then the great millionaires took me to cure a sick person in Lima,' he said. 'Since then, none of my patients have died. All of them have been cured.'

Like many successful shamans and magick workers, Coa knew how to turn on the charm. According to Tierney he was very eloquent and had phenomenal acting abilities. 'He possessed so many voices, he was like a one man theatrical production,' observed Tierney, who found it hard not to be taken in by the shaman's natural charisma. And because Coa used a walking cane, due to disfigurement in his right knee, it was hard not to feel sorry for him. Coa simply did not come across as the callous ritual killer he had been painted as. But as time went on, he confirmed the full horror of his professional vocation. He told Tierney that you could find 'lots of poor girls' in Juliaca, a city of 100,000 located 25 miles north of Puno. All you needed to do, Coa said, was offer them a better job with better pay than their current employment. After a girl's trust was gained, it was just a question of asking her to help with a ritual in the mountains – a task that would be perceived as being given greater responsibility. Once at the place of sacrifice, they would typically be plied with alcohol and cocaine – which may explain why Coa insisted that few resisted or put up a struggle. Describing the usual killing procedure, Coa said: 'She usually lets herself be killed. If the hour isn't right, if it is too early, we just bury her alive. [If we go ahead with the sacrifice] we grab her and cut off her head and with the blood we make holy aspersions around the place. The man [who has commissioned the sacrifice] makes holy aspersions. His wife does too. And so do I.'

## Killing by the Book

In common with many other shamans in Peru and Bolivia, Coa based his magickical practices on the theory and rituals laid down in a number of books. These included the books of *Black*, *White*, and *Red Magic*, and *The Book of Saint Cyprian* (also known as *The Sorcerers' Guide*). The latter book is based on the Western magickal books, or 'grimoires', of the middle ages, which advocated selling your soul to the Devil in exchange for riches and power. Chapter Thirteen of *The Book of Saint Cyprian* is dedicated to making a bargain with the Devil. It instructs the magickian to go to a mountain top (or crossroads near a river or ruin) with various talismans and to draw a magick circle on the ground, from which Lucifer is invoked three times. The first invocation makes no bones about the materialistic nature of the deal:

Emperor Lucifer, owner and lord of all the rebellious spirits, I beg you to favour my request . . . Appear to me tonight in human form, without any awful smell, and grant me, by means of the pact which I am going to present to you, all the riches and gifts that I need.

At this point, according to the book, a demon appears demanding to know why his rest has been disturbed. Then

Lucifer enters the fray, refusing the magickian's request for riches, by saying: 'I can't accede to your demand, except on the condition that you give yourself to me for twenty years, to do with your body and soul what I want.' Following long negotiations, a pact is signed in blood, and Lucifer leads the magickian to the nearest treasure.

South American shamans, however, didn't take to the idea of selling their souls to the Devil in exchange for riches. It didn't make any sense to them. Instead, they took a more pragmatic approach: they sold *someone else's* soul to the Devil in a blood sacrifice.

Considering the amount of faith South American shamans have put in *The Book of Saint Cyprian*, it isn't exactly sophisticated. Most readers in the West would see it as very tacky – magick ritual presented in almost comic-book form – and very hard to take seriously. Yet a report from a teacher in Portugal, Ray Vogensen,[3] shows that, even in the West, the book has a sinister reputation. People take it seriously enough to be scared by it. 'I first heard of it when students of mine told of a girl who had committed suicide in Vila Real by throwing herself off the iron bridge that crosses the Corgo River,' he says. 'According to stories, but believed by my students, *The Book of Saint Cyprian* was found near her body. Students had a genuine fear of the book and advised not to open it.' As far as they were concerned it was an accursed grimoire.

Various versions of the book exist, each claiming to offer the 'true' knowledge of Saint Cyprian.[4] The book is very popular in Portugal and Spain, as well as in South America. In Brazil, it is even available from the well-known department store, Lojas Americans – which is on a par with Harrods stocking it in this country.

The book is divided into three parts. The first part tells the life story of Saint Cyprian; gives prayers for midday, the afternoon, and midnight; offers ways to predict the future; lists the 148 places where enchantments can be found; and ends with ways to deal cards. The second part reveals the 'true treasure' of black and white magick, offers the secrets of witchcraft for good and evil and provides magickal recipes to gain a marriage partner or lover. The third part lists all the treasures that can be found, mainly in the region of Galicia, in northwest Spain.

But who was Saint Cyprian? According to *The Catholic Encyclopaedia* (Volume IV), he was one of the Christians of Antioch, in ancient Syria, who were executed[5] on 26 September, AD 304:

> Christians of Antioch who suffered martyrdom during the persecution of Diocletian at Nicomedia, 26 September, 304, the date in September being afterwards made the day of their feast. Cyprian was a heathen magickian of Antioch who had dealings with demons. By their aid he sought to bring St Justina, a Christian virgin, to ruin; but she foiled the threefold attacks of the devils by the sign of the cross. Brought to despair Cyprian made the sign of the cross himself and in this way was freed from the toils of Satan. He was received into the Church, was made pre-eminent by miraculous gifts, and became in succession deacon, priest, and finally bishop . . .
>
> During the Diocletian persecution [he was] seized and taken to Damascus where [he was] shockingly tortured. As [his] faith never wavered [he was] brought before the Roman emperor Diocletian at Nicomedia, where at his command [he was] beheaded on the bank of the river Gallus. After [the body of the saint] had lain unburied for six days [he was] taken by Christian sailors to Rome where [he was] interred on the estate of a noble lady named Rufina and later [was] entombed in Constantine's basilica . . .

The story ... must have arisen as early as the fourth century, for it is mentioned both by St Gregory Nazianzen and Prudentius; both, nevertheless, have confounded our Cyprian with St Cyprian of Carthage, a mistake often repeated. It is certain that no Bishop of Antioch bore the name of Cyprian. The attempt has been made to find in Cyprian a mystical prototype of the Faust legend: [Spanish dramatist Pedro] Calderón took the story as the basis of a drama: 'El magico prodigioso'.[6]

Most books relating the lives of the saints have two entries for Saint Cyprian: Saint Cyprian of Antioch and Saint Cyprian of Carthage. Both lived in the third century, both were bishops and both were beheaded. To make it even more difficult to distinguish who was who, their festival days are both celebrated in September. But the consensus seems to be that Cyprian of Antioch is the reputed author of the famous grimoire. Of course, there is no record that he himself wrote it; and when the book was first written is still a mystery.

But as teacher Ray Vogensen who looked extensively into the subject, says: 'The facts are meaningless because those who use the book or who believe in Saint Cyprian do not worry about such discrepancies.'

## Breaking the Rules

Sorcerers and shamans are often not averse to making things up as they go along. If the facts don't suit them, they change them. And why not? Especially if it works and other people go along with it. Earl Marlowe,[7] the Voodoo man I was associated with, was expedient in nearly everything he did. Even though he had a Voodoo background, he would mix and match traditions in his spells and magickal workings. He'd borrow ideas from hypnosis techniques or from Chinese Qigong. A good example of this is the main method he used for divining the future. He taught me it one summer's day in the ornate and leafy grounds of Alexandra Palace in north London. We used to spend many an afternoon there, partly because we were inveterate slackers, and partly because Earl, then in his late 50s, used to like to chat up the young women (because he was full of humour and charm, nearly all of them liked his attentions). One of the ways he got their attention was by spreading out a cloth on the grass and laying out a deck of Jack Daniels playing cards, a crystal ball and incense burners. Women of all ages and one or two men would come up and ask, 'Do you tell fortunes?' 'I do,' he'd reply. 'Can you tell mine?' they'd always ask. By the end of the afternoon there would invariably be a crowd of twenty people or more listening to Earl's colourful and outrageous stories, including anecdotes about how he'd performed spells in Highgate Cemetery for a number of high-profile politicians to help them win elections. It was not surprising he always had a large entourage. Once he wearied of that, he'd pull out his tambourine and start singing a haunting blues. I'd plug my red Gibson semi-acoustic into an old, battery-powered Vox busking amplifier and back him up with some slide guitar. Some days a few hundred people congregated around us, which led to us setting up a small generator and using a small PA system to pump out more volume. The good thing was I always used to have a bottle of Wild Turkey bourbon on my amp to swig from. Never once did I have to buy new bottles; replacements would miraculously appear every few days – very touching as a lot of the people who hung out with us were broke and drawing welfare, but they made sure the artists never went short of their 'medicines'.

One evening when most of the entourage had left for the pubs and clubs, Earl was smoking a huge joint (as was his want), and he said, 'You know, Doc,' (short for 'Doktor Snake' which was my stage name) 'all that divination mumbo jumbo with the cards, crystal ball and rituals, it's all for show. You don't need any of it to see into the future. And you can do it for yourself. You don't need a fortune teller. Fact is, it's better not to follow the rules laid down in books on the subject. It's better to do it freeform, improvise like you do on the guitar.' He then showed me a system, which he said had been used by everyone from Voodoo practitioners to hunter-gatherer magickians from distant antiquity. This is how it works:

First off, you enter a state of trance, using the 'sensory systems' method used in martial arts and hypnosis. Simply sit or stand and focus on the input of your senses. Do it in any order, but use the following to start off with:

1. Sight: peripheral vision – what you can see out of the corners of our eyes.

2. Sound: what you can hear – birdsong, the wind in the trees, the distant hum of traffic.

3. Touch: feel the cool breeze on your cheek or the warmth of the sun on your arms.

4. Scent: notice the aroma of the flowers in your garden or window box; or simply become aware of the scents drifting on the air.

5. Taste: this is closely related to the sense of smell – become aware of the sensations in your mouth.

There may be an aftertaste of a meal or drink. If not, just become aware of how your tongue and mouth feel.

This method stills the chatter of the mind and induces a state of deep relaxation. You may need to channel through the senses a few times to get the desired effect. But eventually you will find you can enter trance within a few seconds. Placing your attention on sensory experience will enhance your appreciation of the natural world. What's more, when the chatter of the mind is stilled your imagination is free to seep into your everyday consciousness. Thus when you look up at the clouds, or look at the branches of a tree swaying in the breeze, you will see all sorts of shapes and images. In fact, even when looking at something as ordinary as the weave of a carpet while in trance can produce a powerful visionary state. When I stare at the carpet in my study, I often see faces, animals, mythical beasts, and other images. What is happening is this: when in trance, the imagination comes to the forefront of consciousness and enters into dynamic interaction with the environment.

Earl said this type of visionary experience could be used to good effect in divining: 'It's similar to using a crystal ball,' he said. 'But it cuts out the paraphernalia, which you don't need. First you think of a question, what you want to know about the future. Then go into a trance and stare at some object – the weave of a carpet, clouds in the sky, or the leaves and branches on a tree. When you start seeing visions and images, you work out their meaning according to the nature of the question you asked. If you wanted to know if a friend is deceiving you and you see a fox or coyote, odds are they are deceiving you. But, remember, there's no set rules on this. It all depends on how you perceive given images. If you see the coyote or fox as cunning tricksters, then that is how you should interpret your vision. Don't read books that tell you how to interpret symbols. Make your own rules – that is the route to true magick power.'

## Wizard of the Four Winds

Another shaman with views similar to Earl Marlowe, was Eduardo Calderón, who operated, up until his recent death, on the north coast of Peru, near the city of Trujillo, some 600 miles from Lake Titicaca, where Clemente Limachi and others were sacrificed. Calderón, it should be said from the outset, was a healer and abhorred the idea of ritual sacrifice or violence of any kind. He was the subject of UCLA (University of California, Los Angeles) anthropologist Douglas Sharon's thesis and book, *The Wizard of the Four Winds*, and other academic studies. Calderón also gets a mention in British archaeologist Evan Hadingham's book, *Lines to the Mountain Gods of Peru*.[8] In the book, Hadingham says of Calderón: 'Don Eduardo is a bit of a charlatan, but there's no doubt he has tremendously improved on our understanding of Andean shamanism.' The reason he said that was, like Earl Marlowe, Calderón was highly eclectic in his sorcery; he'd think nothing of mixing and matching concepts from Tibetan Buddhism and biblical imagery with his native belief systems. On many occasions he probably did look like he was making it all up as he went along.

Patrick Tierney also met Calderón and gained a lot of useful information from him – along with many fantastical tales such as how the mountain gods opened up a sacred peak for him and showed him rooms filled with gold. One striking story concerned a black magickian, who he described as a 'brujazo' or 'big witch'. Calderón related how he was at an all-night ceremony being run by

the big witch. At one point the big witch instructed him
to leave the room and spit outside – spitting being a way
to drive off certain evil spirits.

'But when I went outside,' said Calderón, 'I saw this
kind of gorilla, which was half drunk. It scared the hell
out of me, and I bolted back into the house. But when I
got back to the mesa (ritual area), the gorilla was seated
right next to the big witch. The brujazo looked at me and
laughed. "You see him, don't you? This is my guardian
spirit, Chicanga. He does anything I want him to." That's
when I realised he was a black magickian. You'd never
catch me working with a creature like that big black thing.
It was really ugly.'

Calderón went on to tell Tierney that the aim of the
yatiris (shamans) who perform ritual killings is to create
such creatures. 'That's what these guys who perform human
sacrifice are trying to do with the souls of the victims. They
want to control the disembodied soul and make it into a
guardian spirit who will serve them.' He said such entities
are 'thoughtforms' trapped by the minds of magickians,
and used for good or evil. As an example of positive thoughtforms, Calderón cited Jesus and Buddha. 'Thoughtforms
like Jesus or Buddha can go on for eternity,' he explained.
'As long as people think of Jesus, it's like a continually
charging battery. But if people forget him, then, like others
before and since, he'll be dissolved.'

He added that the Peruvian sacrificial victim, Clemente
Lamachi, became a thoughtform that shamans and others
charged up whenever they did magickal workings or
prayers. 'By praying to him, they are giving him greater
potential. They believe he's a saint, which means they've
made him a necessity. He's been crystallised into a deity,
a higher power,' he said.

According to Calderón, one of the arts of shamanism
is to dominate and use these thoughtforms, so they can

be used for good or evil. 'When an animal is sacrificed, and the smoke from the (burnt) offering rises skyward, everyone prays, "Let us have bigger flocks". But it is not the smoke from the animal – it's the united thoughts that rise upwards and produce results. These are thought-forms too. The black magickian concentrates his mind to cause an automobile accident and – THWAACK! It happens. A white magickian also uses these forces. But the forces themselves are neutral.'

## Thought Power

Sorcerers the world over claim they can harness thought and give it some level of form. Tibetan Buddhists who practise 'dream yoga', a form of lucid dreaming, claim they can create physical objects and even living beings, known as 'tulpas', by repeatedly imagining them in their mind's eye. But even for those who create them, the question of whether tulpas have any degree of reality or not is far from cut and dried. Tibetan mysticism states that all the phenomena we perceive – including the world around us – are born of our imagination. Thus to the Tibetan adept the reality or unreality of the tulpa is simply not an issue: both 'solid' matter and thoughtforms exist on the imaginary plane and accordingly neither can be considered real or unreal. To prove that they truly under-stand this bewildering ambiguity, initiates of Tibetan dream yoga subject themselves to a dangerous test – a ritual known as the 'Dance of Chod'. This involves conjuring up, or visualising, a horde of grotesque tulpa demons, along with a tulpa double of themselves. The magickian then has to will the demons to attack his double, and remain completely calm and composed as the hideous thoughtforms rip their double apart and eat it. If the magickian succeeds in staying calm, then the demons cannot harm him because he has truly accepted the dream-like nature of reality and accordingly has no fear of such creatures. But if the magickian continues to see reality in 'nuts and bolts' terms, he empowers the demons and risks insanity or dying of fright.

One of the most famous examples of the creation of a tulpa involved a Westerner – the redoubtable French traveller Alexandra David-Neel, who spent fourteen years in Tibet and wrote over 30 books about Eastern religion, philosophy and her travels (she later became a major influence on beat writers like Jack Kerouac and Allen Ginsberg). Out of curiosity, she set about performing what is known as the 'Dubthab Rite', which reputedly culminates in the tangible manifestation of a thought-form. In *Magick and Mystery in Tibet* (first published in 1931; reissued Thorsons 1997), David-Neel recounts how she chose to create a monk who was 'short and fat, [and] of an innocent type'. After a few months of performing the rite, which consisted of disciplined daily visualisation, she started catching glimpses of the phantom monk. She states: 'His form grew gradually fixed and life-like looking. He became a kind of guest in my apartment.' It got to the point that even when she wasn't consciously thinking of the monk, he would appear anyway. 'The illusion was mostly visual,' she goes on, 'but sometimes I felt as if a robe was lightly rubbing against me and once a hand seemed to touch my shoulder.' In the end, however, the monk's presence became troublesome; it took on a life of its own and changed from being innocent and jolly to being sly and malignant. David-Neel had lost control of the tulpa and, to her dismay, it took about as long to dissolve the phantom creation as it had to create it.

Some occultists have claimed that thoughtforms can be created inadvertently, by a combination of thought and emotion. In *Psychic Self-Defence* (1930), British mystic Dion Fortune (Violet Firth) (1890–1946) describes how she was thinking negative thoughts about someone who had wronged her. Lying in bed in a semi-dozing state, she thought of the Fenris wolf, a demon from Nordic mythology, while at the same time contemplating revenge. 'Immediately I felt a curious drawing-out sensation from my solar plexus,' she says, 'and there materialised beside me in bed a large wolf. I knew nothing of the art of making (artificial) elementals at that time, but had accidentally stumbled upon the right method – the brooding, highly charged with emotion . . . and the condition between sleeping and waking . . .' Although very frightened, she forced herself not to panic, and forcefully ordered the beast out of the house. She would have dismissed the experience as a nightmare, only that same night someone else in the house reported dreaming of wolves, and of seeing the eyes of a wild animal shining in the darkness. The realisation that her creation had been in some sense tangible, and the fact that she did not wish to follow what she described as 'the left hand path' of magick, led her to perform a ritual to 'reabsorb' the creature back into herself.

In the early 1970s, members of the Toronto Society for Psychical Research decided to try to conjure up a fictional spirit,[9] in a process almost identical to the way sorcerers claim to manufacture thoughtforms and tulpas. Under the direction of eminent psychical researcher Dr A.R.G. Owen, the group invented the case history of a seventeenth-century Englishman called Philip, who had an affair with a beautiful gypsy girl. When Philip's wife found out, she accused the girl of witchcraft and saw to it that the girl was burned at the stake. Philip did not intervene and eventually committed suicide in remorse. Having created this story, the Toronto group set about trying to conjure up the spirit of Philip. For several months there were no results. Then one evening, while they were all relaxing and singing songs, there was a rap at the table. They used the standard code – one rap for yes, two for no – to question the 'spirit', which claimed to be Philip, and corroborated and even enlarged upon the story they had invented for him. At later séances, Philip made the table dance all around the room, and even made it levitate in front of TV cameras.

There is also a case on record of a thoughtform entity being created and witnessed by a small gathering of people. Writing in the June 1960 edition of *Fate* magazine, Nicholas Mamontoff recounts how, in 1912, a Russian occult-scientific investigation group, called The Brotherhood of the Rising Sun, invited a mysterious (and unnamed) Tibetan/Chinese-looking guru to instruct them in his knowledge. During the lecture, the guru invited the audience to create an 'egrigor' (thoughtform) using their collective thought power. The guru instructed them to visualise a red-haired puss-in-boots. 'Concentrate! Concentrate! Do not think of anything but the cat,' urged the guru. After a while, according to Mamontoff's father who attended the lecture, the shadowy form of a cat appeared in front of the gathering. When the guru asked them all to stop visualising, the cat faded away. The guru closed the lecture by saying, 'The Western scientists never realise how powerful the human mind is and what miracles it can work.'

Does the human mind really have the ability to create apparently material forms out of nowhere? Clearly some of the above stories are more likely to have been wishful thinking or trickery. But one author and researcher who gives the idea some level of credence is Hilary Evans.[10] He's one of Britain's foremost authorities on strange phenomena and regularly appears in *Fortean Times* magazine. He has investigated alleged ghost and UFO sightings, along with all sorts of other apparently para-normal phenomena. He also helped found the Association for the Scientific Study of Anomalous Phenomena (ASSAP) and is a director of the Mary Evans Picture Library. He has a healthy scepticism, but is open to ideas. So I decided to track him down to get his opinion on the reality or otherwise of thoughtforms. I asked him if he believes it is possible for thoughts to take on an existence beyond that of their creator's imagination.

'I do entertain the idea that people can, up to a point, create something which has physical dimensions. For instance, there's absolutely no question in my mind that people can somehow project themselves into some kind of out-of-body form, which for all intents and purposes could be seen as a thoughtform. And if they visit a friend's bedroom he or she will wake up and see them there – so something has appeared there, it's not just hallucination.' In that case, I asked, can thoughtforms have an effect on the material world? 'Very questionable.' he replied. 'But there is a case on the SPR (Society for Psychical Research) files of somebody's double apparently having a tangible effect in the material world – a husband saw his wife's double go into another room and move an object, and it was moved. We could also take into account the cases of people turning off street lamps, apparently with the power of their minds. That is a projection of power of some sort. So conceivably if this power switched from turning off street lights into projecting some kind of image or entity, then one might well appear.'

I then brought up the Alexandra David-Neel case and asked whether he thought she had really managed to mani-fest a tulpa during her travels in Tibet. 'I'm very dubious about the David-Neel case,' he said. 'It's a very famous story, but to me the tulpa anecdote looks suspiciously like it was brought in to give her a nice climax for her book.

I'm really very doubtful that it occurred, but then that might be cynicism on my part!'

## Is it Really Murder?

Whatever the truth about thoughtforms, one thing is certain: shamans who take the dark path of murder certainly believe the soul of their sacrificial victim can be enslaved and put to use. The fact is, even though their trade involves killing people and cutting them up, professional human sacrificers aren't psychopaths. Nor do they necessarily have a criminal mentality. They don't believe they're doing anything wrong. To them, it isn't murder. As far as they are concerned their practices are rooted in ancient history. What's more, some even bemoan the fact that such practices are now outlawed. During his researches in the 1980s Patrick Tierney spoke to Machi Rosa, an 85-year-old Chilean shamaness, who said: 'There used to be fewer earthquakes and tidal waves in the old days, when they sacrificed orphans. But today a machi (shaman) can't sacrifice orphans. And you know why? Because if she does they'll come and put her in jail.' For Machi Rosa and other shamans in her area human sacrifice is the accepted method of appeasing the bloodlust of an enormous serpent deity which, if allowed to go hungry, causes natural disasters like earthquakes and tidal waves. Not only do natural forces have to be appeased, man-made ones do too. In rural areas of Peru and Bolivia shamans regularly place rocks and boulders on treacherous stretches of road in order to cause fatal car accidents. They believe that blood must be spilled on the road to satisfy the spirit of the highway. This ensures people will be safe from accidents for a while.

Ideas like this can be traced back to Inca times in South

America. Accounts by sixteenth- and seventeenth-century Spanish priests describe how the Incas used to sacrifice children in order to please the gods, whose discontent was considered to threaten Inca fortunes. The children had to be as close to perfection as possible. The ugly or deformed were barred. Selection was considered an honour, as the children were supposed to become gods – a belief still held by some today, as is illustrated by the way Clemente Limachi became deified.

The bloodiest human sacrifices in history were carried out by the Aztecs of Central Mexico. They believed that man was responsible for the maintenance of the cosmos. Therefore if the gods were not fed with enough blood, the world would end. So each day at the temples in Aztec cities people were ritually killed and their bodies were burned with incense in ceremonial braziers. On special occasions the carnage could be enormous. The dedication of the pyramid-temple of Huitzilopochtil, for example, required the sacrifice of around 20,000 victims. Their hearts were torn from their living bodies at the top of the pyramid and their blood was allowed to cascade down the sides.

This kind of thing was normal. It was part of life and was sanctioned by the state. Now the business of sacrifice has gone underground. It has to be done secretly and surreptitiously. Although we in Britain sacrificed people during Viking, Anglo-Saxon and Celtic times, and earlier, we now consider it murder. It clearly is a barbaric practice. But how can you accuse a professional human sacrificer of murder when they don't consider that what they've done is wrong? The motive, after all, wasn't murder, it was sacrifice. It was a gift to appease the gods. By accusing ritual sacrificers of murder we are saying that their belief systems are untrue, and that there are no gods or disembodied spirits (except, of course, for our God, the Virgin Mary and the Holy Ghost). There is a strong element of cultural and religious imperialism in the sacrifice issue, which impacts on law enforcement and the judiciary as much as on religious thinking.

## Devil Doctor of Lagos

Another terrifying – and truly chilling – professional human sacrificer was Doctor Drago, who ran a highly profitable magickal services business out of Lagos, Nigeria, during the 1960s and 1970s. His existence – and the macabre nature of his business – was brought to light in a 1989 exposé called *Blood Secrets*[11] by Isaiah Oke, a practitioner of traditional African religion turned born-again Christian. Although Oke 'joined the other side' and became a Christian – which means he could have been guilty of over-exaggerating certain negative aspects of his native religion – the book does have the ring of truth about it. Oke, a Yoruban Nigerian who was working as a Christian missionary when his book came out, claimed that Juju – an age-old religion involving animal and human sacrifice, curses and the manipulation of good and evil spirits – continues to flourish in modern Africa. Although some scholars say Juju is not the correct term for traditional African religion, Oke insists it is. 'The real name for our religion,' he said, 'sounds humorous to [Westerners'] ears. But we Africans still call it what our ancestors did: Juju. The word is flexible and takes its exact meaning from context. Juju can refer to our religion, to the paraphernalia used in its practise or to the idea of mystical power. But however we use the word, it sounds ominous to us rather than humorous.'

He added that Juju continues to be practised in one form or another by most Africans – even by those who outwardly profess to be Christians or Muslims, who, he says, simply practise in private. When Oke was a boy, like most Central

Africans at that time, his community were still thoroughly Juju but kept it covered up to avoid coming into conflict with the local missionaries. When Oke's parents took him to the local 'Babalawo' (junior priest) for a rites-of-passage ritual, it was found, through divination, that an important ancestor – who was also a demigod – was incarnate in him. Because of this, his mother took him to live in Nigeria with his grandfather, who was an important figure in the Juju religion. He was a 'Babalorisha' or high priest. And it looked certain that Oke would follow in his footsteps – after all the gods themselves had decreed the boy's succession by allowing a demigod to incarnate in him. First, though, Oke had to go through an arduous initiation ritual, which included fasting, drinking the blood of sacrificed animals and meeting the most terrifying spirits (which may have been down to Oke being given psychotropic concoctions). It was touch and go whether he would get through it. But in the end he made the grade and became a 'man of knowledge' destined to become an important figure in Juju.

In the meantime, he had to be trained by his grandfather in the rites and rituals of Juju, most of which regularly involved the sacrifice of animals. Oke's grandfather also brought in a tutor from outside – Mr Olungwe – to teach the boy how to read and write. Oke's people didn't normally hold much with schooling, but his grandfather made an exception in Oke's case. 'It was his long-range plan that I should record on paper the whole Juju knowledge. This had never been done before and he felt that it would make me the most powerful Juju man, not only of Nigeria, but of all Africa,' Oke recalled. Mr Olungwe was under strict instruction not to 'corrupt' the boy with Western thinking. But eventually, Olungwe felt compelled to defy this rule and secretly schooled Oke in history and the ways of other cultures. He also introduced him to the Bible.

Around this time, Oke's grandfather decided the boy

needed extra schooling in the ways of Juju if he was ever to become a high priest of the religion. So he arranged to have the boy sent to Lagos (then the capital of Nigeria) to study with a notorious Juju priest called Doctor Drago. Oke was terrified. Simply leaving his rural village for the sprawling metropolis of Lagos was scary enough for the boy, but studying with Drago made him feel sick to his stomach: 'Drago was a name pronounced throughout the whole of Africa. But only in whispers. They called him the "devil doctor of Lagos". He was also said to be a [Juju priest] of truly exceptional power. There were rumours to the effect that he refused to speak to the spirits, as the high priests do. Instead he commanded them to do *his* bidding. He was supposed to be a truly menacing figure,' he said.

When Oke arrived in Lagos, having walked dust tracks and taken ramshackle buses to get there, he was met by Doctor Drago's chauffeur, 'Speedy', who pulled up in a purple Rolls-Royce. Speedy was very short and wore a peaked cap, knee-high boots and tight-fitting uniform. He was a larger-than-life character who talked fast and loudly, and whose two front gold teeth gleamed whenever he laughed, which was often. Pointing to the Rolls, he said to Oke: 'Only one like it in Lagos; all custom.'

Oke got in the back of the car, and was overawed by its size and comfort. Although gregarious and friendly, Speedy became nervous and tense when he talked about Doctor Drago. 'Just do as he says, Boss, and you'll be okay,' he advised Oke. 'Don't ever cross him, Boss. 'Cause he's a big man, the Doctor. That's right, Boss. A *big man. Big Juju.*'

Drago lived in what Speedy called 'the big house'. It was a large white house, with lots of sprawling outbuildings. The roof of the front porch was balanced on top of four big white pillars, giving the dwelling a majestic appearance. As far as Oke was concerned, it was a palace. 'It was the biggest building I'd ever seen up this close,' he recalled, 'bigger even than the Lagos central bus terminal.'

Once he'd been given a room and settled in, a servant took Oke to meet Doctor Drago, who was sitting at a long dining table. He sat perfectly still, smiling like a statue, but his hands kept crawling around the table 'as if they had minds of their own'. Drago had high cheek-bones and 'his face looked like it had been chiselled from mahogany'. He wore round spectacles and a three-piece suit with a white shirt and necktie. He even had a gold pocket watch in his waistcoat. On every one of his fingers were gold and jewelled rings. He spoke in a high-pitched, raspy voice, and told Oke: 'You will see much during your time here. You will see Juju that is a little . . . different from what is practised out in the country.'

That was an understatement on a par with saying your rabid pit bull terrier has the manners of a poodle.


## A Hard-on for Hell

All went well for a few months. Oke learned lots of new Juju rituals and became a master with the sacrificial knife, having dispatched countless animals on a daily basis. He was like a master butcher; the only difference being the killing and chopping up had a religious or magickal motive. Oke had even got used to Doctor Drago; he was still scary, but familiarity had tapered that off quite a bit. He'd even started to consider himself on a good number. Compared to the village life he was used to he was living in luxury; the food and accommodation were equal to what you'd get in a top-class hotel. Oke couldn't get over the fact that there were bathrooms. Previously he'd only used a flush toilet in bus terminals. But then a sinister visitor turned up at the big white house. It was like the Devil himself had come to town and it changed everything for Oke.

One morning Oke looked out of the window and saw a big motorcade thunder into the courtyard – a huge American stretch limousine with tail fins, followed by two jeeps full of soldiers. Bringing up the rear was a white ambulance with red crosses on its roof and sides. A huge mountain of a man stepped out of the car when it stopped. 'He was as big around as he was tall ... with a moon-shaped face,' remembered Oke. Although he wore the uniform of a senior military officer – complete with a chest full of medals – he was not part of the Nigerian army; nor did his features resemble those of any of the nearby peoples, such as the Yoruba, Ibo or Hausa. He clearly came from another part of Africa.

For the first time during his stay Oke saw Doctor Drago humbled. He bowed before the big man and called him 'Colonel'. The soldiers removed a number of small boxes from their jeeps. They were clearly very heavy because it took two men to carry each one inside. 'Here your fee, Doctor,' the Colonel said to Drago. 'Jus' like we agree on. You like inspec' it?' 'No need, Colonel,' said Drago. 'You are an honourable man.'

While this exchange was going on, two men in white suits removed a stretcher from the ambulance. The body on it was strapped down and was completely covered with a sheet, as if it were a corpse. 'But I could hear some muffled noises and could see movement under the sheet, as if the person were trying to get up from the [stretcher],' said Oke. He concluded it was a case of possession and that Drago had been hired to perform a healing ceremony for a very important person. The entourage went inside, the Colonel chattering to Doctor Drago in broken English and guffawing loudly every so often. Drago and the Colonel went to another part of the house, presumably conducting business of some sort. Two hours later Oke was summoned.

A servant led him to Drago's 'ile-agbara', which meant 'power house' and was his own private shrine. Oke had been in it many times, but only in the central room, the one set aside for sacrifice. Drago required him to do all the sacrificing while he and his subordinate priests negotiated prices with customers in the smaller rooms nearby.

Sacrifice was hard work. 'I've lost track of how many hours I had to labour over the killing table,' said Oke. 'We used a special one made of stainless steel [imported from Sheffield in England]. It had been designated for use in the embalming trade and had little gutters cut into it so the blood and other bodily fluids could drain away into a [container] down at the foot of the table. Sometimes the blood was saved in buckets for use in further ritual. But often, I was liberating so much of it during my day's work that Drago told me to just let it go down the drain. There were times I went to bed with a sore arm from all the ritual killing work I was obliged to do to earn my keep. I may not have been learning as much Juju from the Doctor as I'd hoped, but there was probably no equal in all of Africa for my skill with the blade.'

This time Oke was not working alone in the sacrifice room. He had company. Members of Drago's staff were sitting on the floor softly playing ritual drums. Drago was standing at the head of the killing table, his round spectacles reflecting the fluorescent light. The Colonel stood next to Drago, his huge belly shaking every so often with silent mirth that no one else seemed party to. Everyone was dressed in white, which Oke described as the Juju ritual-killing colour. Two of the soldiers were in the room as well. They were wearing white tunics over their uniforms. The odd thing was, they were huddling into themselves as if badly frightened. One looked like he might faint.

Drago told Oke that the Colonel had personally requested that he and the soldiers be present. The Colonel smiled warmly at them and said: 'I like many witness. Juju too secret, too quiet. But I like many people to know how I do things – to know how I get power, how I use power. So you be witness – tell other Juju men. These men be witness – tell other soldiers.'

Drago then informed Oke that he would be learning something new. He said that during this ritual Oke would be the one doing the killing and that this would be the first time he had performed this particular ritual. Drago added that even he had only had the opportunity to perform the ritual no more than two or three times each year throughout his career. Oke felt honoured and excited. At last he was moving up the more advanced levels of his training. Drago said the ritual was called 'iko-awo' – a term Oke had never heard before, but knew it translated roughly as 'spirit slave'. At that point Drago moved to one side to reveal what was on the sacrificial table. To Oke's horror it was a skinny white man held down with straps. He was completely naked and a tennis ball was stuffed in his mouth to keep him quiet. His eyes were bulged with sheer terror. Oke felt the blood drain from his own face as the full realisation of what was about to happen dawned on him. Even more chilling, he was the one who was supposed to do the killing . . .

'Do you know the ritual of the "two hundred cuts"?' asked Drago. Oke couldn't reply. He was too horrified to speak. So Drago hit him over the head. 'Isaiah! I asked you a question, boy! Do you know the "two hundred cuts"?'

'Oh yes, Doctor,' said Oke fearfully. 'I've seen my uncle do it.'

'But you've never performed the rite yourself, is that correct?' asked Drago.

'Oh, no, sir,' replied Oke, praying that he would be let off the hook. 'I never did. You see, we only did the "two hundred cuts" once a year back home – just before the spring planting.' In his experience, the rite of 'two hundred cuts' had only ever been performed on animals. But it was clear that Drago's plan was to perform it on the skinny white man. The only thing was, Oke had never killed a human before and didn't want to start now.

As its name suggests, the ritual of 'two hundred cuts' involved making 200 cuts into an animal. If done properly, the animal would survive. It was when the 201st cut was administered that it died. The ritual was intentionally cruel and gruesome. According to Oke: 'The more noise [the animal] makes during the ritual the more likely the gods [known as "orishas"] will come to see what all the fuss is about. In between the cuts there was a good deal of celebration, so the whole procedure lasted about twelve hours, from sun-up to sundown.' Finally the 201st cut – across the throat – was administered and the animal would meet its end. The idea is its soul would go to the 'invisible' world to intercede with the gods on behalf of the sorcerers who killed it. Just to make sure it actually did so, its head would be removed and placed in a specially prepared jar, or cauldron (nganga). The head was then held as a ransom until the following year, when a new victim would be chosen.

Oke makes clear that practitioners of Juju generally treat their sacrifices humanely – 'except in those special instances when we want the animal to carry messages for us into the invisible world of the spirits. Then we use rituals like the "two hundred cuts" that are deliberately abusive, painful, inhumane and cruel.' Oke admits that Juju men reason that if the ritual works with an animal, it should be even more powerful with a human victim. 'The [Juju priests] are not fools,' he says. 'They figured that one out ages ago. So they have long believed that the ritual torture and killing of a human being should gain enormous power in the invisible world. But because of the social scrutiny that's a part of tribal life, that kind of murder was really only an isolated problem with us. Until, that is, we Africans found freedom from social judgment in the anonymity of big cities like Lagos.'

Because of his lack of experience, Drago excused Oke from performing the whole 'two hundred cuts' ritual, but insisted he administer the 201st cut – the killing cut. The Colonel chuckled, gleefully watching Oke squirm.

Oke's heart pounded in horror. 'Doctor, I . . . I see no sacrifice here; what animal will we use?'

'Ah,' said Drago, 'as to that, we shall sacrifice the animal that eats salt.'

Oke bowed his head. The phrase 'the animal that eats salt' confirmed his worst fears. It was Juju man code for 'man', the only animal that puts salt on his food.

The Colonel was getting impatient. He stepped forward and said: 'We start now, yes?'

'As you wish, Colonel,' said Drago. He turned to a surgical tray next to the stainless steel table and selected a scalpel. The white man looked on totally helpless as Drago brought the blade down towards his throat. At the first touch of the scalpel the man urinated on himself. Drago slid the flat of the scalpel along the man's neck, almost as if he were about to give him a shave. He then slashed the leather cord holding the tennis ball gag in the white man's mouth. 'Thank God,' gasped the man.

Drago asked him if he understood what had happened to him. 'No,' said the white man. 'I was standing outside the club, waiting for my transport, when a local military vehicle pulled up. Well, I naturally assumed the Embassy had asked them to come collect me. [But] rather than taking the road toward the lake, which they should have done so I could rejoin my unit, the buggers headed for the airport!

This bedsheet was washed up on the southern bank of the Thames in 2001. It had the West African name 'Adekoyejo Fola Adoye' written on it, three times. Police at first thought it might have offered a clue to Adam's murder, but it proved a red herring. It turned out that Adoye lived in New York and his London-based parents had performed a thanksgiving ritual to celebrate the fact that he had survived the 9/11 terrorist attacks.

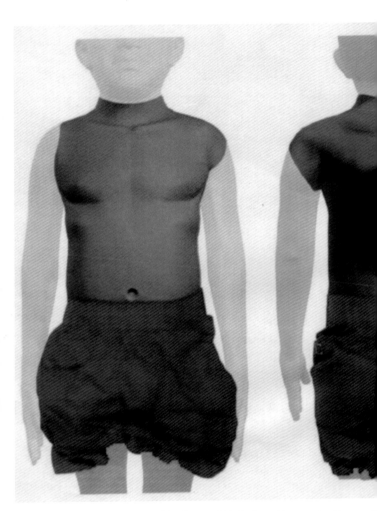

This mock up of 'Adam', created by Scotland Yard, shows him wearing the orange shorts that were found on his limbless and headless torso, which was found floating in the River Thames in September 2001.

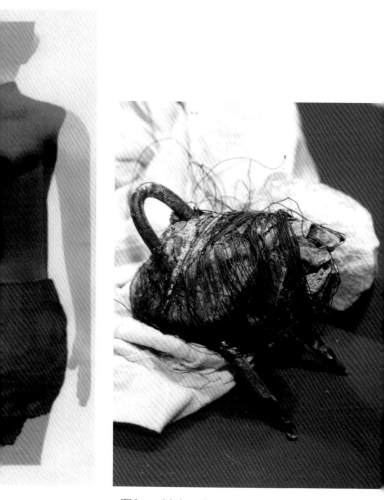

This magickal artefact, recovered by the Metropolitan Police, reveals that Voodoo-like macabre rites of sorcery regularly go on, in and around London.

Nelson Mandela makes a pan-African appeal for people to come forward with information concerning Adam's ritual murder. Alongside him are Commander Andy Baker and Detective Inspector Will O'Reilly of Scotland Yard.

Detective Inspector Will O'Reilly and John Azah (Independent Advisory Group) lay a wreath of yellow flowers from a police launch on the River Thames near Tower Bridge, London, about half a mile away from where Adam's mutilated torso was recovered.

A 'muti' (medicine) market trader in South Africa. Such markets provide the items used by traditional healers in Africa for healing and shamanism. Rumour has it you can pick up human body parts if you know who and where to ask. Otherwise, muti traders are perfectly legitimate.

A female muti market trader, making a talismanic item for use in magick and spiritual practises. Her tiny makeshift unit is the witchcraft equivalent of a 'cash and carry' in Britain.

Jars of herbs and powders used in muti medicine and magick. Such ingredients are often used in rituals that involve creating charm bags - famously called 'mojo hands' in Hoodoo, the folk magick tradition with African roots found in the southern states of America.

Colonel Kobus Jonker, the (now retired) head of the South African Police Service's Occult Related Crime Unit (ORCU) and adviser to Scotland Yard during the early stages of the Adam case. Pictured with an animal slaughtered for ritual purposes.

A costumed shaman uses a rattle to communicate with the spirits during a ceremony in Onitsha, Nigeria.

Juju men (African witchdoctors) in traditional dress. Juju practitioners commune with spirits and the dead during ceremonies. They perform healing magick for the sick and, if the occasion demands, unleash curses on enemies. Renegade Juju men have been known to have committed ritual human sacrifices.

Pre-Colombian sculpture showing a priest wearing the skin of a sacrificial victim and impersonating the god Xipe Totec.

Tribal peoples tie a man to a tree for exorcism. They believe that bad things only happen when an evil spirit enters someone's body and possesses them. To overcome the troubles the spirit has to be beaten out. This can sometimes involve torturing the possessed person.

[I had] six hours on the metal floor of an old Dakota, me trussed up like a Christmas goose! When we finally arrived here, where ever "here" is, they threw me in some sort of old ambulance and . . . well, here I am . . .'

The man, who was clearly a British army officer, then instructed Drago to release him, adding that there was no point holding him, as he wasn't worth much in the way of a ransom.

'No? Then it appears we shall have to find some other use for you,' said Drago with a sinister gleam in his eyes. The blood rushed from the white man's face: 'Now, see here. This is most irregular. I shall be missed, you know,' he said desperately.

Drago told him that this would not be the case; apart from anything else his unit had no reason to suspect he would be anywhere within 2,000 kilometres of Nigeria. He added that Africa was a dangerous place and that 'disappearing here is not the same as vanishing from your Trafalgar Square at high noon. It is likely that your countrymen will feel you've met with some unfortunate mishap.'

At that moment, the Colonel stepped into the white man's view for the first time.

'You!' he shrieked. The Colonel grinned down at the white man. 'Is good of you to reco'ze your ol' frien'.'

'Old friend, indeed!' said the white man indignantly. 'What is your part in all of this?'

'My part? I am the man you will serve,' replied the Colonel.

'Not bloody likely!' the white man responded.

The Colonel roared with laughter, saying that, on the contrary, it was 'very likely'.

Drago elaborated: 'Yes, indeed, Sir,' he said. 'You will truly become the Colonel's servant, his representative. Not here. But in the invisible world. You will become his messenger, his spirit slave – what we call iko-awo.'

The horror in the white man's eyes revealed that he'd heard this term before.

'Ah,' said Drago, 'I see you know iko-awo. That is good. The more you know about this ritual, the better. [That way], the more you will go to the Orisha [gods] in a "charged up" condition.'

The white man gave in to his terror and begged them to let him go – even offering them all his savings. 'You can't do this thing,' he said. 'Especially you, Colonel. Why, your troops are the reason I am in Africa. Don't you remember? I came here to help you.'

'Good,' said the Colonel. 'Now I give you the chance to help me ver', ver' much.' With that he picked up a scalpel and thrust it into the white man's side, making him scream and sending speckles of blood as far as the ceiling.

Quick as a flash, Drago grabbed the scalpel from the Colonel and threw it on the floor. 'Do you wish this man to go to the Orisha having died an ordinary death?' he demanded. 'Can you afford to indulge your anger if it creates such waste?' Drago bent down to inspect the wound. After cleaning it up he said it wasn't fatal, but meant they'd have to work faster. With that he pulled up a chair and leaned close to the white man's ear. 'Listen to me,' he said. 'You will go to the spirits in pain. They will hear you above all others because your pain will be so great. You will plead for good fortune for the Colonel. If you fail him, he will burn your body and scatter the ashes to the winds.'

Drago turned to the Colonel and snapped his fingers. This was the signal for him, as prospective master of the spirit slave, to go and fetch the container in which the remains of the sacrifice would be imprisoned. The Colonel left the room via a doorway into a room at the back of the building. He returned puffing under the load of a portable wardrobe, which he set down at the foot of the sacrifice table, so the white man could see it.

Drago pointed to the cabinet. 'This is your hostage home. Look upon it and know fear.' By this time the white man was delirious with pain and fear. So Drago brought him round with smelling salts, which he rammed up his nose for good measure. He wanted him fully conscious otherwise the ritual would not work.

The two soldiers in the room were as shocked as Oke was. The Colonel, on the other hand, was highly amused by it all. He was also excited. Oke noticed that there was a prominent bulge in his trousers – he clearly had the mother of all erections at the sight of the white man's suffering.

Most people would be shocked and horrified at the idea of becoming sexually aroused at pain, torture and killing. Rightly so. But, chillingly, it may be more common that you might think. A while back, an old friend of mine, actor Richard Bowman,[12] told me an anecdote from his days doing extra work. He was working on a British movie, which was being filmed in London. Extra work tends to consist of hanging about, waiting for the director and film crew to set up scenes and takes. 'It's incredibly boring, just like the way it was depicted by Ricky Gervais in *Extras*,' says Richard. 'At the very least you have to take a book to read. But in the end even that wears thin. So you get chatting to the other extras. There was one chap I used to see quite a lot – I'll call him Joe. He was about 50 and had been into crime on and off throughout his life. You get a lot like that on set. Anyway, one time he said to me, 'Richard, what's the greatest, most profound pleasure you've ever had?' I didn't know what to say to that one. But he said, 'I'll tell you mine, nothing beats sticking a knife into someone. I don't mind telling you I get a hard on and come in my trousers. There's nothing like it. You oughta try it, Richard . . .' Needless to say Richard didn't try it.

*

Drago hadn't noticed the Colonel's erection. Or maybe he had and didn't care. I guess the Colonel was a top-paying client so he wasn't going to let a little thing like a hard-on for torture get in the way of business. Drago then moved even closer to the white man, who was now gasping for air, and told him: 'Pain will be your constant companion for the remainder of your life. There is no way you can change this fact. Think on this and know fear. That is the purpose of this ritual to send you to the spirits in a state such that they cannot help but notice you. Only then can you be effective in pleading the Colonel's case.' Drago then made his first cut. He let the scalpel sink about a centimetre into the white man's flesh, just to the left of his breastbone, and just enough to separate the top layer of skin from the underlying tissue. He drew the blade in a straight line down the front of his body until it reached his pubic hair. A thin trickle of blood oozed up behind the blade as it slid through the skin. Drago then made a number of other strokes, some running parallel to the first stroke. So skilful were Drago's cuts that the white man didn't even scream out. Eventually a flap of skin was hanging loose on the front of the white man's body. Drago turned to Oke and said: 'Isaiah, please remove the first strip from the sacrifice.'

Oke shrank back in horror. Drago glared at him. But the Colonel stepped in, saying: 'I see this before. When we hunt zebra, back home. Often young man afraid to kill first time. We call it "buck fever". Is easy to fix.' With that he grabbed Oke's hand and forced him to remove the bloody flap of skin hanging off the man's chest. Blood and marbled fat oozed between Oke's fingers as he removed the flap. Not surprisingly, he vomited and fell back in horror, while the two soldiers, forced to watch, slumped to the ground in shock. The Colonel, however, continued to enjoy himself, laughing merrily throughout. The white man fainted with pain, but Drago stuffed more smelling salts up his nostrils to revive him.

For the next three hours, Drago cut and Oke pulled. The Colonel spent the time talking to the white man, repeating the purpose of the rite, which was, he revealed, to take over his country. He said he knew it could take ten years but he was prepared to wait. When it came to the 201st cut, the killing cut, Oke – despite his protestations – was forced to do it. He told himself that, by now, he was probably putting the man out of his misery. So he sunk the blade into the white man's flesh and felt a horror and repulsion that he would never forget.

After a short break, they set about removing the man's entrails. The Colonel saved the liver in a plastic box, which had a blue flower on its side. Everything else was discarded. All that was left was a hollow-skinned corpse, which was washed, hung on a hook, and put in the portable wardrobe. When they were finished, the Colonel had his men carry the wardrobe out to the ambulance. Oke followed them with a large carton of herbs and spices that the Colonel would have to apply to the body every week to keep the smell under control. Then the motorcade set off for the airport and the long trip back east.

Oke was ill for some time after his ordeal. He had a fever and couldn't eat. In the end, he recovered and continued to serve his apprenticeship with Drago. Thankfully this involved no more bloodshed and consisted mainly of fetching and carrying things for the Doctor – although he did at one point come close to having to witness Drago sacrifice an unwanted baby, but Drago let him leave the room when he asked to.

When Oke's apprenticeship was up, he returned to his village. He then went to college in Oyo, where various events led to him doubting the efficacy of the Juju religion and magick and spells. He eventually converted to Christianity because, in his words, he 'thirsted for a religion that was positive and valued life'. And who could blame him, given what he witnessed?

Isaiah Oke's story is shocking and horrifying. Yet, in a way, it shouldn't be. Far more people die of starvation, AIDS, genocide and war in Africa than they do of ritual sacrifices. Maybe it's because the victim was British and it raises the understandable – but nevertheless irrational – fear that any one of us could, at any time, become a victim of occult sacrifice – especially since the grim practice has reared its head here in Britain with the killing of Adam. On top of this, the very idea of magick and witchcraft as a motive for murder fills most of us with dread and fascination. But why? Perhaps it's because every culture has, at one time or another, practised human sacrifice, and we have a primal memory of friends and family being dragged off to the sacrificial altar. Or maybe it is just the sheer calculatedness of it all. Professional human sacrificers select their victims in advance, almost like a farmer's wife selecting the plumpest pig to slaughter for Sunday lunch. Then there is the sacrificer's skill with the knife, which is easily on a par with that of a master butcher or even a surgeon. But most troubling of all is the basic idea that a living can be made as a professional human sacrificer – even the most steely-nerved cannot fail to shudder at this. Such people would seem to be the embodiment of all evil – devils incarnate. Professional human sacrificers don't even have the excuse of mental illness or an abusive childhood, which many serial killers could claim. They know exactly what they are doing. It is a career path they have chosen.

## Was it Idi Amin?

As I said at the beginning, when assessing Isaiah Oke's story, it should be borne in mind that he converted to

Christianity and became a missionary and so had a vested interest in painting traditional African religion in a bad light. That said, what he relates does have a strong ring of truth, particularly when you consider the sheer number of news reports about human sacrifice that come out of Africa every year.[13] Had this not been the case, his story could have been dismissed as far-fetched. As it is, we can view his account as a fairly precise blueprint for what goes on in cases of human sacrifice – but with the proviso that victims are usually local and not Westerners. If we take Oke's account as reflecting the facts, one question that comes to mind is: who was the Colonel? Could he have been Idi Amin? Although Oke was careful not to name him directly, many aspects of his account point to the Colonel being Amin. Amongst other things, Oke described the Colonel as a 'tall, mountain of a man': Amin was 6'4' and weighed over 17 stone. He also says he was extremely strong (effortlessly forcing Oke to remove the soldier's skin): Amin was Uganda's national heavyweight boxing champion for nine years. When the sacrifice was done, Oke says the Colonel and his retinue flew back east from Lagos – which would take them to Uganda, Amin's home-land. Then there is the Colonel's stated ambition to become leader of his country, which was the motivation for the sacrifice: Amin had long had his sights on ruling Uganda. All in all, it is almost certain that Oke was implying that the Colonel was Idi Amin. If so, he would have had good cause to believe that the ritual sacrifice Doctor Drago performed on Amin's behalf had worked when he achieved his aim and took over Uganda – especially considering Amin's humble background.

Amin was born in 1925 (some accounts say 1928) in a small tribal village in Uganda, to parents of the Kakwa ethnic group. He was deserted by his father at an early age and brought up by his mother who, it is claimed, was a sorceress. Despite having little formal education, he joined the King's African Rifles in 1946, under the British colonial army. He was one of the few Ugandan soldiers promoted to officer rank before Uganda's independence in 1962. He fast became a close associate of Uganda's first prime minister and later president, Milton Obote. Amin continued to rise through the ranks, becoming chief of the army and air force in 1966. When conflict arose with Obote in 1971, Amin staged a successful military coup, becoming president and chief of the armed forces.

Amin was initially welcomed both within Uganda and by the international community. In an internal memo, the British Foreign Office described him as 'a splendid type and a good rugby player'. However, things were far from rosy; the new leader had become increasingly paranoid, so much so that he had all the military leaders who had not supported his coup rounded up and executed by firing squads and mass decapitations. Rumour had it that he kept the severed heads of opponents and even dined with them, scolding them for not supporting his presidency.

Not happy with simply purging the military, Idi Amin cleaned out the entire government. Next he hired over 15,000 personal thugs to 'keep the peace', which they did by ransacking the countryside, raping, pillaging and spreading fear amongst those who dared to stand up to the dictator. In the cities there was talk of governmental witchcraft and demon contact. Bodies were found with genitals, noses, livers and eyes missing. Prison camps began filling up with common citizens, who here reportedly forced to bludgeon each other to death with sledgehammers. If Amin was the Colonel in Oke's account, all this horror and terror would have been par for the course – he would have enjoyed every minute of it, chuckling, or even getting a sexual kick, at every atrocity.

Amin came to be known as the 'Butcher of Uganda'

for his brutality, and it is believed that some 300,000 people were killed and countless others tortured during his brutal presidency. In April 1979, invading Ugandan nationalist forces, supported by Tanzanian troops, approached Kampala, the capital, and Amin escaped to Libya. He was later given refuge in Saudi Arabia, where he died in August 2003. Shortly after his death, David Owen told an interviewer for BBC Radio 4 that while he was foreign secretary (1977–79), he had suggested having Amin assassinated, but the idea was immediately rejected. Owen said: 'Amin's regime was the worst of all. It's a shame that we allowed him to keep in power for so long.'

Whether Amin was Oke's Colonel or not, it's a shame that David Owen's suggestion wasn't taken up. Countless lives would have been saved as a result.

When I finished looking at professional human sacrificers like Máximo Coa and Doctor Drago, I felt at a decidedly low ebb. What got me most – aside from the sheer horror of it all – was the idea that you can turn someone's soul into a spirit slave, as Doctor Drago is reputed to have done. It's the ultimate defilement of a human being. Whether such a thing is possible or not is highly debatable. But the thought of it is enough to inspire the deepest dread in anyone. It's like something from the stories of horror writer H.P. Lovecraft (1890–1937) – an unrelenting, all-pervading terror that you can't do anything about, and in which you are utterly helpless, as the British soldier was. The human spirit thrives on hope and the thought that – just maybe – you can beat the odds and overcome adversity. The British soldier met an end too terrible for words. He truly had to abandon all hope.

The other starkly grim side of professional human sacrifice is the way human beings are seen as commodities, like meat at a market, that can be offered up to the gods in exchange for worldly reward. Again, this echoes Lovecraft. Many of his stories were inspired by nightmares and concerned the survival of ancient evil and a pantheon of alien, extra-dimensional entities that predate mankind. These entities look upon humans in a less than benevolent light and seem impossible to stop. In a sense, Doctor Drago and Máximo Coa could be seen as representatives of an ancient evil who carry on a tradition born of terrible gods and demonic entities – all of whom, in reality, were created by, and exist within, the human psyche.

As I left behind the terrible tale of professional human sacrifice I had to accept that real, unrelenting evil exists in the world. But it is not a product of external forces, such as demons or bad spirits, it is part of man. As the writer and painter Brion Gysin (1916–86) said: 'Man is a bad animal!' He was right. We have a streak of cruelty, which can erupt into horrifying acts of evil. In the case of ritual human sacrifice, it is born of a belief that more powerful beings than humans exist in our world and that they can help us in exchange for blood and death.

My contention, that there is no god but man (a sentiment I got from the poet and mystic Aleister Crowley), however, was not shaken. In fact I became more sure that this philosophy is the way ahead for humanity. Like Prometheus, we have to steal the fire from the gods and recognise that the time of the old gods (and of God and Allah) has passed. We have to rely on ourselves and take total responsibility for our actions. If we did that, there would be fewer wars (in the name of religion, at least) and no reason to murder people as sacrifices to the gods or spirits.

# Chapter 4: Satan Loves You . . .

A Match Made in Hell . . . Belief in the Unseen
. . . Dark Pact . . . Dead Love . . . Death at the Devil's
Altar . . . Slain But Not Forgotten . . . Turned on
by Rotting Flesh . . . Rock 'n' Roll Can Never Die
. . . Radio Satan . . . His Satanik Majesty's Request
. . . Order Out of Chaos

'The face of "evil" is always the face of total need.'
William S. Burroughs (1914–1997)
*The Naked Lunch* (1959)

Up until now I'd been looking into sacrificial killings
performed by or on behalf of sorcerers. But what about
killings done by Satanists? They often had sacrificial over-
tones, in that murders were often done in the name of
the dark lord or at his behest. The only difference was,
those that have killed in the name of Satan see themselves
more as his followers than as sorcerers or practitioners of
witchcraft. In other words, they don't necessarily commit
ritual sacrifice as an act of causal magick for material gain;
instead, they kill simply to honour Satan. What's more,

Satanic killers are not a part of a living tradition of sorcery. For one reason or another, they have decided to align themselves with the idea of evil, and this has led to them committing murder.

At the same time, the very idea of Satanism is beset with ambiguity. In my experience, those who follow Satanism are a long way from being evil, and have always struck me as far more honourable and honest than many people I've met. So what was the difference between them and those who kill in the name of Satan? Were the Satanists I knew the genuine article? And the murderous variety somehow frauds or psychotic individuals latching on to the idea of Satan as lord of all evil?

The other question on my mind was: why is it some people take spiritual entities, such as Satan, literally and act on what such beings tell them to do even if it involves murder? How is it they can suspend disbelief to the point of taking the life of an innocent person? The story of Satanic murder that caught my attention involved a couple from Germany who viciously murdered a friend of theirs because they thought he would make a good court jester for the dark lord.

## A Match Made in Hell

Frank Hackerts didn't know he'd been selected to be Satan's jester. Nor did he know he was about to die, at 33 years old, in a macabre ritual sacrifice. He thought he was going to have a few beers with his 'colourful' friends Manuela and Daniel Ruda. They'd asked him back to their apartment in the industrial city of Bochum, in the Ruhr Valley, West Germany. By any definition, the Rudas were a pretty wild couple. They were into vampires and the occult, and all things dark, including Satanism.

Manuela was 23. She followed gothic fashions, which are now passé in Britain but still very big in Germany. She dressed all in black and wore her dark hair long, but the right side of her head was shaved to accommodate a tattoo of an inverted Christian cross. It symbolised her allegiance to Satan. Daniel, age 26, whose fingernails were filed down to razor sharpness, was equally into the gothic scene and also felt a strong affinity with the idea of Satanism. But what made him stand out was his eyes. They had a wild, sinister look, like he was capable of anything.

But as far as Frank Hackerts was concerned, the Rudas were fun to be with. He was well aware that many of the disaffected youth in Germany were into the gothic scene and Satanism. Growing numbers mixed this with neo-Nazism too. So it was hardly as if Frank were hanging out with bad company. Admittedly, some of the Rudas' friends now refused to associate with them because of their dark obsessions. But not Frank. He maintained contact. Apart from anything else, he knew Daniel from work; they sold car parts at a dealership in Herten, a city just north of Bochum.

Frank wouldn't have been so keen to party with the Rudas had he known what was going on inside their heads, as they sat on the sofa chatting to him. Had he known, he'd have got out of their apartment fast. As it was, Frank drank a few more beers and made them laugh with his amusing repartee. Manuela later said she and Daniel enjoyed his company because he was 'always so funny'. Maybe they needed to laugh, what with Manuela regularly sleeping in an oak coffin and the apartment filled with imitation human skulls and cemetery lights. Not to mention the poster of a hanged woman in the bathroom.

If there were any indications of the Rudas' intentions on that fateful night of 6 July 2001, Frank didn't see them.

He was nicely relaxed and buzzing after a few drinks. He didn't know that Daniel and Manuela believed that Satan himself had taken possession of them and had given them direct orders to kill. So when Daniel stood up clutching a hammer, Frank wouldn't have thought anything of it – until he saw it careering down on to his head. By then it was too late. The merciless killing spree had begun.

Manuela later recalled: 'My husband struck him on the head twice with the hammer. But he [Frank] suddenly stood up again and walked towards the television. Then my knife started to glow and I heard the command to stab him in the heart.' The command, she said, came from Satan. Without hesitation, Manuela and Daniel stabbed Frank 66 times with a variety of sharp objects, including a small knife, a carpet cutter and a machete. Manuela said that during the killing a powerful force or presence was in the room with them. '[Frank] sank to his knees,' remembered Manuela. 'I saw the light around him fade. That was the sign that his soul had left for the underworld. We said a prayer to Satan. We were empowered and alone.'

When the killing was done, they carved a pentagram, an occult symbol, on his chest with a scalpel, and stubbed out numerous cigarettes on his back. They then filled a bowl with Frank's blood and drank it. After that they consummated their act of ritual killing by making love in Manuela's satin-lined coffin, which had an altar of skulls placed in front of it. Apparently, Manuela could only become aroused in a coffin or a graveyard. The couple later explained that they had had sex after murdering Frank, because they were 'charged by the aura of Satan'.

The Rudas went on the run for a week after killing Frank Hackerts. During their flight they discussed ways they could commit suicide and go out with a bang. One idea was to fill their car with fuel and crash it into a truck.

But the plan was abandoned when they realised they could only afford the cheaper and less flammable type of diesel. It was also said that the Rudas headed for Thuringia, a state in eastern Germany, where a 15-year-old was murdered by three so-called 'Children of Satan' after a black mass. Here they toyed with the idea of killing themselves in a graveyard. More worryingly, Daniel had now purchased a chainsaw just in case Satan gave him new orders. Clearly the two weren't completely set on taking their own lives. In fact, a note was later found in the couple's flat, which police believed listed the names of future victims.

The police were alerted to the Rudas' crime after they got a call from Manuela's concerned parents. They had received a farewell note from their daughter and were worried that something terrible might have happened. So they asked the police to check out the couple's apartment. After knocking and getting no reply, they broke in and found Frank's decomposing body, amidst a collection of murder weapons. One scalpel was still embedded in Frank's stomach and his body was lying beneath a banner that said: 'When Satan Lives'. Recalling the murder scene, the prosecutor said it was 'a picture of cruelty and depravity such as I have never, ever seen'. Such statements were echoed again and again when the Rudas came to trial.

Manuela and Daniel were finally arrested after being spotted at a petrol station in Jena, East Germany. They made no attempt to deny their crime, happily confessing their gruesome deed to police. When they came to trial six months later, in their home town of Bochum, the couple remained defiant. They made rude gestures, rolled their eyes manically, stuck out their tongues and flashed smiles at reporters. Both, however, denied murder on the grounds that they were acting on instructions from a higher authority. 'I got the order to sacrifice a human for Satan,' Daniel insisted in a statement. As far as the Rudas were concerned they had done nothing wrong. 'If I kill a person with a car and half his bleeding head is hanging on the radiator grille, the car is not put on trial,' Daniel went on. 'The driver is the bad one. I have no reason to regret anything because I have not done anything.'

At the beginning of the trial, defence lawyers asked the court to have the windows blacked out. They said Manuela preferred to stay up all night and sleep during the day, and that the sunlight streaming into the court was hurting her eyes. Judge Arnjo Kerstingtombroke was not impressed. He threw out the request but allowed Manuela to wear sunglasses during the trial. She attended court in her usual black garb and made Satanic signs – her index and little finger raised to look like devil's horns – at spectators in the courtroom. 'I signed my soul to Satan two and a half years ago, on the night before Halloween,' she declared. 'That was when I placed myself in, and swore myself to, the service of our Lord (Satan), his will to perform.'

Of the killing, the couple said they were 'answering voices in our heads'. Daniel said he received a vision of the numbers 6667. He concluded that the vision meant he and Manuela should be married on 6 June, or 6/6 (the purpose of the marriage being to guarantee legally that 'our remains could be buried together'). And that they should kill themselves on 6 July, or 6/7, after first carrying out a sacrificial killing for Satan. They chose Frank Hackerts for their victim, Daniel said in a statement, because he was amusing and would be a perfect 'court jester' for Satan. Throughout the trial neither showed any remorse for the murder. They insisted they had done Frank Hackerts a favour because 'he is now beside Satan, the best place that he could be'.

Frank's mother, Doris, was at the proceedings. She wanted to know what kind of people had killed her son and drank his blood. 'I came here each day to look into their eyes to try to see some kind of sorrow or regret. I saw nothing,' she said, fighting back the tears. She was not alone. Nearly everyone in the court (except for the Rudas' supporters, of which there were growing numbers) were shocked at the couple's behaviour and lack of remorse. As, indeed, was most of Germany and the world – the case had seized international media attention.

Kerstingtombroke said the couple's horrific account of their crime made him believe they were more insane than evil. Like most people, he simply couldn't understand how the couple could have killed their friend in such a grotesque manner and feel no guilt – or even consider that they had done wrong. As a result, Kerstingtombroke went beyond the prosecutor's recommendations by a year in each case and sentenced Daniel Ruda to fifteen years in prison, and Manuela Ruda to thirteen years. He stipulated that the couple begin their sentences in a secure psychiatric unit and receive therapy because of the very definite risk that they might kill again.

Unsurprisingly, neither Daniel nor Manuela showed the slightest emotion as the sentences were read out to the courtroom. In fact, they laughed at the judge's decision, pulled faces and made more obscene gestures. When they were led away, Daniel and Manuela cast mocking glances at Frank's mother, Doris, before making a 'V' for victory sign. Admirers of the couple lapped it up. Many were dotted around the courtroom, dressed in black and holding roses. Others were setting up websites paying homage to the murderous pair. Large amounts of fan mail had been sent to the Rudas during the case, leading Kerstingtombroke to declare that he was concerned about the 'limitless stupidity' of many members of the public.

## Belief in the Unseen

The Ruda case brought to light some worrying statistics that revealed an underbelly of disaffected youth in Germany. Experts estimated a hard core of between 3,000 and 8,000 followers of Satanic cults in the country, making it no wonder that Daniel and Manuela had so many admirers. In Britain, however, no one is certain how many Satanists there are, with figures ranging wildly from 200 to 15,000; solid figures are equally hard to come by in the US – suggesting that Satanic groups are either highly secretive in those countries or that it is a bigger and more visible phenomenon in Germany. According to studies, Satanic groups in Germany make their presence known by scrawling graffiti on walls or in graveyards. The most common emblems they use are pentagrams (the symbol the Rudas carved on Frank Hackerts' chest with a scalpel) and inverted Christian crosses. But increasingly they are also using Nazi symbols, mainly because neo-Nazi organisations have been making efforts to infiltrate Satanic and gothic groups in a bid to swell their own followings. Experts say Satanism is often used by young people as a way of defying the adult world, and as a last resort if they see no chance of being successful in more conventional life. Every now and then, goats' heads and black mass candles are found after Satanic rituals in graveyards. This may sound sinister, and in many ways it is. But it should be remembered that the sacrifice of animals, even to this day, remains a legitimate element of religious practice in many parts of the world (though, clearly, the brand of Satanism practised by young people in Germany is far more nihilistic and negative compared to the majority of spiritual paths).

According to studies, most involved in Devil-worship in Germany are jobless and live in the poorer parts of the country. For many, it is probably an affectation. A reaction against poverty, particularly in East Germany, and a rebellion against parents and authority. None of which is necessarily bad in itself. After all, out of rebellion often come great art and music. The problem comes when Satanism is taken to extremes – when the Lord of Darkness is seen as having a life of his own, beyond being a creation of the human mind, and also when believers hold the notion that he is directing them to do negative things.

At the time of Frank Hackerts' death this is what the Rudas believed – that the Devil was real and that they were his tools. While Kerstingtombroke might have seen this as grounds for considering them insane, he was forgetting that the Catholic Church holds a literal belief in Satan too and has procedures for driving the evil one out of anyone it considers to be possessed. In fact, in 1999, the Vatican issued its first updated ritual for exorcism since 1614 and warned that the Devil is still at work. The official Catholic exorcism to drive the Devil out starts with prayers, a blessing and the sprinkling of holy water. The exorcist then lays hands on the possessed person and makes the sign of the cross. The ritual ends with the 'imperative formula' in which the Devil is ordered to leave the possessed person . The formula begins: 'I order you, Satan . . .' and goes on to denounce him as 'prince of the world' and 'enemy of human salvation'. It ends: 'Go back, Satan!'

While the Catholic Church doesn't kill anyone – at least not nowadays – it does share with the Rudas a belief in powerful invisible entities. So it doesn't hold water to dismiss people as insane because they believe in Satan. Otherwise you would have to denounce Catholics and followers of other mainstream religions as equally insane (some might consider this a good idea). And, interestingly, as with Catholics and other spiritual organisations, not all Satanists and Satanic groups hold the same beliefs –

despite the biased and poorly researched reports you read in the tabloid press on both sides of the Atlantic. The most famous Satanic organisation, the Church of Satan, founded in the United States in the 1960s by Anton LaVey (1930–1997),[1] for example, doesn't promote evil, but espouses humanistic values. Read LaVey's *The Satanic Bible* (1969) and you soon realise that he didn't believe in the literal reality of Satan. For LaVey, Satan was simply a convenient symbol for his philosophy, which put humans first and held no place for irrational belief in God or 'gods' or spirits – especially where such systems of belief might lead to harming yourself or others. In many respects, and despite its colourful image, the Church of Satan promotes reverence for both nature and other human beings.

In 2004, the British Royal Navy allowed one of its technicians to register his religion as Satanism. There was some outcry and objection from Christian groups. But the Royal Navy steadfastly held that it is an 'equal opportunities employer and we don't stop anybody from having their own religious values'. The technician is now lobbying the Ministry of Defence to make Satanism a registered religion throughout the armed forces.

## Dark Pact

If some Satanist groups, like the Church of Satan and its offshoot the Temple of Set, promote values that are essentially good for mankind and the planet we live on – what went wrong with the Rudas? What brand of Satanism were they following when they hacked Frank Hackerts to death? Judging by the evidence the couple gave in court, their beliefs were similar to those of any religious extremist who: (1) takes their creed literally, and (2) accepts that whatever image or slice of internal dialogue that enters their mind is real and is a communication from an external spiritual entity. Daniel Ruda indulged in this kind of thinking all the time. He wrote in his police statement, for example, how he realised at an early age that he was Satan's 'messenger of death'. And that after initial visions at the age of 13 or 14, he began to explore the dark side of his soul. Later he said he'd had fantasies of slaughtering people and 'bloody dreams'. Then he discovered what he called 'religious deviation' and LaVey's *Satanic Bible*.

Daniel did a good job of hiding his dark obsessions. At the car parts dealership, where he worked with the couple's victim Frank Hackerts, he apparently did so well at separating his private and professional lives that no one at the store had any inkling about the desires and fantasies he was harbouring. To them he was a regular guy. Daniel later told German magazine *Stern* that he wanted to emulate the deeds of Charles Manson, who killed Sharon Tate, the wife of film director Roman Polanski, and four other people in California in 1969. In fact, Satanic orders aside, Daniel's motive for killing Frank Hackerts might have been partly down to an urge to gain celebrity status. 'I want to get on stage,' he told his lawyer at one point. 'I want that everybody knows me. I want to be as famous as Charles Manson and so I have to kill someone.'

Daniel and Manuela hooked up together after she replied to a lonely-hearts advert he placed in the heavy metal magazine *Metal Hammer*. It read: 'Raven-haired vampire seeks princess of darkness who despises everything and everybody and has bidden farewell to life.' These existentialist words ignited a passion deep inside Manuela and led to a match made in Hell. As Daniel later told *Stern* magazine, it didn't take long for the pair to begin drinking each other's blood and start discussing the idea of making a ritual sacrifice to Satan.

Like Daniel, Manuela embraced the dark side of life early on. Nothing out of the ordinary occurred at elementary school. But at her next school, she dropped out after the tenth grade because 'the others' couldn't deal with her and she couldn't deal with them. As a result, she decided she didn't fit into this world and attempted to kill herself with an overdose of heroin. When this failed she took a number of jobs and went on demonstrations 'against everything'. In 1996, Manuela travelled to the Scottish Highlands, where she worked in a hotel for a few months and enjoyed the emptiness, the cemeteries and the gloomy atmosphere of the low clouds. During this time she visited the Isle of Skye, where she met an eccentric character called Tom Leppard, a 62-year-old man whose entire body was tattooed with leopard spots. Despite his unusual appearance, he was popular with the locals. Leppard claimed he met Manuela when she worked in a Kyleakin hotel bar. Then she visited him four times in his makeshift dwelling. She was clearly fascinated by his way of life. Leppard later said: 'I liked her. She seemed different, if maybe slightly odd. She was an intelligent, focused young woman with varied interests. She was friendly and polite and we walked and went fishing together.'

After leaving Scotland, Manuela headed for north London, where she got a job in a gothic club in Islington. It was during this time that she first got involved in bloodsucking. She joined a group that attended 'bite parties' and indulged in Devil worship. 'We drank blood from living people,' she later told police. 'We slept on graves. One time we dug a grave and I slept in it, just to see what it would feel like.' She also drank blood from men in exchange for sex. 'Men were always trotting after me,' she revealed. 'I made them pay for their affections with their blood. That's all I wanted from them – to drink their blood. I tolerated them. They were my blood donors.'

Returning to Germany in 1997, Manuela led an increasingly isolated life. Ironically, one thing she discovered at this time could, in my view, have been her salvation (although I'm sure psychologists wouldn't agree). This was Chaos magick, a postmodernist and eclectic brand of occultism that offers ideas and psychological techniques that can have a very balancing and emancipating effect on the mind. One of the tenets of Chaos magick is that if you don't care for your lot in life, or consider some aspect of your personality to be detrimental to your life, you set about changing it using sorcery. One of the methods used by Chaos magickians to make changes in themselves and/or in the external world is sigil (or glyph) sorcery. The crafting of sigils goes back to prehistoric times, when shamans would paint their magickal desires in symbolic form on cave walls. In modern times the great exponent of sigil sorcery was Austin Osman Spare[2] (1886–1956), an obscure British artist and magickian whose work and ideas have been a major influence on Chaos magick. Spare, whose unkempt hair and intense gaze made him fit perfectly into London artistic circles, considered the subconscious mind to be the 'greatest magickian' and used sigils as a direct means of communicating with this far more powerful aspect of the self. In his *Book of Pleasure* (1913) Spare asserted that: 'All desire, whether for pleasure, knowledge or power, that cannot find "natural" expression, can by sigils and their formula find fulfilment from the subconscious.'

A magickal sigil to bring "fame and fortune" in the
style of artist Austin Osman Spare.

To give a clearer picture of what sigil magick entails,
here's a simple working designed to bring fame and
fortune, a popular desire in modern times:

1. Come up with a short phrase that encapsulates
   your desire. E.g. 'fame and fortune'.

2. Eject all repeated letters, so 'fame and fortune
   becomes 'fame nd ortu'.

3. Now arrange the letters in the form of an aesthet-
   ically pleasing gylph or sigil. The idea being that
   the original phrase or desire becomes unrecog-
   nisable, but its 'energy' remains within the image
   – and bear in mind that magick is *not* a science,
   it is an art (in other words, you need to put your
   scepticism to one side).

4. Enter trance, either by gazing at a stillpoint or by dancing and drumming, and stare at your sigil until you feel confident it has been transmitted to your subconscious, which is considered to be the powerhouse of sorcery in the Chaos magick paradigm.

5. You now just have to wait for your desire to come to fruition, while at the same time ensuring there is an earthly channel for it to manifest. That is, you work on honing your skills and talents and set about promoting yourself, confident in the knowledge that your magickal working will assist you to be 'in the right place, at the right time'.

Like Spare, Chaos magickians see the subconscious as a powerful intelligence that can cause the apparently miraculous to occur. They don't generally take spirits or gods literally. In other words, while they might practise the magickal arts, they aren't religious, unlike pagans or those that follow Voodoo or traditional African religions. As Dave Lee,[3] a leading figure in Chaos magick and author of the acclaimed *Chaotopia!* (2006), told me: 'Paganism is a religion. It's a matter of rules which if you accept the religion make sense; if you don't, they're just arbitrary. I think magickians in general, and Chaos magickians in particular, are deeply irreligious people who just can't relate to religion.'

For Chaos magickians, the key ingredient for sorcery to work is that the practitioner truly believes in what he or she is trying to do. But this is far harder than it sounds as Peter J. Carroll,[4] one of the founders of organised Chaos magick, explains: 'It's very difficult to maintain a belief in the reality of magick in the context of a modern technological society, which vehemently denies it,' he says. 'That's why the magickian puts on a black pointed hat and carves a rune staff, because it does at least help you to feel a bit more confident about what you are trying to achieve.' In other words, dressing for the part helps you believe that you are actually capable of having an effect on reality using magick.

Another method used by Chaos magickians to kick-start and maintain belief is to use modern archetypes rather than those taken from conventional mythology. Traditional magickians and witches, for example, will often invoke gods and goddesses from the Roman, Greek or Norse pantheons, whereas Chaos magickians may choose to invoke characters from the TV series *Star Trek* (Mr Spock for logic, Scotty for emotion, Uhuru for communication, etc.). This is seen as more effective magickally because the characters and images are contemporary and familiar – and are thus far easier to visualise.

But how could Chaos magick have been Manuela's salvation? Had she had the discipline to follow its tenets she would have been able to take an objective view of the workings of her mind. She would have seen how the internal chatter and pictures that flow incessantly and involuntarily through our minds dictate our actions and behaviour. She would also have found that we have the power to control this flow. With effort and discipline we can still the inner dialogue, for example, and we can create and manipulate inner visions and can dissolve or banish those we don't like. In other words, we can be captain of our mental ship and we don't have to be thrown this way and that by the waves.

But to follow the path of Chaos magick – or any other system of magick – demands a resolute and balanced mind in the first place, otherwise you get sucked down the road of illusion and self-importance. Clearly, anyone who is even a touch neurotic or has mental health problems of any sort should see a qualified psychologist before going anywhere near magick, otherwise their mind is likely to become even more unbalanced. But I think it is interesting to note that, by studying Chaos magick, Manuela had some very powerful tools and ideas at her disposal (arguably far more powerful than those you find in conventional psychology) to psychoanalyse and make changes in herself – changes which might have prevented her from turning homicidal.

As it was, Manuela left Chaos magick behind and got into vampirism, a growing subculture that is popular amongst those who gravitate towards gothic and dark culture. To quench her new-found taste for blood, she soon located willing blood donors on the Internet. 'Givers are happy to offer their arms or legs for a bite,' she said. '[But] you just have to be careful not to hit an artery.'

When Manuela and Daniel teamed up, they practised their macabre interests in earnest. 'At night we visited cemeteries, ruins and woods and drank blood from voluntary donors,' Manuela said. They then gravitated to sacrificing chickens and goats in local woodland, before turning to human prey – when they cut short Frank Hackerts' life in the name of Satan. But why did they commit ritual sacrifice? It's easy to say they were insane or that they were seeking to achieve notoriety, or that some event during their childhoods traumatised them. Any of these factors could have influenced their desire to kill. But maybe they also had a need to do it in the same way a shaman or sorcerer does – to gain rewards from the gods or spirits. In this case their chosen deity was Satan.

Clearly, you could argue that the Rudas were hardly typical shamans or sorcerers; Daniel, after all, was a car parts salesman. The truth is, however, shamans and sorcerers turn the proverbial dollar in many different ways.

They also come to the path of magick from various directions. Some are born in cultures where shamanism is
common and are initiated by family members. Others
might start out, say, as Christians or Muslims and be drawn
to it. It should also be remembered that individuals and
groups into witchcraft and the occult, in the vast majority
of cases, are decent and honourable people – often holding
strongly environmentalist views. It is only a tiny minority
who turn to human sacrifice as a means of achieving their
goals – maybe it is a throwback to a time when it was
once practised by nearly every culture in the world.

To say that Daniel and Manuela could not have been
genuine practitioners of magick and witchcraft because
of their 'average' (suburban working-class) backgrounds
doesn't hold water. Manuela, for instance, studied Chaos
magick, a comparatively recent strand of the occult arts
that approaches magick more scientifically and doesn't
hold to any set belief system. This means she and Daniel,
who also studied various types of magick, would have
gained a clear understanding of practical occultism – the
art of trying to manipulate reality to your own ends
using spells and rituals. This, combined with vampirism
and Satanism, led to them making what they considered
to be real contact with a spiritual entity – namely Satan.
They may well have prayed to the lord of darkness and
dedicated many rituals to him. All of which could have
led to them becoming possessed, in the same way that
devotees of spiritist religions like Voodoo and Santeria
do.

None of this is to say that Satan or any other spiritual
entity is real. It's just that magick and the occult, if practised with dedication, will eventually bring curious results.
Magick and the occult are very similar to hypnosis. They
have a profound effect on the unconscious mind, which
can produce visions and other phenomena that seem as

real as everyday life. This is why anyone of an unsound mind or who is emotionally unstable is going to run into trouble when they practise magick. Apart from anything else, they will be likely to take the visions and voices that can occur, as a result of rituals and meditations, as real and act on them. In the case of the Rudas, this had deadly consequences.

## Dead Love

> 'Any man has to, needs to, wants to once in a life-time, do a girl in.'
>
> T.S. Eliot (1888–1965)
> *Sweeney Agonistes* (1932)

It was a warm July evening in 1995. Pretty 15-year-old blonde Elyse Pahler was lying on her parents' bed, watching TV, when the phone rang. It was some guys from school inviting her to a nearby eucalyptus grove to smoke some 'wicked weed and drop some acid', as they put it. The three young men she would be meeting – Royce E. Casey (age 16), Jacob W. Delashmutt (age 15) and Joseph Fiorella (14) – were heavily into drugs and death metal. Elyse's friends dismissed them as weird. But she had decided they were probably okay once you got to know them. And besides, she'd always had an innate curiosity about everything, and now this curiosity extended to drugs. So she looked in on her parents and said, 'I love you and I'm going to bed.' She then slipped from the house unnoticed.

Elyse lived with her parents in their comfortable four-bedroomed house on the edge of the small Californian town of Arroyo Grande, which lies on the coast between

San Francisco and Los Angeles. It's the kind of place teenagers always want to get out of, a suburban wasteland where the only way to keep your hopes and dreams alive is to get a one-way ticket out – preferably the same day. Which might explain why Casey, Delashmutt and Fiorella's main pastime was cranking up on methamphetamine and smoking marijuana, while listening to death metal band Slayer at ear-splitting volumes. For them, it was the next best thing to a ticket out of Arroyo Grande. It addled their brains. But, what the hell, it was rock and roll. And their main ambition was to be big rock stars like Slayer. So the drugs and loud music were part of the apprenticeship.

Their aspirations to hit the big time were not idle. They'd already formed their own death metal band called Hatred, and had written their own songs. They'd even had the wherewithal to invest a few hundred dollars to make a demo and had 200 copies printed, with a view to selling them to death metal fans in Arroyo Grande. Those who heard Hatred said the music was thunderously loud with searing, overdriven guitar and heavy, pounding drumbeats. The words of their songs extolled the merits of Satanism and sacrificing virgins – in other words, what any self-respecting death metal band sings about.

The only thing missing in their wannabe rock and roll lifestyle was the sex. It might have worked out if they'd been living in LA, but in the small town of Arroyo Grande, there weren't enough girls into death metal. Which meant Fiorella, Delashmutt and Casey were not exactly a catch for local girls. They didn't have the right 'uniform'. Most considered the three boys weird because of their death metal obsession, and were probably put off by their long greasy hair and baggy, grunge-style clothes. Although to be fair, Royce Casey, who was seen as the most level-headed and civilised of the group, did date the occasional girl from Lopez High School, on Mesa View Drive, which

he attended. The other two, who went to Arroyo Grande
High School, had never been seen with girls.

As you might suspect, the three youths had another
obsession too – the occult. Fiorella had built up quite a
library on the subject, which apparently covered one whole
wall of his black-painted bedroom. Amongst his collection he had pamphlets by Aleister Crowley, the much-
maligned English mystic, poet and mountaineer who,
despite his reputation as a 'black magickian', can be cred-
ited as among the first to popularise yoga and other Eastern
philosophies in the West. In one of the pamphlets owned
by Fiorella, Crowley described a ritual in which a toad
was crucified after being kept all night in an ark or sacred
chest. It was supposed to be a factual description of a
ceremony Crowley had devised and performed himself.
The toad finally met its end after being stabbed in the
heart with a dagger by the magickian, who says: 'Into my
hands I receive thy spirit.' The animal was then cooked
and eaten as a sacrament. Crowley had a dry sense of
humour, so he may or may not have actually sacrificed
the toad. What is certain is that Fiorella was fascinated
with the idea and took it seriously.

With access to the Internet, which was then just taking
off, Fiorella and his friends looked further into the occult
and developed a strong interest in Satanism. They logged
on to websites proclaiming 'Hell, the Online Guide to
Satanism', 'Altar of Unholies' and 'Satan's Playground',
amongst others. Similar websites that exist today include:

*Superhighway to Hell: the definitive guide to Satanism online*
www.purgingtalon.com/sth/
and
*Joy of Satan*
www.angelfire.com/empire/serpentis666/HOME.html

The youths also came across the Church of Satan (www.churchofsatan.com) and duly joined it – devouring books by the Church's founder, Anton LaVey, including *The Satanic Bible* and *The Satanic Rituals*. Fiorella, Delashmutt and Casey were also fascinated by the 1986 movie *River's Edge*, which featured the then little-known Keanu Reeves and veteran Hollywood star Dennis Hopper. The story centres around a high school kid in small-town America who murders his girlfriend and shows the body to his friends, who decide not to tell the police. One of their favourite lines came when the boy who killed the girl says: 'I get into a fight I go fucking crazy. Everything goes black and I fucking explode, like it's the end of the world. Who cares if this guy wastes me because I'm gonna waste him first.'

The three used to watch the movie while smoking joints, emulating the characters in the film. They would also repeat lines from the film, which they knew by heart, having watched it so often. The other big attraction of the movie was that it featured the Slayer tracks 'Tormentor', 'Captor of Sin', 'Evil Has No Boundaries', and 'Die By The Sword'. The stock-in-trade of the veteran thrash band, from Huntington Park, California, were lyrics glorifying killing, suicide, ritualhuman sacrifice and necrophilia. The song 'Necrophiliac' on the 1985 album 'Hell Awaits', for example, talks about draining the life out of a virgin and succumbing to a terrible and insatiable urge to have sex with a corpse.

It would be easy to condemn such lyrics as irresponsible because of the potentially bad influence they could have on the young. But the truth is they're cartoon-like and tongue-in-cheek and are not a road map for would-be killers. The other big thing people forget is that lyricists from bands like Slayer often write in the first person. They put themselves in the shoes of unpleasant characters like serial killers (or, in this case, a necrophile) and write in their voices – very much as a novelist might write from the point of view of a child murderer or rapist, for example. It doesn't mean the author *is* that person. Nor does it mean they desire people to emulate the terrible deeds that might be described in their books. Many modern art forms portray evil acts and shocking events. The only problem is, a tiny percentage of the population take such art seriously and strongly identify with it to the point that they want to act it out. This is what happened with Fiorella, Delashmutt and Casey. And Elyse Pahler was about to get a starring role in the re-enactment . . .

## Death at the Devil's Altar

After slipping away from the house, as arranged, Elyse met up with Casey, Fiorella and Delashmutt. The foursome walked about a mile to a eucalyptus grove called the Nipoma Messa, an area the boys believed was a naturally occurring 'Devil's altar'. The group sat around talking and smoking weed, just like kids into dope do everywhere. It was a good place to hang out, far enough off the beaten track to avoid being spotted by passersby or patrol cars. Then, at one point, Delashmutt got up and walked behind Elyse. He removed the belt from his trousers and looped it around her neck, pulling it taut. As she struggled, Casey held her hands down. Fiorella pulled out a six-inch, antler-handled, hunting knife and began repeatedly stabbing Elyse in the neck. After he was done, he handed the blade to the others to take their turns.

Elyse lay bleeding on the ground, praying to God for

help and crying out for her mother, while the boys stomped on the back of her neck to silence her. They then dragged her body by the feet to the edge of the grove, where she soon bled to death from the twelve to fifteen stab wounds inflicted on her. Casey later told investigators that the boys had planned to have sex with the corpse, but decided not to go through with it. Police and prosecutors, however, were strongly convinced they did because when Elyse's body was discovered her legs were spread and her genitals were exposed.

Judging by the way the killing unfolded, it seems likely that Casey, Fiorella and Delashmutt planned it down to the last detail. It was almost choreographed. First they lulled Elyse into a false sense of security with the friendly chat and drugs. Then, at what must have been a prearranged moment, Delashmutt got up to strangle her with his belt. What is that certain is that the youths took their dedication to Satan and evil to the limit. They mounted a frenzied, rabid wolf attack on Elyse; then, when she was lying dead and broken, allegedly took turns to commit necrophilia on her. It seems beyond belief that three teenage boys (or anyone else, for that matter) could kill someone and then have sex with the corpse. Apart from anything else, you wonder how they could possibly have got aroused over the pallid, bloody corpse that lay before them. But maybe the drugs, the *River's Edge* obsession and endless Slayer songs – along with the sheer excitement of committing evil – were enough to loosen their grip on reality and blur the lines of right and wrong. This probably was the case, but only up to a point. After all, getting wasted on drugs is not a rare thing amongst teenagers; nor is listening to death metal, watching cult movies and identifying with Satan. Plenty of kids do all these things, without taking a kamikaze dive into murder and necrophilia.

The truth is, Casey, Fiorella and Delashmutt had another motive driving them – namely Satan and what he could offer them if they performed a ritual sacrifice in his name. As Casey wrote in his journal, three months after the murder:

> I'm fighting on the other side now. Allied with the darkened souls, satan's arised and shall conquer and reign . . . In the bible it says that in the end Lucifer will bring out his best in everything, music, love, murder . . . All the psycho serial killers and rapists don't know that if they would just build an alter of sacrifice and kill the person on the alter and then [have repeated sex with] the corpse. Virgin meat is the ultimate sacrifice.

Casey and his friends had found their 'virgin meat' in Elyse (she apparently had never slept with anyone). By all accounts – and as unbelievable as it may seem – she was an offering to Satan who, they hoped, would reciprocate by giving them a leg up on the ladder of fame. One of the chief investigators, Doug Odom, put it this way: 'It was to receive power from the Devil to help them play guitar better. By making this perfect sacrifice to the Devil, [the boys thought] it might help them go professional.'

In other words, they were making a pact with the Devil. In the grand old tradition of rock and roll, they were selling their souls in exchange for fame and musical prowess. This notion goes back a long way. Legend has it that celebrated blues man Robert Johnson made a pact with the Devil to gain fame and expertise on the guitar. One night, so the story goes, he went down to a lonely crossroads in the Mississippi Delta, near where he was staying. Out of the darkness came a man, dressed in shabby black top hat and tails, who took Johnson's guitar and tuned it in a special way – to the 'Devil's tuning'. He then gave it back. After the encounter, Johnson, whose musical abilities had previously been described as a terrible racket by fellow blues man Son House, became a highly proficient and outstanding guitarist, often moving audiences to tears. He also shot to fame (or at least he became as well known as was possible as an itinerant blues artist in the 1930s), which added fuel to the rumour that he had made a diabolic pact. When Johnson died young in 1938 (he was still under 30) people said the Devil had taken his due. But the reality was that Johnson was most likely poisoned (his whiskey spiked with strychnine) by a jealous husband whose wife had succumbed to Johnson's notorious womanising. As to the Faustian pact at the crossroads, this can be traced back to a religious initiatory rite in African religion and magick. When this religion was transported to the southern states of America by slaves it came to be known as Voodoo and Hoodoo (the later being the folk magick side of the religion).

Whether you believe the tale or not, one thing is certain: the myth of making a pact with the Devil at the crossroads underpins rock music, which came out of the blues. It is also the reason why both rock and blues have often been described as 'the Devil's music'. Everyone who takes up electric guitar playing seriously is aware of the Robert Johnson story to some degree. Obviously, only the most impressionable believe in the literal existence of the Devil. Nevertheless, the idea that only the Lord of Darkness can teach you how to play 'kick ass' guitar – and bring you fame – is a powerful one. Anyone struggling to make the big time, or even simply trying to get a decent sound out of their guitar, will at some point think: 'What if it's true? What if you really can achieve your dreams by going to the crossroads and making a pact with Satan?'

But most would-be rock stars don't take this notion too far. Of course, they adopt an outlaw attitude and ally themselves metaphorically with the Devil to get their creative juices flowing and to take a 'rebel stance' in society. Other than that, they don't take it literally. But some do. Some take it all too literally – just like Royce Casey, Jacob Delashmutt and Joseph Fiorella did. For them, only a blood sacrifice to Satan would help them achieve their dreams of rock stardom. And the truth is, an act like the slaying of Elyse Pahler was bound to happen one day. Rock and roll – in common with nearly all aspects of popular culture today – is an art of excess; it can only survive by pushing the boundaries of what is acceptable ever further. In the vast majority of cases this is a good thing; it drives artistic development and encourages the kind of stinging social commentary you get from the most talented rock lyricists.

However, Casey, Delashmutt and Fiorella's band, Hatred, was not exactly a vehicle for social commentary. If the band had a message, it was simply that killing, necrophilia, the dark side of the occult and torture were a good lifestyle choice. Hatred wasn't even like the three youths' rock heroes Slayer, who, if nothing else, had the virtue of comic-book irony. No. Casey, Delashmutt and Fiorella formed Hatred for one reason: to glorify Satan, who they believed in as literally as a sermon-spitting, born-again preacher. The only difference being, they'd taken Satan's side and believed that by committing the ultimate crime against God – killing a virgin – they would earn themselves a one-way ticket to Hell.

## Slain but not Forgotten

After the killing, the three boys would go back now and then to look at their handiwork. They'd stare down at

Elyse's decomposing body as it lay propped against a
fallen branch in the middle of the eucalyptus grove – and
they'd laugh until they couldn't stop. They were like a
pack of drooling, crazy-eyed hyenas, loping around their
killing field, overawed by what they'd done. Had Satan
been there with them, he'd probably have despaired at
the sheer imbecility of his followers. But the youths' return
to the scene of the crime, prosecutors later said, was not
merely to gloat. It was to make sure that no one could see
Elyse's body from the nearby road. Casey, Fiorella and
Delashmutt weren't stupid. They knew that if the body
were found and they were charged with the murder they'd
get a heavy-duty sentence. Worse still, the tables could
be turned on them during their jail term: big, nasty,
tattooed guys, long deprived of sex, were likely to welcome
the 'long-haired, pretty boys' with open arms and would
most probably show them what being used as meat was
like. So all the youths could do was pray to Satan that no
one would stumble across Elyse's body. And Satan went
along with the deal for a while. No one could find Elyse's
body. Her anxious parents reported her missing. They
told police that Elyse had once been expelled for five days
in junior high for drinking alcohol, and had later attended
drug rehab. But despite these minor problems, which
were born of Elyse's daredevil nature, they were certain
she was happy at home. They said they knew that their
daughter hadn't just gone off with some guy . . . She
wouldn't have done that . . . They were sure something
terrible had happened to their daughter.

The cops, on the other hand, were just as convinced
that Elyse was yet another runaway and put the case on
the pending file. To be fair, they did follow up a number
of leads – people claiming they had spotted girls who
looked like Elyse – but these obviously led nowhere.
What brought Elyse's body to light, however, was a full

confession from Royce Casey. Racked with guilt, he had been attending the New Life Ministry in nearby Pismo Beach. During a question-and-answer session he asked one of the ministers whether God could forgive anything. 'Of course he can forgive anything,' came the reply. It made Casey feel better for a while. But he just couldn't get the night of the murder out of his mind. The image of her dead body lying amongst the broken branches haunted him. He couldn't concentrate on anything and his school work was suffering badly. So on 13 March 1996, eight months after the killing, Casey walked into Arroyo Grande police station and told them everything. He said he was afraid the urge to kill might surface again. He also admitted to being worried that he might become the next victim of Fiorella and Delashmutt. He could well have been right in his fears; he'd seen a lot less of them in recent months and they no doubt saw him as the weak link, the one most likely to cave in to guilt and go crying to the cops.

As Casey led police to the eucalyptus grove where Elyse's body lay rotting amongst the foliage, squad cars were sent to the homes of Fiorella and Delashmutt to pull them in. The game was up. Satan had finally turned his back on his followers and left them to their fate. But he hadn't reneged on his bargain because the three youths were about to achieve the notoriety they craved. By May 1996, the case was being covered by the media across the USA, with headlines focusing on the fact that a teenage girl had been murdered as a sacrifice to Satan. It wasn't rock stardom. But maybe any kind of fame was enough for the three youths. The media coverage meant the police department was inundated with inquiries about the case. But it wasn't just reporters who were calling. Police said dozens of 'Satanists' phoned at all times of the day and night asking obscure questions about the more grisly details of the case. 'The weird thing was that these people would call up as if it were perfectly normal to contact us with bizarre questions about Elyse's murder. I was sickened by it,' said one Arroyo Grande officer.

And who could blame him? When I speak to cops off the record and bring up the subject of what humans are capable of, their faces almost always harden and they'll say things like: 'People are assholes, it's hard to believe that they can be such fucking scum . . .' Five minutes before, they may have been enthusing about the positive side of policing, telling amusing stories and so on. But get them on to the dark side of human nature and their whole demeanour changes. That's not surprising, of course, as they work at the raw edge of society and see what people are capable of. But it isn't just the murderers and rapists that get to them, it's everyday people too – especially the types that loiter at crime scenes, like vultures, trying to catch sight of something grisly. Maybe it's just grim fascination or simply taking satisfaction in the fact that someone has met a worse fate in life than they have. It might have been the same with the so-called Satanists who called up the Arroyo Grande police desk to find out the gory details of how Elyse Pahler was killed. Either that, or they got a sick kick out of it, or worse, they were looking for ideas. What is certain, however, is they were unlikely to have been Satanists. Describing the callers in this way was probably prejudice and ignorance on the part of the police. The fact is, taking a morbid interest in grisly deaths and human misery is a condition of the average person. You don't have to be a Satanist or occultist to get a kick out of gore and horror. With that in mind, you can't help but empathise with the sentiments of the character played by Harry Dean Stanton in the 1984 movie *Repo Man*, who memorably said: 'Look at 'em, ordinary fucking people, I hate 'em.'

# Turned on by Rotting Flesh

On 19 June 1996, juvenile court judge Michael Duffy threw out the special circumstance charges of rape, torture and stalking against the two youngest defendants, Fiorella and Delashmutt, which had been pushed for by the prosecution, who wanted them to be tried as adults. He ruled that the youths, aged 14 and 15 at the time of the murder, were too young to be charged with special circumstances. Special circumstances would have raised the potential punishment from life in prison to life in prison without possibility of parole. Seventeen-year-old Royce Casey, however, was facing life without the possibility of parole if convicted. The special circumstances charges apply to defendants aged 16 or older and, if proven, add to the severity of their sentence. In the end, though, Casey, Fiorella and Delashmutt pleaded no contest to the murder charges against them and were given sentences of 25 years to life.

During their trial an investigator for the local District Attorney's office, Rick Conradi, told the court that Delashmutt had admitted to a friend at Arroyo Grande High School that he and his three accomplices had had sex with Elyse before and after she died – adding strong weight to what officers at the crime scene believed had happened. 'Delashmutt said they had sexual intercourse with her before she died and after she died,' Conradi testified, adding that Delashmutt had even gone as far as admitting that they would regularly 'return to her body and have sex with her'. Another investigator told the court that Joseph Fiorella's mother told him that her son admitted, after his arrest, that he and Casey both had sex with the girl after she was stabbed.

These testimonies seemed to remove all doubt that the three youths practised necrophilia on Elyse. And the press lost no time in reporting this aspect of the case to a shocked world. What they didn't cover, however, was the fact that necrophilia is not uncommon. A quick scan through the online press archives I subscribe to, for example, reveals that in August 2002, an undertaker in Thailand admitted committing necrophilia with the corpse of a woman he had long admired, after helping dress the body before the funeral service. Sakchai Thammasri was arrested at his home after an abbot at a temple in suburban Bangkok informed police that the coffin of Thippawan Charoenkasemsuk had been pried open and her body left naked. Police said Sakchai, who had been infatuated with the victim, left a note admitting he had sexually violated the body and apologising to Thippawan's family. 'She is the only one I raped,' Sakchai later said, on Thai television, following his arrest. He was charged with destruction of property, and police said they were investigating whether Thailand had any specific law against necrophilia.

Thankfully, Sakichai didn't kill anyone. He did something that most of us would find too hideously repugnant to even contemplate. But not all of us. In the days when I used to play guitar in rock bands, I remember being confronted with something that sent a shiver of disgust through me. There was a trainee undertaker who used to be a regular at gigs. He looked the part even when he went out, always wearing a black tie, crisply ironed white shirt and a high collar, and a black funerary suit. Amazingly, he always had very attractive girls on his arm. But, to be fair, it was the early 1980s and the gothic fashion was at its height. So being an undertaker probably meant he was quite a catch. I often used to sit down and have a drink with him. On one occasion, after a gig, I was packing up my gear and he said: 'Why don't you come back to my parlour, I've got some fine single malt and some good coke?' I said, 'Okay, why not.' Once my gear was loaded in the van for the rest of the band to drop off at the rehearsal studios, I left the venue with the undertaker.

We walked about a quarter of a mile through winding city streets until we arrived at the funeral parlour where he worked. He ushered me into a back room and pulled out the bottle of whisky he had promised, along with a bag of coke, which he tipped out onto an oak coffin. As the night wore on we exchanged all sorts of stories. His, it has to be said, usually involved graveyards, coffins and corpses, but then his life was spent predominantly with the dead, so I could have expected little else. At one point I said to him, 'You're a very lucky man. You always seem to get the girls – how do you manage it?' He looked me in the eyes and said, 'Well, to be honest with you, I think most of them are on the make. They're looking for a guy with a steady income and prospects. And in my trade you don't have to worry about custom dropping off and going out of business. But to be honest with you, I can take the girls or leave them. Most of them don't do a lot for me.'

He got up and said, 'Come along with me, I've got something to show you.' He led me into a back room. To my horror (although it was no more than you would expect in a funeral parlour) there was a body laid out on a large table. On it was a very attractive and very dead middle-aged woman. 'This is what I live for,' he said. 'I was working on her today. You can't beat the feeling you get making a stiff pristine and presentable for a good send-off.' I had no problem with that. It was good to see someone taking a pride in their work – just as I did, when it came to playing the guitar. It was the next thing he said that made me think I either needed to snort the rest of the coke lying on the coffin in the other room (in a desperate bid to enter oblivion) or hurl myself out of there like I'd got an enraged rhino on my tail. Instead I froze when he nonchalantly informed me that the 'real prize is shafting a stiff'.

'Er . . . did you say what I thought you said?' I asked, certain I must have misheard.

'Yes,' he replied. 'There's no greater turn-on on this earth than fucking a dead woman.' He then asked me if I'd like to try it. 'You're welcome to her,' he said. 'That is, if you don't mind the fact that I've already done her three times today.'

As you can imagine, I hurriedly made my excuses and got out of there. To this day, I don't know if it was some sort of elaborate joke. But I wouldn't bet on that. I'm 99 per cent certain I ran into a necrophiliac that night. This was pretty much confirmed some years later when I became a journalist, writing freelance for newspapers and magazines (as I still do now). An assignment I was on involved interviewing a retired mortician in a pub on the Holloway Road, north London. We got on well and spent most of the afternoon drinking, by which time I'd plucked up the courage to relate my story. He didn't laugh. He just went very quiet for a moment, then said: 'It's more common than you think in our industry.' The afternoon didn't recover after that.

The reason I related that story is to show that people do very weird and very ugly things. They might appear ordinary on the surface and make a good show of appearing so, but you can't know about everything that is going on in their lives. Even a good friend might indulge in the most hideous depravity, completely unbeknown to you. Indeed, maybe you shouldn't risk turning your back on your best friend; how do you know they won't one day hack your head off and feed it to the dog, then sodomise your headless corpse? Lurking behind closed doors could be a nightmare world that would make a psychopath look tame. And you can never tell when that nightmare world is going to break out and unleash its horror on the world.

This is what happened with Casey, Fiorella and Delashmutt – their own personal nightmare erupted into a blaze of horror on that fateful night in 1995 when they sacrificed Elyse Pahler to Satan, the dark deity that had so fired their imaginations. They might have been out of it a lot of the time, but no one could have predicted they would turn into rabid, murdering beasts and rapists of the dead. Yes, they were deeply into death metal, Satanism and drugs. But, as I've already said, these are not exactly uncommon interests with teenagers. It would be interesting to know what pushed the youths over the edge. Did their parents have sociopathic tendencies? Did they have terrible upbringings? Considering what the three boys did, you would be forgiven for thinking that their parents must have been on a par with Norman Bates, possibly with dead parents in the attic to boot. But this was not the case. While not models of perfection (who is?), they weren't monsters either. Fiorella's mother, Betsy Leo, for example, was the executive director of the local Meals on Wheels programme. In a local newspaper interview, she admitted that in her younger days she had been interested in ESP, hypnotism and astrology. This was promptly seized upon by some who saw it as damning evidence that she was involved in diabolism. Betsy Leo vehemently denied this, saying she had never practised Satanism or witchcraft and that she prided herself on being open about her religion and her moral and ethical values to both her sons. However, in a savage twist of irony, Betsy

Leo's older son Anthony was convicted of an unrelated murder in January 1998. He's now serving 50 years to life.

Jacob Delashmutt came from a well-to-do family and was the youngest of six children. His parents were devout Mormons, whose other children included a missionary and a teacher. It soon became clear Jacob was not going to follow in their footsteps – he was expelled from school twice for possessing drugs and yelling obscenities at a teacher. His parents tried to make sense of the killing of Elyse Pahler. 'We're as shocked as anyone,' said his father; while his mother described him as brilliant and artistic, a gifted writer who composed music but got bored at school. 'Jacob is totally naive and delicate, easily persuaded,' she added.

There was nothing particularly unusual about Royce Casey's parents either. His father was a school custodian and his mother a housewife. Both, however, refused to comment on the case or on what might have driven their son to commit such heinous acts.

One of the saddest aspects of the killing of Elyse Pahler is none of the three youths showed much remorse for what they'd done. During an interview with a local newspaper, Fiorella, who now had closely cropped hair, smirked arrogantly as he explained how he wanted to get away from the case and draw a line under it. 'It's no one's business except for my own,' he said. 'I'm not like what they say. I'm just a regular kid.' Fiorella didn't even seem concerned that he would be spending the next two decades of his life in prison. 'Whatever happens, happens,' he said with a shrug. 'It's not like I'm going to be living on the streets.' Then, as he stood up to leave, he said, almost as an afterthought: 'Of course, I feel bad that she's dead.'

Of course, Elyse's parents were utterly devastated,

especially when they discovered the sheer brutality and depravity of the events that surrounded the murder of their daughter. During the trial of Fiorella, Elyse's father, David, felt moved enough to address the sullen youth directly. He wanted to make him understand the terrible pain and anguish he and his friends had caused. As Pahler got up to speak, the courtroom fell into silence. 'Joseph, it's a parent's worst fear and lifetime pain to outlive their child,' he said. 'It's even worse knowing that she was murdered, tortured, and raped as a virgin sacrificed on the altar of Satan so that (you) can earn a ticket to hell.' Elyse's grandfather, Richard Walter, also made a speech to Fiorella directly, saying much the same thing as his son-in-law. After he'd finished, Fiorella leaned towards his lawyer and muttered, 'That's bull-shit.'

The Pahlers got no emotional resolution from any of the three youths. None would discuss the details of the case or give any indication as to why they did what they did. On balance, it looks like they really did offer Elyse as a sacrifice in an extreme version of the rock and roll Devil's pact – a perverted and depraved distortion of the Robert Johnson legend. But the Pahlers wanted more. They wanted someone to blame. So they turned to the music.


## Rock 'n' Roll Can Never Die


'They're the nicest people. It's a matter of opinion how you take their music, but I think it's fiction, period. They're nice, conservative people, believe it or not.'

Chris Ferrara, Slayer publicist, 2001.

During his confession, Royce Casey had admitted that Elyse's murder was a Satanic sacrifice inspired, at least in part, by the lyrics of death metal band Slayer, whose song 'Altar of Sacrifice' includes the lines 'High priest awaiting dagger in hand/Spilling the pure virgin blood'. To Elyse's parents – David and Lisanne Pahler – this sounded like a blueprint for their daughter's killing. And who could blame them? Slayer's lyrics do deal with shocking and horrific themes and the thundering, speed metal riffs pound into you like an industrial hammer drill – and would make anyone unused to such music think they'd died and gone to Hell. So it was no surprise that the Pahlers decided to sue Slayer and the companies that distributed their music for contributing towards their daughter's death. 'This case isn't about art,' said David Pahler. 'It's about marketing. Slayer and others in the industry have developed sophisticated strategies to sell death metal music to adolescent boys. They don't care whether the violent, misogynistic message in these lyrics causes children to do harmful things. They couldn't care less what their fans did to our daughter. All they care about is money.'

Slayer's drummer, Paul Bostaph, dismissed the lawsuit, saying in 1999 that: 'They're trying to blame the whole thing on us. That's such nonsense. If you're gonna do something stupid like that, you should get in trouble for it.' He went on to observe that, if Casey, Delashmutt and Fiorella had been inspired to kill by the band's lyrics, they 'hadn't done their homework properly; they had failed to follow the rituals of necrophilia sacrifice set out in the songs'. Quoted later in *Entertainment Weekly*, Slayer's lead singer, Tom Araya, showed more sensitivity towards the Pahlers, but also denied that the band should be held responsible in any way. 'We totally understand the tragedy of the situation

Well known South African traditional healer Credo Mutwa, wearing a healing talisman around his neck while attending the XIII International Aids Conference in Durban, South Africa in July 2000. Credo was consulted by Scotland Yard when they visited South Africa during their investigation into the murder of Adam.

The late Anton Lavey, author of 'The Satanic Bible' and founder of the Church of Satan, an organisation aligning itself to the Lord of Darkness, but whose members, typically, are honourable, outstanding citizens (contrary to media hype). Lavey is seen standing beneath an inverted pentacle, a five-pointed star.

Manuela and Daniel Ruda in romantic embrace. Manuela had met Daniel via a lonely hearts ad he placed in a heavy metal magazine. Getting together led to their hacking a friend to death and drinking his blood in a grisly human sacrifice.

Daniel Ruda in a typical pose showing no remorse for killing his friend Frank Hackerts. In a statement, Daniel said he and Manuela chose Hackerts as their victim because he was amusing and would be a perfect 'court jester' for Satan.

The late Idi Amin, President of Uganda, (1971 - 1979) is believed to have extensively employed black magick-ians working in the African sorcery tradi-tion. One account claims that Amin abducted a British soldier, and then employed one of the most powerful sorcerers for hire in Africa, at the time, to slowly skin the abductee alive in a ritual to capture his soul, and make it a slave for Amin.

Liberian President Charles Taylor sitting on a throne with a traditional dancer at his feet during a cere-mony in Monrovia. Human sacrifices allegedly took place in Taylor's house, and during Liberia's 14-year civil war (1989-2003) there were countless cases of gun-men, some of them child soldiers, eating their victim's hearts and other body parts.

US Forensics experts remove a Nganga cauldron after a raid on a Palo Mayombe temple in New Jersey. Inside the cauldron were decaying animal parts and human remains that had been stolen from local cemeteries.

This skull in a plastic bag was used as evidence in a trial known as the 'bones case' in New Jersey, in which two individuals were prosecuted for handling stolen human remains for use in Palo Mayombe rituals.

A Palo Mayombe practitioner on trial in New Jersey for tomb robbing and handling stolen human remains, which were used to contact the dead and other discarnate spirits in magickal rites.

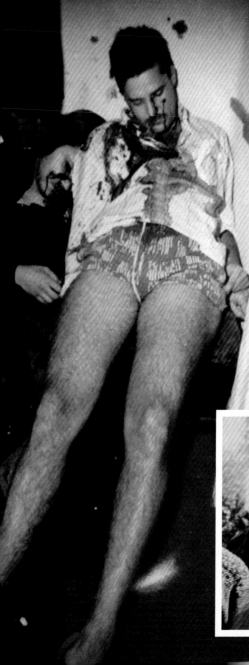

Adolfo De Jesus Constanzo, a Cuban American cult leader known as 'El Padrino' or 'Godfather', laying dead with another gang member in an apartment in Mexico City, following a shoot out with police. Constanzo and his deadly cult notoriously murdered American student Mark Kilroy in Matamoros in 1989 and were thought to have been involved in at least sixteen ritual murders, all involving children or teenagers. The inset shows Constanzo as a young adult.

Police escort some of Constanzo's accomplices to their arraignment in Matamoros, Mexico, in 1989, where they were charged in connection with a string of brutal ritual killings.

A portrait of murder victim Elyse Pahler left in a jar along with a ribbon in 1996, near where her body was found in Arroyo Grande, California. Three high-school youths, who formed a death metal band to glorify Satan, drugged, raped, tortured and viciously murdered the 15-year-old girl in the hope that a virgin sacrifice would propel them to fame and earn them a ticket to hell. It was also alleged that the three had sex with her corpse.

Peruvian shamans stab a picture of Brazilian football player Rivaldo during a ceremony to help Peru beat Brazil in a play off that would see the victor qualifying for the World Cup in 2006. Hexing in sport, particularly football, is becoming increasingly common - and has even been seen in Britain and Germany.

When US forces invaded Panama in 1989, resulting in the imprisonment of General Manuel Noriega, they found some unusual items in his mansion – including a large table covered with glass-cased candles, strange-looking statues, and little cloth bags containing various powders, which were assumed to be drugs. When analysed the powders were found to be a mixture of herbs and incense. Later it was discovered that General Noriega employed sorcerers of Brazilian, Cuban and Puerto Rican extraction to perform hexes against the Americans to thwart their efforts in capturing the general.

and sympathise,' he said. 'But we just don't understand how or why we can be held responsible for someone else's actions, especially actions we never would have intended.'

David Pahler, however, was adamant: 'Elyse would be alive today if it wasn't for the music. [These kids] drenched themselves 24 hours a day in this music and the lyrics. They were just acting out what they learned.' Lisanne, Elyse's mother, concurred, saying: 'I don't believe they were born killers. I don't believe that. We know the music is not the only thing, but it was the last straw.' The Pahlers' lawsuit stated that: 'The distribution and marketing of this obscene and harmful material to adolescent males constituted aiding and abetting of the criminal acts described in this complaint. None of the vicious crimes committed against Elyse Marie Pahler would have occurred without the intentional marketing strategy of the death metal band Slayer.'

Lawyers for the band and their music companies – which included Def Jam Music, Columbia Records, Sony Music Entertainment and American Recordings – said that Slayer's work was protected by the right to free speech enshrined in the Constitution. Civil liberties groups, however, weren't so confident. 'We're kidding ourselves if we don't think the cultural climate doesn't affect judges and their decisions,' said Peter Eliasbert of the American Civil Liberties Union. 'We're getting to the point, if we let these cases go forward, that someone can say [the blaxploitation movie] *Shaft* glorifies vigilantism. There is a really serious danger to decide to not make a movie or not write a book.' That danger was highlighted in a report from the US surgeon general's office, published in January 2001, which claimed to have identified a 'scientific link between graphically violent television and increased aggression in children. Research to date justifies sustained efforts to curb the adverse effects of media violence on youths. Although our knowledge is incomplete,' said the paper, which was commissioned by the White House after the Columbine shootings, 'it is sufficient to develop a coherent public health approach to violence prevention that builds upon what is known, even as more research is under way.' Speaking to a police counsellor a year after Elyse's murder, Fiorella added weight to the report's findings (albeit inadvertently). '[The music] gets inside your head,' he said. 'It's almost embarrassing that I was so influenced by the music. The music started to influence the way I looked at things.'

In the end – on 25 January 2001 – the Pahler lawsuit was thrown out. San Luis Obispo (California) Superior Court judge Judge E. Jeffrey Burke ruled that Slayer's music was neither obscene, indecent nor directly harmful to minors, and so the marketing of such music to children was therefore considered to be legal. Allen Hutkin, attorney for the Pahlers, however, predicted the case might eventually be decided in the appellate courts based on the First Amendment concerns inherent in it. The Pahlers currently maintain a website in memory of their daughter (www.elyse-marie.org) and have set up a foundation to 'provide information and public education concerning the protection and welfare of children, and to assist families and law enforcement officials in resolving cases of missing persons'.

Their sadness will never die. But neither will rock and roll, and nor should it. According to Jeff Arnett, an American research professor, heavy metal – and its offshoots, death and speed metal – generally have a positive influence on the young, despite their dark nature. For his 1996 book, *Metalheads: Heavy Metal Music and Adolescent Alienation*, he talked to a large cross-section of teenage heavy metal fans. What he found out surprised him. 'The subjects of violence and suicide have been part of the criticisms against heavy metal,' he says. 'But what these kids had to say didn't fit the stereotypes very much. The fans told me they listened to it when they were very angry, and it calmed them down. It purged their angst.' He goes on to say that heavy metal also acts as an outlet for alienation. 'It's striking to me that the shows are a celebration, although the lyrics to the songs aren't celebratory. With the harder bands, most of the lyrics are pretty gloomy. The show has become the collective expression of that. It's a mass expression, so it becomes celebratory.'

Difficult though it would no doubt have been, the Pahlers might well have benefited from talking to the band and their fans. They would have discovered that the music, along with the mock Satanic lyrics, on the whole, brings young people together. It doesn't encourage them to kill. Attacking Slayer meant the band and their lawyers had no other choice but to dig their heels in because they felt unjustly accused.

## Radio Satan

To get a better take on the minds of Satanic killers I took the opportunity to interview the true crime writer, Carol Anne Davis, on my occasional 'True Crime Hour' radio show. She tends to delve into the psychology of murderers and looks deeply into their backgrounds, which often brings a better understanding of why some people are driven to commit unimaginable acts of slaughter and cruelty. What follows is a transcript of the interview with Carol.

*Programme theme: Satanic killings*

Future Radio[5]; 3/11/2005; TRUE CRIME HOUR
Time: 6.00–7.00 p.m.

*Track 1: Keith Richards, '999', from 'Main Offender'
(1992)*

JIMMY LEE SHREEVE, host: Greetings! We've got an
interesting guest on the show tonight. British crime
writer Carol Anne Davis. Carol is something of an
expert in strange and gruesome killings, having
written several books on the subject. Titles include
*Couples Who Kill*, *Children Who Kill* and *Women
Who Kill*. We'll see if she's on the line now. Welcome,
Carol . . . are you out there?

DAVIS: Hello Jimmy, nice to talk to you.

JLS: And very nice to talk to you. Now as an experienced crime writer, I'd value your opinion on a
couple of stories I'm covering in my upcoming book
*Blood Rites*.

DAVIS: Okay, fire away.

JLS: Well, the first one is a particularly brutal case.
That of the killing of Californian girl Elyse Pahler
by three local boys.

DAVIS: Yes, I know the one.

JLS: Okay, well, the three youths that murdered
Elyse – Royce Casey (16), Jacob Delashmutt (15)
and Joseph Fiorella (14) – seem to have been influ-

enced by a mix of death metal music (Slayer, etc.), the *River's Edge* movie and drugs. Well, I can certainly relate to them on the rock music front – when I was about 12 I got into Alice Cooper and other rock and roll bands. I then started learning the guitar. And I mimicked the rock lifestyle and attitude, which meant I was more than a little rebellious. I didn't really do bad things, just bucked the system and led the school a merry dance if I could. As it happened the rock music influence turned out fine. I got good on the guitar and played in bands until I was about 29, when I got into journalism – but, actually, it was the influence of far-edge cult writer Hunter S. Thompson (*Fear and Loathing in Las Vegas*) that prompted me to become a journalist. So, again, there is another 'bad' motivational influence that turned out okay.

Going by my story, it could be argued that rock music can have a strong influence on young people and even dictate their behaviour. I personally defend free speech and the right of artists to express themselves how they will. But the band Slayer did write lyrics about necrophilia. Maybe they were putting themselves in the first person like a novelist does. Who knows? The problem is, it looks like the three youths who killed Elyse took the lyrics literally. What do you think about the influence of rock music – particularly genres like death metal?

DAVIS: Well, I suspect that this is one of those chicken-and-egg situations – that is, it's the unnurtured or misunderstood child who turns almost exclusively to music for validation. He's getting negative (or no) feedback from his family and teachers, so listening to the lyrics of alienation make him feel less alone. There was a case a few years ago where two teenagers listened endlessly to death metal then attempted suicide with a gun. One of the boys succeeded, but the other put the gun in his mouth and pointed it downwards, so he blew off the lower half of his face and survived. His family blamed the music and tried to sue the band, but violence expert Gavin de Becker testified that the teenager should have turned the scrutiny on himself, his family and even society. Clearly, if music could cause such colossal personality change in a vacuum, we'd all turn into homicidal maniacs every time we heard an Alice Cooper track on Radio Two. In *Children Who Kill*, I look at all the scapegoats that society uses when a youth becomes violent – the media blame everything from vampire novels to horror videos, whereas the reality is usually that the child's primary carers have put him through hell.

JLS: What about the victim Elyse Pahler? To me she sounded like a nice girl who was looking for excitement in small-town America. She had a wild streak that manifested in an interest in drugs – she did dope, meth and a bit of acid. She apparently had not yet had sex. Much was made of her being a virgin; in fact, it was used to emphasise her innocence and set it against the youths' apparent embodiment of evil. One thing's for sure, had she got into sex she wouldn't have hung out with Casey, Delashmutt and Fiorella. She'd have gone for the more popular and smarter boys. What do you think about Elyse Pahler? Was she a typical victim?

DAVIS: Well that' s a complex one – yes, she put herself into classic victim mode by hanging out with three drug-taking youths without telling anyone where she was going. But she thought that she was safe because she knew them and society erroneously gives the impression that stranger danger is the one that we should fear. The reality, as I'm sure you know, is that we're most at risk of violence from family, friends and acquaintances, as this unfortunate teenager found to her cost.

Ironically, the fact that the youths were also virgins probably contributed to her death – advertisers tell us again and again that we're worthless if we're not sexually active, and it's a message that hormone-tormented youths are especially open to. There's also a pack mentality in such gang rapes, whether they happen pre or post mortem. Usually the most dominant male makes the first sexual assault, and the others follow, as they want to appear macho, keep their status in the gang. The gang has become a surrogate family and most of their validation comes from it.

JLS: Yeah, that's interesting, I believe it was the youngest of the three, Joseph Fiorella – only 14 at the time – who emerged as pack leader. In fact Jacob Delashmutt's mother described him as easily led, he was maybe trying to keep in with the crowd like you point out. But do you think there was any way that Elyse could have avoided being a victim? Is it possible for people to recognise this trait and overcome it? Or is it just luck that you avoid a nasty end?

DAVIS: Yes, I think sometimes people are just in the

wrong place at the wrong time – one victim of torture killers Bittaker and Norris, both of whom I profile in *Couples Who Kill*, was coming home from a church group when they abducted her in broad daylight. But other victims indulge in risky behaviour such as street prostitution or escort work. The murderer often has to psych himself up to commit the homicide, and it's easier to do this with a working girl as he can convince himself that she cheats men or spreads disease, that he's cleaning up the streets. The other high-risk group is hitchhikers, even male ones – again, the killer can convince himself that he's being used and that the freeloader deserves to die.

Sadly, the young girl who has been victimised by her own family is at risk of remaining a victim because she gives out signals of low self-esteem, and violent men pick up on this. They'll work hard at alienating her from whatever support system she has, and then the beatings start. Killers can also go into a bar and recognise the one girl who is likely to leave with them. It's a predatory thing. But yes, victims can and do change, especially if they find something that they're good at and which builds their self-confidence. Once they are seen as powerful, self-aware and self-respecting individuals, most killers – who want an easy life – will leave them alone.

JLS: Yeah, maybe there was something about Elyse that the three guys homed in on – or maybe it was simply that she was known to be a virgin. Nasty story though . . . The next case I want to ask you about isn't any prettier. Now, I know you covered this in *Couples Who Kill* – it's the case of the vampire-obsessed killers Manuela and Daniel Ruda. Okay, so in your book you suggest that Manuela meeting up with Daniel was a catalyst that created a deadly combination – a match made in Hell, much like the Moors Murderers, Ian Brady and Myra Hindley. But could Manuela have eventually committed murder had she never met Daniel? Or would she have turned out fine, got a job, and eventually settled down?

DAVIS: Well, I think that . . . Manuela was so damaged that I doubt if she could have recovered of her own volition without intensive psychiatric counselling and probably some kind of medical intervention – remember that this was a girl who was biting strangers in the street at age 14! She also left her home country at an incredibly young age, so this was someone who was desperate to both escape her past and reinvent herself. But she took her demons with her, and the rest is history. Manuela was an accident waiting to happen – drinking strangers' blood and having lots of casual sex made her a potential victim. And she further victimised herself by slashing her own wrists. If she hadn't met Daniel, she'd have found someone else who was equally disenfranchised and, as sociopaths tend to escalate their antisocial behaviour when they join together, they'd probably have gone on to commit increasingly violent acts.

Ironically, Daniel might not have killed if he hadn't met Manuela. Though his attitude was racist and homophobic, he rented his own home (whereas Manuela drifted from place to place and even slept in graveyards for a time), was holding down a job and had even been promoted. He might have eventually grown up and softened in his attitude. If he'd met a more balanced girl, he could well have taken the approach of 'because you're mine, I'll walk the line'. But he chose to place his existential advert and attracted the deeply disturbed Manuela.

JLS: Yeah, he kind of sealed his fate there, didn't he? He was obviously keen to explore his darker side and meeting Manuela certainly helped him with that. So, Carol, what do you make of Satanism? This is of course a religion that the Rudas took to the extreme. I personally think it is fine; obviously it is dark culture, but Anton LaVey, author of *The Satanic Bible* and founder of the Church of Satan, was closer to humanism and rationalism in his views than to the occult. In some respects, his views were similar to those of Ayn Rand (1905–1982), the author of *Atlas Shrugged* (1957) and proponent of objectivist philosophy, which put reason above all else. There are kids who adopt Satanism, but it seems like a childish stance, albeit a nasty one. They don't seem to look at it with any intelligence at all – their Satanism seems to come out of death metal and Dennis Wheatley. I'd say that those who kill would kill anyway. If they were into stamp collecting they'd use that as the excuse. Anyway, what's your view?

DAVIS: I can, believe it or not sympathise to an extent with those disaffected youths who join Satanic cults – I almost wrote off to one when I was 16, having seen an advert in a newspaper! I'd been told every day of my childhood that I'd never amount to anything, that they'd got the wrong one at the hospital, so I was desperate for power, for revenge. Now, as a rational adult, Satanism seems puerile – but so does reality TV, the Queen's speech and numerous other things that grip parts of the nation. Putting one religion above another is simply saying 'my magick good, your magick bad'.

Satanism can be a short-term outlet for a practitioner's anger and frustration: presumably they ditch it when they find that it doesn't work. Obviously it becomes dangerous when it involves animal sacrifice – or human sacrifice, as in the Elyse Pahler case. That said, I suspect that the desire for excitement and sex was stronger in these boys than the desire to sacrifice a virgin to Lucifer – that excuse probably came later as they knew that it would be happily seized upon by religious adults. As with someone who claims to be homicidally interested in death metal music, I think that the unhappy childhood comes first and the obsession with a criminal level of Satanism follows. Happy and strong people don't need an external belief system.

I agree that there's a lack of intelligence amongst some youthful Satanists, but, in fairness, they live in a dumbed-down culture. Many have grown up in religious households where the maxim is 'ours not to question why'. There's also a great deal of ignorance amongst some new age practitioners – one best-selling book on self-healing suggests that we all choose our parents for the lessons that we can learn from them. In that case, there's a phenomenal number of us choosing to starve to death in Third World countries within weeks of being born. Similarly, when Princess Di separated from Prince Charles, numerous so-called psychics predicted that she would remarry and have more children. None of them foresaw her early death – yet they are still in business today.

I remember a fellow crime author saying that, after her husband died in a road accident, she contacted a famous psychic and had to wait weeks for an appointment. But when she saw him, he told her things that only someone familiar with her life could know. She was impressed until she spoke to a distant relative who said: 'I was interviewed about you a few weeks ago for a newspaper.' The so-called psychic was simply employing researchers to find out background information about his clients. I know of another girl who started work on a newspaper and was asked to make up the horo-scopes. When she refused, she was sacked. So, laugh at the Satanic youth if you will – but you also have to laugh at his parents for their own belief systems. Alternately, you can feel sympathy for adults who are so unhappy that they have to turn to magickal belief systems to get through the day.

JLS: Yeah, these belief systems – they're out of control. But I have to say that the tenets of an occult system called Chaos magick involve harnessing the power of a belief to get a magickal working done, then you totally discard that belief – finito! So a slightly different and highly iconoclastic perspective on belief there.

I'd like to ask now, Carol, your opinion of our law enforcers when dealing with the sort of crimes we've been talking about. Do you think the religious beliefs of individual police officers can influence murder investigations which have an occult or Satanic element?

DAVIS: It's certainly true that some policemen are very conventionally religious – just look at how poorly Colin Stagg was treated when he was investigated for the murder of Rachel Nickell in 1992. The police found that Colin, an artistic youth with time on his hands, had drawn pagan deities on the walls of his spare room and had a small altar dedicated to ancient gods in his bedroom. They were immediately convinced that he was their man, and their early questions included: 'Is it the type of religion where sacrifices are made?' Stagg was simply a lonely and somewhat lost young man, but they were so determined to nail him for the murder that they spent untold thousands in a honeypot sting operation. Thankfully, the judge threw the case out.

But the media continued to suggest that he was guilty and had 'gotten away with it' and the very few of us who'd studied the case in detail, and who believed in his innocence, found it almost impossible to get articles published in the press. Fortunately, David Kessler co-wrote a brilliant book on the subject and I managed to interview him for a feature in *True Crime Monthly* magazine. DNA evidence has now shown that the killer is almost certainly a man locked up in Broadmoor for a double murder – but that's little comfort to Colin, who has spent more than a decade being verbally and physically attacked by an ignorant public, so that he now lives like a recluse. He'd have been treated very differently by the press, public and police if he'd been a Sunday school teacher rather than a pagan.

JLS: Okay, interesting stuff, Carol – just shows how your beliefs can be held against you. To find out more about Carol and her books go to www.carolannedavis.co.uk. Okay, folks, that's it for this week's show. Tune in next week . . . or forever burn in the fires of Hell . . . presuming, of course, that your personal belief system goes along with the idea of eternal damnation in an alternate dimension.

*Track 2: The Bottle Rockets, 'You Can't Hide A Redneck (Under That Hippy Hair)', from 'Songs of Sahm' (2002)*

## His Satanic Majesty's Request

When I got home after the show I made myself a coffee, put on Ralph Vaughan Williams' *Symphony No 3, A Pastoral Symphony*, on the stereo, and lay down on my back on a rug on the floor to relax. Despite the gentle, swirling tones that evoked the best of our green and pleasant land, I couldn't seem to quiet my mind. I kept thinking about Satanic killers and how absurd it was that they committed terrible murders in the name of an invisible entity. But I had no answers and didn't want to think about it any more. To stop my mind racing, I used all the internal-dialogue stilling techniques I'd learned from magick and Indian mysticism. None of them worked. Still the thoughts and images raced across my consciousness, incessant and adamant, like spoilt children demanding attention. Then, just as I was about to give up in despair, a strange feeling came upon me. Everything went quiet and I felt a strong tingling sensation in the small of my back. There was also an odd smell, like sulphur, and a fly or mosquito buzzed irritatingly close to the back of my head. I tried to swat it, but found myself completely unable to move. My heart pounded in fear – had I become suddenly paralysed? Had I contracted some terrible condition? It was then I felt myself descending into the earth, into some underground cavern. I looked around me. Flaming torches lit up strange sigils that were scrawled over all the walls. To one side, sprawled out on a chaise longue was a dapper-looking middle-aged man in top hat and tails, and sporting a precisely trimmed goatee beard. It was clearly Satan himself. It looked like I'd at last got the chance to sell my soul for fame and fortune. But I was to be disappointed.

'Ah, Mr Shreeve . . . do sit down, old man,' he gestured to a chair made of dark wood and carved with rows of copulating couples, all joined to each other in an orgy of carnal embrace. On a table next to the chair was a bottle of Plymouth gin, mineral water and a glass made of sparkling crystal. 'Your favourite tipple, I believe,' he said, playfully stroking the silver snake's-head handle of the walking cane he held in his hand. 'Good choice. It's popular with most of those who follow the left hand path, otherwise known as the way of the serpent from the Garden of Eden.'

I poured myself a drink and asked him what he wanted with me.

He smiled, shifting slightly on the chaise longue. 'I thought it was about time I put my side of the story across. I get blamed for much of the blood spilt in the world. Lowbrow books and the gutter press are particularly keen to evoke my name in relation to deranged, and let's face it, tacky and uncultured, killers – people I'd hardly be seen dead with – not even at the Café Royal.'

Satan got up and poured himself a drink, then let out a long sigh and said: 'The biggest irony is I was but a mere bit part actor in the Bible. I didn't even get to kill, maim or torture anyone, more's the pity. All I did was put a little temptation before Christ, and God knows he needed it – such a pious fellow. Yet they blame me for the atrocities committed by plebeian maniacs, people who I wouldn't even have washing up at my selective members' club.'

Satan walked over to me and patted me on the shoulder. 'Could you see your way to painting me in better light, old man? That's all I ask.'

With that, Satan was gone. But he had left his snake's-head walking cane propped up against the chaise longue. I picked it up and called, 'You've left your cane behind . . .' He didn't reply. The scene faded and I found myself rising from the underworld back up to the surface. I opened my eyes. Not only was I no longer paralysed, but the Vaughan Williams symphony was still playing on my stereo and my coffee was still warm enough to drink.

## Order out of Chaos

Although I was disappointed to have missed out on making a Faustian pact, I felt that Satan had a point. He really was little more than an extra on the biggest religious show on earth. Yet so-called Satanic killers, believing they are doing his work, have launched frenzied, bloodthirsty attacks on innocent victims. Where are they taking their lead from? Certainly not the Bible – Satan's role was way too small. In my view they take their lead from the popular *idea* of Satan as lord of all evil, which was built up in the West during medieval times in a bid to keep the populace under control and faithful to the Church. In a sense, Satanic killers create their own version of Satan. They mentally envision him and his terrible works until eventually Satan becomes as good as real to them. Aligning themselves with the Devil in this way would be an unconscious process, possibly brought about by a damaged child-

hood or a general dissatisfaction with life, and the resulting
need to identify with a creed that holds the promise of
excitement and is frowned upon by society.

Interestingly, the *conscious* act of identifying yourself
with a deity (or archetype) and letting it possess you is a
part of magickal tradition going back thousands of years,
possibly as far back as prehistoric times. In Voodoo and
Santeria, and pagan African spirituality, possession is a
key part of religious practice. Devotees go into deep trance
states and are overtaken by gods, spirits or ancestors.
Their belief system holds that such entities are real and
influence events in our world. Because I'm deeply irreligious (like those who follow Chaos magick) I personally
cannot accept the literal reality of gods and spirits, and
do not see any value in subscribing to one set belief pattern.
But I do see possession and identifying with deities as a
positive act, so long as you never believe in them long
term and move from one pantheon to the next – say from
the Voodoo gods to the Greek gods, and then to the Celtic
gods (or even to the dark deities from horror writer H.P.
Lovecraft's *Necronomicon*). The secret is being able to use
belief to gain knowledge of the vast terrain that makes up
the unconscious mind, but not to become stuck on one
track. It's a delicate balance and not something that should
be entered into by anyone lacking a strong will.

This is where Satanic killers fall down. They become
obsessed by Satan and allow the dark archetype to possess
them completely. They then come to believe that they are
being guided by the lord of all evil. And if he tells them
to kill, they will kill. This is probably what happened with
the youths who killed Elyse Pahler. The mix of drugs,
death metal and diabolic led to them becoming almost
literally possessed by the idea of Satan – an idea which
they had created with their imaginations. Again, one of
the inner secrets of magick is the use of imagination to

create internal pictures and visions which stimulate the deep mind or unconscious to bring knowledge that is beyond words (some might describe this as 'enlightenment'). Almost invariably, this is felt as a peak experience or a feeling of profound inspiration. But in the wrong hands the use of the imagination in a magickal way (be it consciously or unconsciously) can lead to negativity and destruction, or at worst killing.

Daniel and Manuela Ruda probably fell into the same trap as the killers of Elyse Pahler. So profoundly did they identify with the concept of Satan as the Lord of Darkness that they were overwhelmed by it. Their identities were eclipsed by the diabolism they created with their imaginations. Yet, as I said earlier, Manuela was exposed to Chaos magick, which offers you the concepts and mental tools needed to gain control of your psyche. But she either studied the subject superficially or interpreted it according to her growing belief in the objective reality of Satan. If she had been able to digest and take on board the ideas of Chaos magick she would never have taken the concept of Satan literally. This is because one of the key tenets of Chaos magick is to use belief as a very powerful engine to power magickal workings and/or transform yourself for the better. Once a belief has served its purpose, it is then discarded. A new belief might then be adopted by the practitioner for some other end, or he or she might 'run on empty' for a while, with no creed or ideology in place.

Clearly, had Manuela Ruda acquired these abilities when she practised Chaos magick, she would have gained control over her mind and arguably would have recognised her weaknesses and homicidal tendencies – even overcome them. What's more, she would not have been prey to her beliefs; instead she would have controlled them and 'plugged' them in (like a piece of software) when and if they proved useful. She might well have worshipped Satan on occasion. Why not? Satan is a figment of our imaginations and can be moulded to fit our outlook on life. As it was, Manuela had a total and unswerving belief in the literal existence of an invisible entity. And this led to a demented and deranged murder.

But it is important to recognise that it is not Satan that is bad; it is the *misuse of belief*. After all, plenty of people have killed others in the name of God or Allah, both of which, arguably, have been created by the human imagination. Personally I think the mystic and magickian Aleister Crowley had it right when he said: 'There is no god but man'.[6] How we use our godlike power is the important thing.

The main lesson I learned from looking into Satanic killing was that is crucial for society to differentiate between the two types of Satanist – the bona fide and the pretender. Bona fide Satanists tend to be intellectual, artistic and cultured, along with respecting nature and other human beings. Satan for them is more a symbol for libertarianism and the 1960s ideology of doing what you want. The pretenders, on the other hand, become obsessed (or even possessed) by the idea of Satan as lord of all evil. This could be a reaction to abuse that occurred in childhood or simple dissatisfaction with life. The upshot is they approach life in a negative and destructive way, and some go as far as committing murder. These could well have existing psychological problems and are essentially 'time bombs' waiting to explode. All it takes is a catalyst, which could be anything from another person to drugs or a flirtation with the idea of Satanism.

This is why I think society at large needs to recognise that bona fide Satanism is a valid spiritual path and is not bad or evil. That way, those who follow bona fide Satanism are less likely to be persecuted, and the pretenders will be seen for what they are – people with severe mental problems, some of whom may have the potential to kill.

Accepting that Satanism is not evil could clearly be difficult for anyone who believes in God and his traditional diabolic adversary. But if we are to move into the future and finally offload the religious prejudices inherited from the Middle Ages, we need to accept that God and Satan, along with the many pantheons of pagan deities are creations of the human mind. And that, while not 'real' as such, they are very powerful archetypes that can be used by the human mind to develop consciousness and enter transcendental states. This won't happen overnight. But eventually we will evolve more sophisticated systems of spirituality. And I'd even go as far as saying that Chaos magick – along with the seminal influence of artist and magickian Austin Osman Spare – might one day be looked back on as a key instigator of this evolution.

Just as I was typing up this thought there was a knock at the door. It was the postman delivering a package that had been sent via airmail. It was from my Canadian shaman friend, Dr Crazywolf. I signed for the parcel, then carefully cut it open with my Swiss army knife. Inside was a black walking cane, with a silver snake's head ... Considering I hadn't mentioned my vision of Satan in the underworld to Crazywolf, I couldn't help but wonder whether I was just a pawn in some invisible entity's divine plan ... it's just I couldn't work out whether it was the guy upstairs or the one below stairs.

# Chapter 5: Death Dealers

Dead Babies . . . Hexing in High Places . . . Driving the Tractor on the Death Farm . . . Tantra: The Yoga of Killing? . . . Money for Nothing? . . . Sacrifice: The Art of Giving Something Up . . . A Necromancer in the Family

'For the Angel of Death spread his wings on the blast,
And breathed in the face of the foe as he pass'd;
And the eyes of the sleepers wax'd deadly and chill,
And their hearts but once heaved, and for ever grew still!'

George Gordon, Lord Byron (1788–1824)
*The Destruction of Sennacherib* (1815)

Those who deal in ritual death walk amongst us. They live in our cities and towns, use our buses and subways, and shop in the same food stores as we do. But would we recognise them? Would we see tell-tale signs that they're set on putting the grim reaper out of a job? Probably not. Most of us naively believe that our fellow humans are innately good – we try to see the best in people. This is a good attitude and will serve the majority of us all our lives. We won't run into trouble, or, worse, walk into the wolf's lair like a lamb to the slaughter. But some do. It might be a small minority, but they meet an end few could dream up in their worst nightmares.

It's down to fate who will be a victim. But out there in the crowd are people who are almost inhuman in their cruelty and grotesque practices. You would have to be a saint or completely mentally deluded to see the good in them. If we were able to enter such people's lives – even for one day – it would be like going on a holiday to Hell with a pack of demons as our tour guides.

Sometimes it is only chance that brings such evil people to the surface and marks them out from the crowd. Take the so-called Palo Mayombe 'witch' from New York for example. If fate hadn't intervened, the dark and appalling secret in her apartment may never have come to light . . .

## Dead Babies

When Margaret Ramirez left her Washington Heights apartment she wasn't to know that the short walk, covering only a few blocks, would be her last. Nor was she to know, as she walked down the sidewalk, that fate had turned its deadly and sinister gaze on her. She wasn't about to be murdered. Her death would be a genuine accident. She would simply be in the wrong place at the wrong time. Her fatal accident would not even be viewed as particularly tragic because the 74-year-old Ramirez was not popular. She was a recluse. A misfit who lived with her son Michael Grajales, age 54, a Vietnam veteran with long yellowed hair and beard, who was also an outcast from conventional society. If the truth be known, many in the neighbourhood would think it was a good thing that Margaret Ramirez got hit and killed by a car while crossing the street near her apartment on West 164 Street in Washington Heights, New York, on 17 July 2000. Not because she didn't fit in. But because she seemed like a crazy woman. She was a self-confessed witch, obsessed by the occult, and most likely did bad things to people, like cursing and hexing them.

One thing is for sure, the cops who went to Ramirez's apartment to give the standard family notification were in for a big shock. They would walk into a scene of unimaginably macabre horror. They banged on the door and eventually roused Michael, Margaret Ramirez's son. On learning of his mother's death, he became so unstable he had to be led away in handcuffs. The apartment was clearly strange. It reeked of incense which, at least up to a point, covered up the gut-wrenching stench of decay that pervaded every room. The police officers steeled themselves. Instinct – and the terrible smell – told them they were about to find something ghastly. They weren't wrong. The first items they found were two skulls, one from an adult, the other from a 1- or 2-year-old child. The child's skull was in a cauldron and was coated with rotting flesh, dried blood and candle wax. Rank-smelling dirt, which investigators later came to believe had been gathered from a local cemetery, was scattered on the floor. And statues of Catholic saints were in every corner of the room. Chillingly, police also found a jar filled with pieces of flesh, floating in murky formaldehyde.

Then they opened up a closet. What they found left them dumbfounded. 'What the *fuck* is this . . .?' they probably breathed as they stood staring at the gruesome sight that confronted them. Preserved in a knee-high jar of formaldehyde was a fully formed, perfectly preserved newborn girl. She had olive skin and straight black hair and was floating head up. She still had her umbilical cord – and a clamp, like those used in hospitals, was attached.

Her tiny hands had been inked for prints, as is the common procedure in US hospitals, even to stillborn babies. How the baby girl got in the jar in the Washington Heights apartment, no one knew. She had no name and presumably had no one to mourn her death. Detectives theorised that she may have been stillborn, her body stolen for some reason or sold out of a hospital morgue. Far worse, she may have been born alive, then sold or kidnapped. Or she could have been given away for ritual sacrifice. 'We haven't ruled out homicide, but we're hoping the baby was stillborn,' said Lieutenant George Menig. 'It's too creepy to think that it could have been a human sacrifice.'

It didn't take investigators long to conclude that Ramirez, and possibly her son Michael Grajales, were, at the very least, using body parts and other remains in the practice of Palo Mayombe, an Afro–Cuban religion and dark relative of Santeria, a popular spiritual path similar to Voodoo. Followers of Palo Mayombe, known as 'Paleros' or 'Ngangaleros', believe human body parts can be used to contact and enslave the spirits of the dead. With the body parts acting as a psychic connection, the shaman or sorcerer goes into a trance, much as psychics and mediums do, and travels in the realm of the spirits. Using magickal signs and formulas, the dead are then compelled to do the sorcerer's bidding, be it to bring money or other worldly wants, or to hex enemies. Such practices can seem horrifying to the uninitiated: 'These people, these Paleros, redefine evil,' said one horrified investigator. 'You're dealing with the Devil himself.'

Ramirez's son, Michael, was locked up in a psychiatric ward at the New York Veterans Affairs Hospital. He denied all involvement with his mother's witchcraft.

Meanwhile, the police discovered Ramirez's notebooks, which she used in the study of her magickal arts. They contained intricate renderings of skulls, arrows, crosses and other symbols that are drawn on the floor by practitioners of Palo Mayombe to conjure up spirits. The notebooks also contained clues to the identities of other Palo Mayombe initiates. According to one unnamed source Ramirez was a 'very high-roller'. To others, she was plain weird and scary. According to the building superintendent, Luis Pena, who lived across the hall from Ramirez and her son, great clouds of choking incense would waft out from under Ramirez's heavily deadlocked door. 'The apartment smelled like a dead body, I tell you,' he recalled. The mother and son lived in their first-floor apartment like recluses for 30 years, he went on, not once allowing anyone inside to decorate the place. Ramirez was paranoid about privacy. She not only kept her windows boarded up, but, according to Pena, she was reluctant to use the garbage cans outside her building; instead she put her trash into manageable small bags and carried them around the corner to dump them in cans belonging to another building. Pena went on: 'She'd tell me, "Don't look at me! I'm a real witch!"' She also told him she could 'fly in the night'.

But how would Ramirez have used the baby in her rituals? One person who had a theory was Dr Charles Wetli, the chief medical examiner of Suffolk County in New York and a Palo Mayombe expert from his days as a coroner in Miami, where the practice is found among the large Cuban population there. He said that 'she could have enslaved the baby's spirit. Or maybe her "fumbi" [the enslaved spirit of the child whose skull was in the cauldron] was lonely, and asked for a companion.' A Palo Mayombe priest from the Queens district of New York, who knew Ramirez, was quoted in the *New York Post*. He said: 'Everybody in New York using Palo heard about her. She would use the body to make an agreement with El Diablo, with the Devil. But it gave her no power. She didn't know what to do with it.' Getting knocked down and killed by a car, he said, was proof that she was out of her depth. Her spirits – possibly even the spirit of the baby girl in the jar – turned against her. 'That could have happened, that the baby killed her,' he said. 'She may have paid with her life.' He dismissed Ramirez as a novice who dabbled in dangerous dark magick when she should have stuck to tarot cards. But neither he, nor any other local practitioners of Palo Mayombe, was likely to have admitted to having any dealings with her – especially considering investigators had not ruled out homicide.

In the end, though, police were unable to prove whether the baby girl had been sacrificed in a black magick ritual or not. Margaret Ramirez was dead and her son Michael was in no fit state mentally to offer reliable information. But detectives knew this case was not a one-off. However crazy Margaret Ramirez had seemed to those acquainted with her, they knew that she was only one of many practitioners of Palo Mayombe across America. Every now and again, as reported by the press wires, body parts are found – sometimes with the rotting flesh still on them and usually with ritual items, such as candles or signs and symbols surrounding them. Chillingly, some of these remains are not stolen from graves; they are taken from people, most likely killed in ritual sacrifices. The only problem is, there has never been enough proof to gain a solid conviction – except in one terrifying case, in which at least 24 victims were killed and mutilated in ritual sacrifices by Palo Mayombe devotees. But we will come to that shortly. In the meantime, let's take a closer look at what Palo Mayombe is and what it involves.

Palo Mayombe is an Afro-Caribbean religion with roots in the African Congo. Like many others in Africa, large numbers of Congo tribespeople were forcibly taken to the Caribbean to work as slaves. Uprooted from their homeland, they had no choice but to adapt their cultural and religious beliefs to fit in with the culture and Catholic religious tradition of the new land. Besides Catholicism, the Congo slaves incorporated some of the beliefs, symbols and rituals of Santeria, a religion predominantly practised in Cuba, but with roots in the Yoruba tribes of south-western Nigeria. The result of this spiritual mix and match was Palo Mayombe. The term is derived from the Spanish 'Palo' meaning 'wooden stick' or 'branch' and refers to the pieces of wood practitioners use in their magick spells.

Initiates of Palo Mayombe are known as 'Paleros'. The source of the Paleros' power is the cauldron where the spirits of the dead are supposed to reside; the African name for this sacred cauldron is 'nganga', which is a Congolese word meaning dead, spirit or supernatural force. Items commonly kept in the cauldron are human skulls, bones, graveyard dirt, herbs, insects and animal and bird carcasses. The nganga does what its owner orders it to do, and working with it is referred to as 'playing' with it. When the spirit of the nganga carries out a Palero's wishes, he or she gives it blood as an expression of gratitude. This would normally involve the sacrifice of an animal or bird. Paleros also serve their own ancestors, all the other dead, and the spirits of nature.

It is said that for a fee, some Paleros will carry out rituals to inflict mental or physical harm, even death, on a victim. A black magick spell, known as a brujeria or bilongo, can be unleashed in many different ways – including by spiking a person's food or drink with a magickal preparation or by sending a spirit of the dead to cause torment and misfortune. Other kinds of black magick include leaving animal carcasses, such as decapitated roosters, dead goats, or human skulls, at the entrance of a business or home; or stuffing dolls with ritual items like pendants, herbs or the names of people scrawled on parchment. These are then kept at home to do their malevolent work.

But it is important to recognise that Palo Mayombe is

not necessarily all bad; there is, after all, good and bad in all religions. In her book, *Santeria: The Religion*, cultural anthropologist Migene González-Wippler[1] points out that many Paleros perform rites of healing and spells for the good of their local communities. And Felix Mota – a Voodoo practitioner in Passaic, New Jersey, who owns a store selling supplies used in Palo Mayombe ceremonies – stated in an interview with the *New Jersey Herald News* that: 'I know people from Palo who practice good.' He also said that the practice of Palo Mayombe is growing to the point that he has difficulty keeping up with the demand for books on the subject. He did, however, admit that he knew several practitioners who used bones stolen from graveyards.

And this is the problem. It is hard to get away from the dark side of Palo Mayombe. Even as far back as 1903 there is a record of a Palero sacrificing a young girl in Cuba in a Palo Mayombe rite. And in more recent times, you can find numerous incidents pointing to murder and black magick rituals. Back in 1986, for example, a baby in Miami was found murdered, its tongue and eyelids cut off and offered to various deities. The same year, in Fort Myers, Florida, a search of a drug-dealer's home and shrimp boat turned up a cauldron with two human skulls – from black males – that were not medical specimens. What's more, flesh was still attached to the skulls, along with human organs that had not been embalmed – making it pretty clear they were not got through grave robbing but through murder. All too typically in cases like this, homicide could not be conclusively proven.

Then in 1988, while investigating a child pornography ring, the Port Authority in New Jersey uncovered a ritual altar to protect the illegal operation – along with a large container filled with human blood. Investigators suspected that the blood came from one of the children used in the ring's pornographic movies – the child had disappeared not long after filming – but they couldn't prove it. Had they been able to do so, the child pornographers would have been charged with the fatal draining of the child's blood. As it was, the child was never found. But if a child was killed, then it could well have been part of a ritual with roots in Palo Mayombe. Equally, though, the child pornographers could have used the excuse of dark magick to justify murder. Even when altars and magickal paraphernalia are involved it isn't always cut and dried that the motive genuinely involved ritual sacrifice.

In March 2005, police in Florida launched a manhunt for six armed people after discovering human skulls and bones inside a shed. The items were covered in blood. They also found two kinds of cocaine, twelve handguns, a goat's head and live chickens, pigeons and guinea pigs. 'It gives me the creeps,' one neighbour said. Police said they believed the six followed Palo Mayombe, having arrived in the US as Cuban immigrants.

## Hexing in High Places

'Every dictator uses religion as a prop to keep himself in power.'

Benazir Bhutto, two-time prime minister of Pakistan, and first woman to lead a Muslim country (1953–): Interview on *60 Minutes*, CBS-TV, 1986.

Even those in power are not immune to the lure of gaining dark spiritual power. When Panamanian military dictator General Manuel Noriega, walked out of the Vatican embassy in 1989 and into the custody of US drug agents, various items on his person gave away the fact that he was a devotee of Afro-Caribbean sorcery. Not only was he grasping a crucifix, wearing a cult necklace and carrying a magickal amulet in his pocket, he was also wearing red underwear – all apparently to ward off demons. American soldiers also uncovered a collection of occult shrines in Noriega's various headquarters and residences. The US Army took all this very seriously. They called in Chief Warrant Officer James R. Dibble, an expert on the occult and head of the general crimes team at Fort Campbell, Kentucky. The Army wanted Dibble, then aged 38, to analyse the discoveries and help develop a psychological profile of Noriega.

It turned out that for protection against his enemies Noriega had invoked the aid of various spiritual creeds, including Santeria and Condomble (the Brazilian equivalent of Santeria and Voodoo), Brujeria (diabolical witchcraft), Egyptian mysticism, Voodoo and Palo Mayombe. The largest trove of occult items was uncovered in Noriega's headquarters at Fort Amador outside Panama City. Inside was a freezer containing more than 30 'trabajos', blackmagick totems directed at Noriega's enemies. Among these were George Bush Senior, Ronald Reagan, Henry Kissinger, Panamanian Archbishop Marcos McGrath, Senator Jesse Helms and Miami judge William Hoeveler, who presided at Noriega's drug-trafficking indictment in 1988. A photo of Reagan was covered in red candle wax, which was meant to immobilise the former president. 'The trabajos were put into the freezer as a means of freezing the actions of the person,' Dibble told reporters from *People Weekly*.

In another room was an altar to St George, which held a lock of Noriega's hair, a ritual stone, called an otane (said to contain the spirit of a Santeria saint) and other personal items. 'This altar was to grant [Noriega] power,' Dibble went on to explain, adding that Noriega and cult worshippers like him believe spirits can manipulate the fate of mortals. According to Dibble, the majority of Latin American

drug traffickers arrested in the United States are found to
be practitioners of either Santeria or Palo Mayombe. 'They
use it in a malevolent manner to protect themselves not only
from police but also from rival drug dealers,' said Dibble.
'If we discount or do not give credence to their religious
convictions, we have underestimated the enemy.'

## Driving the Tractor on the Death Farm

> 'All right, then, I'll go to hell.'
> > Mark Twain (1835–1910)
> > American humorist, writer and lecturer

Most of us refuse to believe it possible that people – even
children – can be sacrificed in brutal occult rituals to gain
power or wealth. It's hard to imagine how anyone, other
than a deranged serial killer, could target an individual and
lure them to a quiet spot to sacrifice them to spirits or deities
in the hope of gaining favours. Surely it's ancient history?
It can't be going on now. But it is. And the truly horrifying
thing is: it is going on far closer to home than any of us can
feel comfortable with. Yes, the practice certainly occurs in
far-flung corners of the globe, but it also happens on our
doorsteps in the USA, Britain and Europe. As I have shown,
it forms part of the dark underbelly of civilised society. And
because of this the unwary can walk into it – *completely
inadvertently and at random* – and meet an end they wouldn't
wish even on their worst enemy.

Every year at spring break, in the US, more than 50,000
college students cross the US–Mexican border to indulge
in some well-deserved R&R in the slum town of
Matamoros. They hit a ramshackle strip of bars and clubs
sandwiched between whorehouses and drug dens,

surrounded by a tundra of poverty and violence. Spring break is a national event and the subject of endless teen comedies. Parents don't normally worry too much about their kids crossing the border to party; they might rather they didn't go because they know deep down their kids will do everything they did when they were younger – perhaps a whole lot more too. But they don't think anything truly terrible is going to happen.

Like lots of other students, Mark Kilroy, who was studying at the University of Texas, was eagerly looking forward to cutting loose during the March vacation. A friend who went with him recalled: 'The whole semester, that was all he talked about.' Nobody suspected the dark-haired and fresh-faced Kilroy could come to harm. All he was going to do was spend a few nights drinking and having fun across the border. College kids had been doing it since the 1930s. You work hard on your grades; you're entitled to let loose.

On the first evening, Kilroy and three friends, all former classmates at Santa Fe (Texas) High, met some girls from Kansas. They drank beer, laughed a lot and swapped addresses. At the end of the night, they returned safely to their rooms at the Sheraton Hotel on South Padre Island, Texas, twenty miles away. Their second night of beer drinking and revelry went equally well. At around 2 a.m. in the morning of 14 March, the four young men decided to call it a night. They began walking towards the river, a fifteen-minute stroll that would take them over the bridge to the US side of the border, where they had parked their car.

Two of them walked ahead. Kilroy and Bill Huddleston (age 21) followed about twenty feet behind. Huddleston paused to step into an alley to relieve himself. Kilroy waited on the street, kicking his heels. By the time Huddleston came out, Kilroy had vanished. There were no sounds. No witnesses. He was just gone. 'Hey, Mark, stop fucking around,' shouted Huddleston. 'Come out, we gotta get back.' He got no response. The cops were called. Kilroy's family had various connections, including an uncle in customs. So no stone was left unturned trying to locate him. A $15,000 reward was put up for information leading to Kilroy's safe return or the arrest of his abductors. But no useful leads came in. Kilroy's whereabouts remained a mystery.

A month later, however, an unexpected incident put investigators hot on the trail. In the bleak, brown plains of Mexico's Rio Grande valley – some twenty miles from where Kilroy disappeared – drug smuggling is as common as a coyote's yowl. Which is why Mexican authorities, every so often, mount anti-drug campaigns, erecting roadblocks at random and sweeping border districts for unwary smugglers. One such roadblock was smashed through by the lackey of a local drug baron. The cops pursued him to a rundown ranch nearby. A quick search turned up 75 lbs of marijuana. No big deal. A routine seize. But the investigation took a darker turn when the authorities, as a matter of course, showed the ranch's caretaker a photo of the tall and reasonably good-looking Mark Kilroy.

Kid disappeared a month back, said the cops. Had he seen him?

'Yeah,' the worker recalled, 'I saw him.' He then pointed to a rust-coloured wooden shack in the corral, 400 yards away.

There, under a grey, misty sky, the police made a ghastly discovery. In and around the corral, they found several makeshift graves. The stench of decaying flesh was overpowering. After extensive digging, they uncovered the corpses of twelve males (later a thirteenth was unearthed). One was as young as 14. Several of the victims had been slashed with knives; others bludgeoned on the head. One had been hanged, another set on fire. At least two had been pumped with bullets. Some had been tortured with razor blades or had their hearts ripped out.

Nearly all had been severely mutilated: ears, nipples and testicles removed, the eyes gouged from one victim, the head missing from another. Amongst the victims police discovered the corpse of Mark Kilroy. When officers finally entered the darkness of the 15-by-25 foot shack, they found a squat iron cauldron. Its contents suggested that more than just a band of ruthless killers had been at work. Inside the pot, resting in dried blood, was a charred human brain and a roasted turtle. Other containers held a witch's brew of human hair, a goat's head and chicken parts.

Mexican police arrested and questioned four suspects, including the drug baron's lackey who had led them to the ranch. The horrifying truth soon became clear: the cops were dealing with a quasi-spiritual cult of drug smugglers who believed that orgies of human sacrifice would win diabolic protection for their 2,000 lb a week marijuana-running operation to the US. 'They felt that all the killing would draw a protective shield around them,' said Texas Attorney General Jim Mattox. 'It was religious craziness.'

Kilroy – like all but two of the victims – was picked at random. Fate dealt him a bad card. His spring-break revelry led to his blood-curdling demise. Further questioning of suspects revealed what happened to him. At 2 a.m. he was lured towards a pickup truck by a thin, scar-faced man who offered a ride. Two thugs threw him into the back and sped off. Five blocks away, Kilroy attempted to escape, but was recaptured and driven to the ranch. There he was gagged and blindfolded with heavy grey tape and hurled into the darkened shack. Kilroy's captors brought bread and water. They assured him there was no danger. But twelve hours later he was abruptly led outside and executed with a machete slash to the back of his neck. The man who wielded the weapon was the cult's ringleader, Adolfo De Jesus Constanzo, age 26, a lanky, red-haired Cuban American. He inspired such fervent loyalty among his followers that he was known as El Padrino, the Godfather. It turned out that Constanzo had commissioned Kilroy's abduction by ordering his followers to 'go out and bring in an Anglo male'.

Constanzo grew up in South Florida, where he practised Santeria, the religious path with roots in the Yoruba tribes of Africa and related to Voodoo. He was well versed in other aspects of the occult too, including tarot card reading. A few years before Kilroy's murder he had become involved in Palo Mayombe. As we've seen, the majority of those involved in the religion do not condone human sacrifice. Nevertheless, they do regularly use the bones of the dead in rituals (usually obtained from dubious sources). Constanzo's sect, however, embraced human sacrifice wholeheartedly. In the killing fields, police found dozens of long candles as well as garlic, peppers and scores of half-burned cigars – paraphernalia that goes with Palo Mayombe. To gain the favours of the dark spirits of Palo Mayombe, Constanzo and his followers boiled the brains and hearts of their victims, mixing the concoction with leg and arm bones and animal heads. So vicious were the cultists that it took two pathologists labouring at a Matamoros mortuary almost four days to piece together the bodies and complete the autopsies. Several victims remained unidentified, but, as well as Mark Kilroy, at least one other young man may have been an American kidnapped from neighbouring Brownsville, Texas. Several shocking revelations began to emerge at this time too – including the fact that as well as torturing his victims Constanzo had sodomised them.

Besides Constanzo, authorities sought three other

suspects, including the Godfather's companion, Sara Maria Aldrete, age 24, a Mexican honours student at Texas Southmost College in Brownsville. Searching Aldrete's home in Matamoros, police found a blood-spattered altar and candles. The four cult members who had already been picked up pleaded guilty to the grisly deeds, but showed little remorse. When paraded before reporters in Matamoros, the shirt of one suspect was pulled back to show a series of scars in the form of inverted crosses, an apparent sign that he was selected to kill. Later, police dispensed their own brand of justice. Having discovered from their interviews that there was one further body buried at the ranch, they hauled one of the dope traffickers back to the grave site and forced him to dig in the blazing sun, without water, until he uncovered it.

Lawmen scoured the border in vain for Constanzo and what remained of his entourage. On 17 April, however, they arrested another gang member, Serafin Hernandez Rivera, in Houston. Searching the house where he had been hiding they seized weapons and cash, but found no occult paraphernalia. Constanzo and his closest aides, meanwhile, had moved on.

On 18 April 1989, in the small apartment where he was now staying with Aldrete and his other trusted gang members, Constanzo, ever the occult believer, read betrayal in his tarot cards. He knew informers must have sold out Rivera, and now he eyed his friends more warily. He kept an Uzi close to hand and rarely slept for more than a few minutes at a time. Increasingly, he threatened those around him with a power exceeding that of the police. 'They cannot kill you,' he boasted, 'but I can.'

Then, on 22 April, the Mexican authorities set about fighting bad magick with good magick. They burnt Constanzo's bloodstained ritual shack to the ground and performed their own psychic cleansing of the area.

Comandante Juan Benitez (age 35), head of the Mexican anti-narcotics squad, who was heading the hunt for Constanzo, muttered darkly under his breath: 'You'll see, I'll bury the son of a bitch. I'll kill him. I'll kill him.' His fine Indian features and slick black hair shone in the dancing light of the flames. He and other operatives freely admitted it was an act designed to 'drive Constanzo crazy'.

The next morning, bang on cue, Constanzo flew into a rage, watching on television as police conducted a full-dress exorcism at the ranch, sprinkling holy water over the graves and smouldering ashes. Constanzo stormed about the small apartment, smashing lamps and over-turning furniture. He was a man possessed.

On 24 April police arrested another cultist, Jorger Montes. Like the others arrested before him, Montes spilled everything he knew, naming Constanzo as the mastermind and chief executioner in a string of chilling homicides. Three days later, Constanzo and his four remaining cohorts settled into their last hideout, an apartment house on Rio Sena in Mexico City. Aldrete, fearing for her life, penned a note on 2 May and tossed it from a bedroom window to the street below. It read:

> Please call the judicial police and tell them that in this building are those that they are seeking. Tell them that a woman is being held hostage. I beg this, because what I want most is to talk – or they're going to kill the girl.

A passer-by found the note moments later. He read it, but kept it to himself, believing it was someone's lame attempt at a joke. Upstairs in the crowded flat, Constanzo began laying plans to flee Mexico with his now tiny band of disciples; perhaps they'd start afresh somewhere else where no one knew them. 'They'll never take me,' he assured his followers. His plans were blown on 6 May, when police arrived in Rio Sena. They were doing door-to-door inquiries, asking questions everywhere. Unbeknown to Constanzo, it was an unrelated case. They were searching for a missing child. So when he glimpsed the cops from a window, he panicked and opened fire on them with his sub-machine gun. Within moments, 180 policemen surrounded the apartment house, returning fire in a fierce exchange that lasted some 45 minutes. Miraculously, the only person wounded was a cop who was struck by Constanzo's first shots.

When Constanzo realised that escape was impossible, he didn't hesitate. He handed his weapon to another gang member – El Duby – and told him to take him out, along with another leading member of the cult. As El Duby later told police: 'He told me to kill him . . . told him I couldn't do it, but he hit me in the face and threatened that everything would go bad for me in hell. Then . . . I just stood in front of them [Constanzo and the other cult member] and shot them both with a machine gun.'

Constanzo was dead when police stormed the apartment. He was dressed in shorts as if for a day at the beach. There were three survivors, including El Duby and Sara Aldrete. They were promptly arrested and rushed off to jail. In custody, El Duby cheerfully informed police, 'The Godfather will not be dead for long.' Mexican authorities were less concerned with Constanzo's impending resurrection than with making charges stick against the surviving cult members. El Duby's case was open-and-shut: his confession recorded on two murder counts. But Sara Aldrete was posing as a victim, claiming the gang took her as a hostage. She later betrayed herself by inadvertently disclosing intimate knowledge of the cult's bloodthirsty rituals.

In the wake of the Mexico City shootout, fourteen cult

members were rounded up. They were indicted on various charges, including multiple murder, weapons and narcotics violations, conspiracy and obstruction of justice. Sara Aldrete continued to protest her innocence. She said she never practised any religion but 'Christian Santeria', and that the television reports about the murders at the ranch had taken her completely by surprise. Jurors were not taken in. In 1994, Aldrete and four male accomplices were convicted of multiple slayings at the ranch. Aldrete was sentenced to 62 years. The others drew prison terms of 67 years. Should they live long enough to be released from custody in Mexico, US authorities stand ready to prosecute them all.

Their evil, however, may not be vanquished, even now. A grisly list of cult-related crimes remains unsolved in Mexico. From prison, Sara Aldrete told reporters: 'I don't think the religion will end with us, because it has a lot of people in it. They have found a temple in Monterey that isn't even related to us. It will continue.'

Between 1987 and 1989, police in Mexico City recorded 74 unsolved, suspected ritual murders, fourteen of them involving infant victims. Constanzo's cult is thought to have been involved in at least sixteen of those cases, all involving children or teenagers. But authorities lacked sufficient evidence to press charges. Referring to those cases, prosecutor Guillermo Ibarra told reporters: 'We would like to say, yes, Constanzo did them all, and poof, all those cases are solved. And the fact is, we believe he was responsible for some of them, though we'll never prove it now. But he didn't commit all of those murders. Which means someone else did. Someone who is still out there.'

A lot of paranoia surrounded the Matamoros case, which is not surprising considering the sheer horror of it. But were Constanzo's compatriots really out there looking to kill again? Were they really that set on murder and organised enough to hold a secretive cult together? No one can say for sure. What is certain, however, is that much of the paranoia was exacerbated by the general wave of 'Satanic panic' that was coursing through the United States at the time. As Jack Sargeant, author of a string of acclaimed books on avant-garde and underground culture, says in his essay, 'Blood and Sand'[2]:

> Satanic rituals, and the belief in a massive Satanic underground and other similar conspiracies formed the basis for numerous right-wing evangelical fundamentalist Christian witch-hunts in the eighties and nineties. Numerous Christian groups believed that a massive Devil-worshipping occult underground was operating across America, but, despite numerous accusations, no evidence was ever found to substantiate such beliefs, which lay purely in the overactive imaginations of fundamentalist zealots. Despite this lack of evidence – and sometimes *because* of this lack of evidence – the fundamentalist belief in a Satanic conspiracy continued to flourish. For some fundamentalist Christians and self-appointed cult watchdogs, Matamoros represented the proof they wanted for the existence of the Satanic underground.

Sargeant is undoubtedly right. In some ways the Matamoros killings were like a gift to fundamentalist groups. It validated their views and brought such groups a level of credence they didn't previously have.

That said, in October 1989, after the memories of the Matamoros killings had begun to fade, FBI agents working on a drug case in Brownsville made a sinister discovery. While serving a search warrant on a suspected drug dealer's house, they found a back room with walls and ceiling painted crimson red. This could have been written off as simply bad taste in interior decor. That is, if it hadn't been for the refrigerator standing at one end of the room, which was giving off an ungodly stink. Inside were vials of blood and noxious fluids. Each contained a tiny piece of paper, which had the name of a person scrawled on it, along with a curse or spell of control. At the other end of the room was an altar. On it were three figures, made from twigs and painted black, with pins sticking in them. Next to them were three blue, votive candles, encased in glass, with the words 'Law Be Gone' on each one. Chillingly, at the centre of the altar was a black-and-white photograph of Comandante Juan Benitez Ayala of the Mexico anti-narcotics squad, the man who hunted down Constanzo's gang. A hatpin had been thrust through the photo, pinning it to the altar.

The officers who made the discovery stood back in horror, reportedly voicing the fear that Constanzo's un-relenting evil really was living on. But, the truth was, the people behind the crimson sorcery room may not have had anything to do with Constanzo. According to press reports, many drug dealers follow the religion of Palo Mayombe and perform spell workings designed to protect themselves from being caught. Cursing the police goes hand in hand with this.


## Tantra: The Yoga of Killing?

'. . . the follies of Vamacharya (debauchery)'
                    Aleister Crowley (1875–1947),
                    writing in the *Equinox* (1909–1919).

Magick, like anything, can be used for good or bad ends. It's always down to the individual. I became fascinated by the occult at around 8 or 9 years old, which some might consider a bad thing, but I would say turned out to be very positive in that it engendered in me the belief that you can be and do anything you want in life (all you need is the imagination). My interest was sparked by UFOs and aliens and accounts of supernatural phenomena. Then, shortly after leaving school at 16, I discovered magick. Although a voracious reader, I didn't have a single qualification and had the unenviable task of finding a suitable job (and, more to the point, an employer who would appreciate and understand my eccentricities). The school careers officer had given up after his first talk with me. But later I was directed to a specialist careers officer in Northampton where I lived. He looked over my poor school record and the horrifying lack of even one CSE. He then asked about my interests. I told him at length about my heroes, the people I emulated and admired, who included Lord Byron, Shelley, SF writer Philip K. Dick, the Sex Pistols, Malcolm Mclaren and style and culture commentator Peter York. Rather surprisingly, he looked up and said: 'I've got just the position for you.' Within minutes he'd organised an interview, which he said I could attend right away, if I liked. So I did. I walked across Northampton's main shopping area and along the quaint St Giles Street to an antiquarian bookshop. Piles of books were stacked outside in a '10p' rack, and in the window were leather-bound titles that clearly went for high prices. The sign above the shop read: 'J.S. Billingham's, fine antiquarian books, founded 1878'.

I went in and met the manager, Bob Marriott, who was in his late 20s and besides being an expert in collectable books, played keyboards in a band. We hit it off right away and within minutes, he said: 'When can you start?'

It looked like my luck was in. 'Whenever is convenient,' I said.

'Can you start now?' he asked.

I didn't hesitate. I took the job. I knew it would suit me down to the ground. And, besides, I was all too aware that this was the only job I was likely to get in the whole of Northamptonshire. But I also liked the old lady, Agnes Billingham, who owned the place. She'd sit at the back of the shop, chain-smoking – in fact, she smoked so much that she had her cigarettes delivered in bulk (thousands of packs) every month to keep her going. It suited me too. Whenever she offered me a cigarette, she'd say, 'Take the whole pack.' Later, when she was in hospital for months on end, Bob and I kept the shop going. But without Agnes' direction we fell into playing cards and drinking whisky all day. I tended to be so inebriated on a daily basis that I often couldn't work out which bus to catch home. Clearly, I'd found my true vocation in life. But it didn't last. A few years later, when Agnes went into care and the bookshop changed hands, I was forced to look for new employment – but discovered I was totally unemployable. I couldn't find a single employer who would accept my need to drink and gamble on the job. So it's no surprise that I eventually became a freelance journalist . . . But that is another story.

The biggest thing the bookshop did for me was give me access to thousands of books; I read voraciously on many different subjects. When a set of first editions by the English mystic Aleister Crowley came in, I bought them and read the lot. This gave me a thorough grounding in the occult and mysticism – as well as the deeper levels of yoga, which Crowley was very well versed in. Crowley, however, earned himself a terrible reputation, what with his 'scarlet women' and having sex with male and female partners in magickal rites. The climate in which Crowley lived was not ready for such behaviour. At one point the press were describing him as 'the wickedest man in the world'. Because he was something of an exhibitionist Crowley relished the epithet. As for me, well, Crowley sounded like a man after my own heart – being around 17 at the time mixing magick and sex sounded like a damn fine idea. I thought if I declared myself a sex magickian it would bring me lots of girls. Sadly, it had the opposite effect (but you can't blame me for trying). Anyway, as my researches progressed further into the yoga field I came across Tantra, a branch of mysticism believed to have originated in India between the fifth and ninth centuries AD, and subsequently practised around the world by esoteric sects of Hinduism, Buddhism and, to a limited degree, Jainism. I also found that it involved lots of visualisation, breathing exercises, and prolonged sexual marathons, sometimes lasting eight hours, earning it the title the 'yoga of sex'. Of course, I thought I'd discovered the Holy Grail at the time. 'This is for me!' I thought; but there was a major problem – I didn't have a partner to test it all out with. I contemplated going to India to join a Tantric sect, but I couldn't be sure whether they provided you with willing partners or not. In the end, I got back to playing guitar in rock and roll bands, which proved a far more successful way of attracting members of the opposite sex.

Years later I noticed in some tacky celebrity magazine that Sting and his wife Trudi Styler had revealed they were followers of Tantra. Sting had even boasted of being able to 'last eight hours' while entangled in passionate embrace with Trudi. To be fair, Sting later confessed that he exaggerated a little, after a drunken night out with his mate Bob Geldof. 'I think I mentioned to Bob I could make love for eight hours. What I didn't say was that this included four hours of begging and then dinner and a movie,' he said.

I wonder if Sting and Trudi are aware that Tantra, which is dismissed as airy-fairy new ageism by much of the popular media, has a dark, terrifying and bloody side, which involves human sacrifice?

This side of Tantra was highlighted in a village in

Jharkhand state, India, in April 2002. Devotee Khudu Karmakar was about to perform a ritual he believed would bring him awesome power. But for his wishes to be granted by the bloodthirsty goddess Kali, his sacrifice of a virgin had to be done just right. The victim had to be willing; she had to know what was happening. She also had to watch the knife and not try to stop it. However, things were not going to plan. Even the tranquillisers Karmakar forced down 15-year-old Manju Kumar's throat were not enough to stop her putting up a desperate fight for life. In his confession to police, Karmakar said his wife, daughter and three accomplices were forced to gag Manju and pin her to the ground in front of the shrine to Kali. During the ritual, Karmakar wafted incense over Manju, tore off her blue skirt and pink T-shirt, shaved off all her hair, including pubic hair, and then sprinkled her with holy water from the Ganges. After that, he rubbed cooking fat over her body, chanted the necessary mantras to Kali, then sawed off her hands, breasts and left foot. He then placed the body parts in front of a photograph of a blood-soaked idol of Kali. Police said the arcs of blood on the walls suggested Manju bled to death in minutes.

India is no stranger to human sacrifice. Two hundred years ago a boy was killed every day at a Kali temple in Calcutta. With the law against killing people strongly enforced today, artificial substitutes now stand in for humans when sacrifice is required. Most Kali temples have settled on large pumpkins to represent a human body; others slit the throats of two-metre-tall human effigies, or of animals such as goats. While Kali is generally considered to be destructive and to have an insatiable appetite for blood, she actually has a long and complex history in Hinduism. She was first conceived of as a creature of indiscriminate violence and wrath, but some Tantric devotees consider her to be the 'ultimate reality' or 'source of being'. And one comparatively recent movement even thinks of Kali as a benevolent mother-goddess.

A small number of Tantric sects today, however, have no truck with this benevolent side of Kali, and continue to believe in the efficacy of human sacrifice. They say Kali looks after those who look after her; bringing riches to the poor, revenge to the oppressed and fertility to the childless – if she's paid with blood. During the year Manju was murdered, police recorded at least one case of ritual killing a month. In February 2002, two men in the eastern state of Tripura beheaded a woman on the instructions of a deity they claimed had appeared in their dreams, promising hidden treasures. Then in May, police dug up the remains of two sisters, aged 13 and 18, in Bihar. They had been dismembered with a ceremonial sword and offered to Kali by their father. Later, on the outskirts of Bombay, a seller of maize cut off the head of his neighbour's 9-year-old son to save his marriage, on the advice of a practitioner of Tantra. The maize seller said: 'He promised that a human sacrifice would end all my miseries.'

According to *Time* magazine, which did a report on the subject, Tantra and Kali worship are becoming increasingly popular in India; each year millions of devotees flock to the two main Kali centres in eastern India, at Kamakhya and Tarapith. Sociologist Ashis Nandy told the magazine that this is what happens when the 'rat race that is India's future' meets the superstitions of the past: 'You see your neighbour doing well, above his caste and position, and someone tells you to get a child and do a secret ritual and you can catch up.' In other words, in a desperate bid to 'keep up with the Joneses' people waste a kid, sometimes even their own. A local expert on mysticism, Roy Chakaraverti, backs this up, saying this sort of practice has nothing to do with genuine spirituality – 'It comes down to pure and simple greed,' he said.

In 2003, hundreds of Hindu monks pledged to fight the 'ancient barbaric rituals of human sacrifices' that still occur in the country. 'A very minuscule cult still believes that to achieve supernatural magickal powers one needs to sacrifice a child at the altar,' 45-year-old Hindu mystic Biswajit Giri told news agencies in Pakistan. 'The practice of human sacrifice . . . has not died down completely and is being carried out in many select temples secretly.' Giri was among some 50,000 monks that had assembled at the temple of the Hindu mother goddess, Kamakhya, in Gauhati, the capital of the northeastern state of Assam. They were there for the five-day ritual of Ambubachi Mela, which occurs every year, and marks the 'annual menstruation' of Kamakhya.

The Kamakhya Temple is the principal seat of Tantrism in India. Scholars and practitioners alike are drawn to the Ambubachi Mela. Most, however, will not talk to non-Tantrics about it because Tantrism is considered 'a secret affair' between gurus and disciples and is thus kept under wraps. Some devotees who gather at the temple claim they can perform wonders – make childless couples conceive, bring back lovers or spouses who have left, or put curses on others. But there are those who go further and consider the Ambubachi Mela as an ideal time to commit ritual killing. Around the same time as the Hindu monks were protesting against sacrificial slayings, a self-proclaimed mystic called Amritlal Mazumdar, who dressed in saffron robes and wore vermilion beads on his forehead, almost managed to sacrifice his 18-month-old daughter at the Kamakhya temple. He was slicing his daughter's neck with a razor when her screams of pain alerted devotees, who rescued the baby from a grisly end. 'It seems the man was a lunatic and we managed to save the child from being sacrificed. The man was arrested by police later,' a temple official was quoted as saying. 'We have deployed special volunteers at the temple to prevent any such bad things from happening.'

One follower of Tantrism, however, bemoaned the demise of human sacrifices, saying they were an essential ingredient to 'appease the goddess and get her divine blessings. But then nowadays you don't get volunteers for the sacrifice and hence, as something symbolic, devotees perform the ritual using 6-foot effigies made of flour.'

Had Madan and Murti Simaru taken the effigy option in the autumn of 2003, a six-year-old child would still be alive. The couple – who lived in a village some 100 miles north of New Delhi – were desperate for a son, but nature hadn't obliged. They already had a daughter, but, like countless other couples in India's male-dominated society, yearned for a son to look after them in old age and carry on the family name. In the end, the impoverished field worker and his wife consulted a Tantric, as many Indians do. Unfortunately, they selected a practitioner for whom only bona fide human sacrifice would do. Acting on the Tantric's instructions, the Simarus arranged for their six-year-old neighbour, Monu Kumar, to be kidnapped. Then, while the Tantric intoned mantras and directed them, the couple mutilated and killed the child, on the bank of an irrigation canal. Murti Simaru allegedly completed the fertility rite by washing herself in the child's blood.

'I was never expecting such a heinous crime against any child,' said the victim's 22-year-old father. 'This is not a matter of Monu only. These Tantric practices must be stopped.'

He was referring to a spate of similar killings that had occurred in the area around that time – an unofficial tally compiled by the *Hindustan Times* put the figure at 25. The sheer level of sacrificial slayings led to a police crackdown on Tantrics. Four were jailed and many others were forced to shut up shop and pull their advertising from local newspapers and television stations.

To be fair, despite its dark side, Tantra is generally benign and is practised across a wide spectrum of Indian society, as well as in other parts of the world. Practitioners advertise their services on billboards in New Delhi and other cities. Some enjoy near-celebrity status in India, hosting seminars at top-class hotels and hanging out with film stars and politicians. But oddly, even though it is so popular, it is difficult to pin down just exactly what Tantra is. 'No one really knows what it is,' says Sudhir Kakkar, a psychoanalyst who has written widely on Indian mysticism. Some Tantrics believe the road to enlightenment lies in shattering taboos – involving sex, diet and habitual behaviour – in order to 'uncondition yourself from all the conditioning you have had,' Kakkar explained. Followers of one particular Tantric cult near the Hindu holy city of Varanasi, however, are said to eat charred human flesh stolen from crematoria. As we've seen, others seek to appease the goddess Kali through blood rituals involving the sacrifice of animals and, occasionally, people. Commenting on cases involving infertile couples, Kakkar said the idea is that 'if you want a child, you sacrifice one to get another life back. You give it to the goddess and the goddess gives it back to you.'

## Money for Nothing?

'Pennies don't fall from heaven. They have to be earned on earth.'

Margaret Thatcher (1925–):
in the *Observer*, 18 November 1979.

I don't think Margaret Thatcher would have been too impressed by the notion that you can gain divine gifts through sacrificial rites – not even the harmless variety using effigies. But in Malaysia in 1999, an American woman fell victim to a worshipper of Kali who thought the route to a lottery win lay in the dark art of ritual killing. Carolyn Bushell's mother said she was 'just too trusting'. She was probably right. But her daughter was also desperate. She was 10,000 miles from Minnesota, where she grew up, and had a divorce looming with little likelihood that she would win custody of her three children. Being something of a new age believer, she sought the help of an Indian spirit medium who promised that the rituals and prayers he prescribed would put everything to rights. That's why, on the night of 8 November, she walked into the darkness with the spirit medium and three other men she hardly knew, down the maze of dirt tracks on a 1,000-hectare plantation of towering oil palms.

They took Carolyn to a palm tree that had a crude scarlet 'X' slashed into the bark. She knelt for the ceremony, which she believed would help solve her marriage problems. But on that fateful night the men, supposedly there to help Carolyn, had ideas of their own. They were going to pay homage to the fearsome Kali, goddess of destruction. And Carolyn was to be their sacrificial victim. So instead of the garland of flowers she had been expecting, she felt the bite of a nylon rope cut into her neck and squeeze the life out of her.

The men constructed a ramshackle temple to the goddess, a few hundred metres from where Carolyn was strangled – and just beyond her shallow grave, which was finally discovered by police after a tip-off. The spirit medium and the three other killers conducted a gruesome set of rites upon Carolyn's corpse – an otherworldly ceremony they believed would bring them winning lottery numbers. It's not clear exactly what the ceremony involved, but Nithiyanantha Gurukkal, one of Malaysia's most senior Hindu priests, said some devotees of Kali believe that 'human body parts and especially blood will be given to these demigods'.

After making the offering, police sources say the spirit medium fell into a trance in the makeshift Kali temple and intoned a four-digit sequence of numbers. He then drove straight to a betting shop and put down a few hundred dollars, carefully repeating the sequence. But Kali let him down; the numbers proved to be losers. Had they been the winning numbers, the sacrifice of Carolyn's life could not have been any less in vain.

The fact is, despite its 30 years of breakneck development, Malaysia remains a land of spirits. Commenting on a survey revealing that 90 per cent of professionals said they had consulted spirit mediums for marital, health or work-related problems, Hairudin Harun, from the University of Malaya, said: 'Most of these [mediums] are harmless. It is like watching David Copperfield.' But he added that the regular reports in Malaysian newspapers of ritual dismemberment and the discovery of skulls and other body parts used in occult rituals testified to the continuing popularity of a much darker side to the Malaysian faith in the spirit world.

The deadly variant of Kali worship that involves ritual killing is found in other parts of the world besides India and the Far East. In 1997, in Trinidad, for example, police unearthed the remains of three children, after a couple had been charged with the murder of an 18-year-old relative as part of a macabre 'get rich quick' ritual. Kenrick Lunden (age 35) and his wife Chandroutie (age 22) were pulled in and charged with strangling Chandroutie's sister, Meena Sookdeo, who had been missing for a week. Police said the couple kidnapped Meena near her home in Esperanza, central Trinidad, and took her to a nearby sugar cane field, where they tortured and strangled her – she was covered with cigarette burns. Intensive interrogation of the couple revealed that they had done more killings. They led the cops to the back of their small wooden hut, also in central Trinidad, where the bodies of three of their four children – aged between 3 months and 3 years – were found buried in a shallow grave. The fourth child remained unaccounted for. None of the children had been registered at birth, and there was no evidence they had ever existed.

Chandroutie told the police she had killed the children as an act of worship to Kali, believing that making human sacrifices to the Hindu goddess would make them wealthy. Neighbours described her husband, Kenrick, as a 'weirdo man, who dabbled in witchcraft and made late night visits in the nude to a [nearby] cemetery'.

Hindus make up the second largest religious group in Trinidad and Tobago after Roman Catholics. But leaders of the biggest Hindu organisation in the country, the Sanatan Dharma Maha Sabha (SDMS), which has around 110,000 members, denied that Hinduism had any connection to human sacrifice. Worshippers of Kali – who, in her guise as destroyer of evil, is represented with swords and knives – claim they are vegetarians and do not engage in blood sacrifices. SDMS General Secretary Satnarayan Maharaj said Hindu sacrifices include flowers, fruits, and vegetables: 'We do not believe in animal sacrifice and we do not believe in human sacrifice,' he said. 'Extremists and fundamentalists, once they perform evil acts, they try to cover these evil acts under the name of religion . . . it happens in every religion. It happens in every continent of the world.'

But Steve Rampersad, spiritual leader of the Maha Kali Shakti Temple, in Gasparillo, southern Trinidad, told local news agencies that he had heard of children being abducted and sacrificed at sea. He said that in the Hindu faith, 'such sacrifices were unholy and performed only for evil gains'.

People who have lived in Hindu communities have told stories of the raising of black flags at the time of Kali Puja (invocation of the fearsome goddess) and of vagrants being fed and later sacrificed, or family members being sacrificed in staged car 'accidents' so as not to arouse suspicion. They say that the followers of 'the evil path' insist a blood sacrifice is mandatory to gain or maintain wealth. If there is any truth in these persistent rumours, it is another sign of how the old world is meeting the new. If you're living in a shack in the developing world, but you know of people nearby who are making good money – maybe they got into IT or some other skill useful to the industrial world – you are going to feel very envious. If you had some knowledge of witchcraft you might well perform a few money spells. If that failed, you might sacrifice an animal as part of a ceremony. If that didn't work you might contemplate killing a human being on the principle that, although generally considered the blackest form of sorcery, it is also considered by some as the most powerful. Or maybe you'd rather remain poor than contemplate such acts.

Apart from the odd rogue individual, most cultures today consider human sacrifice to be abhorrent and try to stamp it out. But in some very remote areas the practice is not only still acceptable but a central part of life. Trouble only occurs when victims are picked from further afield, away from their tribal areas. In a recent case, six indigenous tribesmen from the remote Seram Island in Indonesia were sentenced to death in February this year for the sacrificial slaying of two men. The six, who were members of the Naulu tribe, had been ordered to bring back two human beings for a ceremony. In the hunt they came across two men out fishing and, in line with tribal custom, killed them and took their heads, hearts, tongues and hands. Such rites have been conducted by the tribe on the island, which lies some 1,740 miles east of Jakarta, for centuries, especially during a change of tribal leadership. Ritual sacrifice is even required as part of the tribal marriage contract; the groom has the unenviable task of handing over a human head from another tribe to the bride's family. The last known sacrifice occurred in 1994, when two residents of nearby Masohi, out hunting in the forests, were mutilated by members of the Naulu tribe. How many have not come to light is anyone's guess.

During the tribesmen's trial their defence lawyer, Janes Manubun, argued that the men should not be condemned to death because they had no idea that killing people was illegal. 'The government has never given them an explanation about laws, so we had hoped that the verdict would be based on more equitable considerations,' he said.

He had a point: how could they be condemned to death if they didn't know they were committing a crime? Clearly, the dead men's family would have wanted to see justice done. But in this case 'justice' was meted out to placate the relatives of the dead and the Indonesian public. The better policy might have been to put the Naulu tribe wise to the ways of the rest of the world. Hands up who would like to volunteer for that job . . .

## Sacrifice: The Art of Giving Something up

Looking back over the cases I'd investigated, I couldn't help but feel that many of my worst fears had been confirmed. Magick and the occult were being used in the most unbelievably nefarious manner – way beyond what I'd previously considered bad, such as cursing and hexing for no good reason. I realised that this was the reason I'd been haunted by the Adam case from the very beginning; I'd been appalled by the way people had used something I considered good in an evil way. I couldn't stop thinking about how the little boy had been mercilessly dumped in the Thames after being used in a vile corruption of the magickal arts. Of course it didn't end with the killing of Adam. There was the prevalence of human sacrifice in Africa – along with the gruesome trade in body parts that goes along with it. But what was supremely grim in its unrelenting evil was the callous and workman-like attitude of professional human sacrificers; the mere idea that such people existed was enough to shock me to the core, as it would anyone. As if this wasn't enough, there was the frenzied, almost ecstatic, killings done in the name of Satan by the Rudas and the killers of Elyse Pahler. Not to mention the string of gut-wrenching sacrificial murders conducted by Adolfo De Jesus Constanzo – surely he was the epitome of evil incarnate?

And what were all these killings about? They were about trying to alter reality and influence fate using spells or by petitioning gods and spirits. It was causal magick with an injection of horror that would make the Texas Chainsaw Massacre seem tame.

Around the time I was musing on all this I met up with an old friend of mine – craggy-featured character actor Robert 'Bob' Goodman (seen in Luc Besson's *Joan of Arc*, in which he played a necrophiliac rapist, and in *The League of Extraordinary Gentleman*). Like me, he has studied and experimented with various forms of magick over many years. Over coffee in the New Piccadilly café, central London, I told Bob about how the cases of human sacrifice I'd investigated seemed to be all about using spiritual means for material gain. I wanted to get his take on it all. He leaned back in his chair, his expression turning from light-hearted amiability to a deep frown. He then said: 'I think these people who sacrifice humans – and indeed animals – as part of their low magick rituals are getting mixed up,' he said. 'Christians, for example, practise Lent. They give something up. And when you give something up, or *sacrifice* something, you create a space, and this space can be filled with whatever you choose.' Bob gave the example of when he gave up cigarettes; he did it to be healthier. He *sacrificed* the cigarettes and filled the space or gap created with fitness and well-being. 'If you want something to sacrifice,' he added, 'a human being is the wrong thing. If you want money or material gain, why not sacrifice your laziness?'

But for Bob all this is in the domain of low magick, which is the term he uses to describe causal magick. As far as he is concerned, at its highest, magick is about attempting to achieve spiritual enlightenment. 'The purpose of high magick is to know God, which is a concept, or indeed a being, that is viewed in many different ways,' he explained. 'God is the one thing that doesn't come from us. Everything else, even the universe itself, is contained within us. So demigods, demons, yetis, and the Loch Ness monster, to cite some of the more colourful examples, all come from us – which doesn't make them any the less real because, after all, our imaginations and subconscious minds are real. Therefore the mission of the true magickian is to experience God.'

When you look at cases of human sacrifice, the higher ideals of spiritual attainment are sadly lacking. This was made clear to me yet again when, a couple of days after meeting up with Bob, I visited the central library in Norwich to research the press archives for stories of human sacrifice. I picked years at random to see what would come up. Disturbingly, there weren't many years that didn't have some mention of the practice.

One story that caught my eye was reported by *The Times* in January 1962. Police in Liverpool, investigating the murder of Maureen Dutton (age 27), who lived in the Broadgreen area of the city, called on Interpol to assist with information on the South Sea worship of the Polynesian god Tiki. Although they were following other lines of inquiry too, they had suspicions that the murder had a ritualistic motive. Another story, also reported by *The Times*, this time in 1977, revealed how a religious sect in northeastern Brazil hurled eight small children into the sea in a mass human sacrifice 'to appease God'. The children were aged between 8 months and 5 years. Some of the older ones who struggled to the shore were thrown back until they could fight no more, and drowned. The police arrested 21 people, including the parents of the victims. The killing ceremony took place on a beach near Salvador, north of Rio de Janeiro.

More recently, in February, 2004, the news wires reported that a decapitated baby boy had been found on a hilltop near Lake Titicaca in Peru. The 7-month-old infant was thought to have been killed in a sacrifice ritual. Investigators suspected the killing was meant to appease a pre-Columbian earth god, because the body was found on the hilltop surrounded by flowers, liquor bottles and containers of blood. Highland Indians in the area consider many Andean hilltops to be the homes of deities, and tradition has it that the first Inca rose from Lake Titicaca.

Police were led to the remote rural site by villagers upset and shocked by the killing. Peruvian anthropologist Juan Ossio told reporters that human sacrifices date back to the Chavin culture, which flourished in Peru between 900 and 200 BC, and remained an official part of Peruvian cultures until the Spanish conquered the Incas 500 years ago. 'Sacrifices were made for more than a thousand years and it is hard to get rid of deeply rooted beliefs,' he said. 'Anthropologists occasionally encounter reports of human sacrifices while conducting research in Peru, although it is more common to hear about old people being buried alive in an effort to appease the earth gods.' What he didn't mention was that professional human sacrificers – often commissioned to do ritual killings by drug dealers – have been known to operate in the Lake Titicaca region, and may still be doing so (see Chapter 3).

# A Necromancer in the Family . . .

'I am the family face; flesh perishes, I live on,
projecting trait and trace through time to times anon,
and leaping from place to place over oblivion.'
Thomas Hardy (1840–1928) *Heredity* (1917)

After I'd finished my library research, I adjourned to a
café for a coffee and a much-needed break from reading
about people meeting gory ends. I sat back and picked
up the latest edition of *Country Life* that happened to be
lying on my table. I started reading a piece on agricul-
tural policy, which reminded me of my Uncle Bernard –
a farmer and landowner in Warwickshire – who I knew
would have something less than complimentary to say on
the subject. Then I remembered that, because of newspaper and book deadlines, I hadn't been in touch with
him for a long time. I'd sent him a card at Christmas,
but hadn't had a chance to speak to him. So I took the
opportunity of a quiet moment to give him a call on my
mobile.

'Jimmy, old chap,' he said 'How's the book going?'

'Well, I'm *doomed*,' I said. 'Even as we speak, I can
hear the thundering hooves of the four horsemen of the
apocalypse. They'll be upon me any minute. We don't
have much time.'

'Ah,' he said. 'In that case, why don't I tell you about
this little case of witchcraft murder I unearthed round
here . . .' Bernard proceeded to relate the story of how, in
the fourteenth century, a minor favourite of King Edward
II, Robert de Sowe, died in Coventry under mysterious
circumstances: he was allegedly killed by witchcraft. This
was what Bernard told me:

It all started on a snowy night shortly before the Feast of St Nicholas [6 December] in 1324. Twenty-seven wealthy tradesmen, merchants and landowners from Coventry and Warwickshire went to see one John de Nottingham, who was a cleric and necromancer. Before telling him what they wanted, they swore Nottingham and his assistant, Robert Mareschal, to secrecy. They then complained bitterly about the crushing taxes they had to pay to the King; the Prior of Coventry; Hugh le Despenser and his sons (both favourites of the King); and the Earl of Winchester – Robert de Sowe, a lackey for the Prior, came in for their wrath too.

Anyway, they offered John de Nottingham and his assistant good money if they would kill the King and the others by means of wizardry and the black arts.

Nottingham agreed and the deal was sealed. Seven days after the Feast of Saint Nicholas, Nottingham and his assistant set about making wax dolls of the King and his cronies. Rather than try and hex the King first, Nottingham decided to prove his skills on one of the lesser men – Robert de Sowe. He cast a spell over the doll, then ordered his assistant to stick a lead spike through its head. They then went to bed.

The following morning, Nottingham sent his assistant to Sowe's house to see the results, if any, of their sorcery. Robert de Sowe, he discovered, had gone mad in the night, shouting and screaming around his house. What's more he couldn't recognise any of his family or retainers. He apparently remained in this condition until the Sunday before the Feast of the Ascension. With the agreement of the wealthy chaps who commissioned the spell, Nottingham removed the spike from the head of the wax doll of Sowe and

pushed it through the heart. Sowe stopped his ravings
and dropped dead within days.

This panicked Nottingham's assistant and he
shopped the lot of them. The conspirators were
arrested and sent to a preliminary hearing. Such was
the feeling against the King and the Prior, however,
that many people in Warwickshire put up the bail
money for the traders, but not for the necromancer
who later died in prison. Once out of custody some
of the conspirators fled from justice. When the case
was came to court, those remaining were acquitted
by a jury of local people, who either considered the
tale too far-fetched to be true or sympathised with
those accused.

At first I thought Bernard might have made up the story
(which I wouldn't have put past him). But it turned out
that someone else had been digging into it too – Lyn
Clarkson from the Coventry Writers' Group.[3] '[It is]
thought to be England's earliest trial for witchcraft,' she
says on CWN.org.uk, a Coventry and Warwickshire news
and web portal. 'It greatly embittered the citizens, who
afterwards hated the Prior even more and took every
chance to do him harm.'

But then came the sting in the tail. After relating the
witchcraft story, Bernard informed me that John de
Nottingham was an ancestor of ours. He'd found the story
while researching our family tree: 'Who'd have thought
we'd have had a necromancer in the family . . .'

'Good God,' I said. 'That seals it, we'll be burnt at the
stake before we're done.'

I was secretly quite pleased to have a necromancer in the
family. But, to me, John de Nottingham seemed more like
a Robin Hood figure with an esoteric twist than a black

magickian. After all, he had used his sorcery to strike down oppression. That being the case, I wondered what he would have made of Adolfo De Jesus Constanzo's sacrificial rampages or the ritual sacrifices in the name of Kali? Despite his alleged use of witchcraft to kill, I think he would have frowned on the ritual killers as epitomising the degradation of the magickal arts, which, like alchemy, ought to have the ideal of turning base metal (unenlightened consciousness) into gold (enlightened consciousness).

Focusing on causal magick, even without the sacrificial element, is often seen as an absurdity even by those involved in the occult. As my friend, actor and esoteric expert Robert Goodman, said: 'Causal magick is all well and good, but the same results can be achieved by normal methods. Take love magick, which I personally consider unacceptable – but if people must do it, wouldn't a bunch of flowers and a meal work just as well?' He also cited money magick, saying that hard work and 'worldly effort' will normally bring financial rewards.

So why is it that people such as the spirit medium in Malaysia – who sacrificed an American woman to the goddess Kali to gain winning lottery numbers – are willing to take the idea of causal magick to terrible extremes? Why couldn't he stick to earthly means to gain money? While his chances of winning the lottery would have been extremely slim, it's likely he could have earned a reasonable living by using his skills in a more positive way.

Perhaps the answer to this lies in the story of Aladdin's lamp from the *Arabian Nights*,[4] a medieval Middle Eastern literary work considered by Aleister Crowley and similar occultists to be a valuable storehouse of oriental magickal lore. The tale relates how Aladdin, an impoverished young man living in Arabia, was recruited by a greedy and unscrupulous sorcerer to retrieve an oil lamp from a booby-trapped enchanted cave. After the sorcerer tries to double-cross and kill him, Aladdin keeps the lamp for himself, discovering that it summons up a genie that will do the bidding of anyone who owns it. With the aid of the genie Aladdin becomes rich and powerful and marries a princess – all of which the sorcerer had hungered for.

Eventually Aladdin's domestic bliss is shattered when the sorcerer returns and gets his hands on the lamp by tricking Aladdin's wife, who has no idea about the lamp's power. Aladdin, however, discovers a less powerful genie that can be summoned by a ring that had been loaned to him by the sorcerer, but forgotten about during the double-cross. With the help of the lesser genie, Aladdin gets back his wife and the lamp.

Apart from being a classic rags-to-riches tale of a street kid made good, the Aladdin's lamp story highlights how the evil sorcerer was willing to stop at nothing in his pursuit of riches and power. His greed knew no bounds. Not only did he trick Aladdin into helping him get the magick lamp from a hazardous cave, but he planned to kill him or leave him for dead. He then relentlessly pursued Aladdin to get his hands on the lamp, which he believed was rightfully his.

The sorcerer was eaten up with greed but, more importantly, he was mesmerised by the idea that a magick lamp could fulfil his desires for power and riches. He was consumed by the promise that everything he wanted could be gained without hard work or effort. But, for him at least, it proved to be fool's gold – just like it was for the Malaysian Kali worshipper who was mesmerised by the notion that sorcery could provide him with winning lottery numbers . . . and a fool's paradise.

# Chapter 6: Tomb Raiders

Boneyard Blues . . . Commercial Magick . . . Loose Talk . . . Cops Turn Sorcerers' Apprentices . . . Ain't Never Gonna Stop . . . Death of a Palo Priest . . . Dem Bones, Dem Bones Gonna Walk Aroun' . . . Shake, Rattle and Roll . . . Ancestor Power . . . Gimme Some Head

'The cemetery is an open space among the ruins, covered in winter with violets and daisies. It might make one in love with death, to think that one should be buried in so sweet a place.'

Percy Bysshe Shelley (1792–1822)
*Adonais* (1821)

Sacrificial killing revolves around the concept of life after death. But for the victims it is not about living on in a heavenly paradise; it's about spiritual enslavement by a sorcerer, who uses their disincarnate souls to help him influence the material world or liaise with the gods. But such practices don't just involve murdering the living to make them slaves in death. Some nefarious sorcerers in the US raid graveyards to collect people's remains for use in rituals and as ingredients in witchcraft cauldrons, which also include animal carcasses and various herbs and potions. It's a gruesome business; and also an illegal one. After all, who wants the remains of their loved ones dug up and used in baleful sorcery?

Besides looking at how bones and whole skeletons have been stolen from tombs and put to use in magick, I wanted to find out if the worship of the dead is all bad. Can followers of legitimate religions which practise ancestor worship do so without fear of breaking the law? Or is ancestor worship a throwback with no place in the modern world?

Back in 1999 in New Jersey two men had no doubt that what they were about to do was illegal. But the magick – and indeed the spirits of their religion – demanded they break the law and violate the resting place of the dead . . .

## Boneyard Blues

It was a cold winter's night in January. The thirteenth of January to be exact. Whether this was significant or not – what with the number 13 being considered lucky by some who hold occult beliefs and unlucky by others – is hard to say. But two men with a very definite interest in the dark side of the occult were keeping to the shadows as they walked briskly through the shabby, grey streets of Newark, New Jersey. Their breath wafted like fog in the cold air. One of the men was clearly nervous. He kept peering this way and that, keeping his eye out for passing patrol cars. He had reason to be wary. The two were on an illegal and macabre mission that would involve breaking into the Holy Sepulchre Cemetery, a sprawling sea of Victorian Gothic that lay in the heart of the smog-choked cityscape, just off Central Avenue, one of the main thoroughfares that cuts through Newark.

Once they had scaled the iron railings and jumped down into the murky stillness of the cemetery, the two men crept past the rows of gravestones and crypts. Eventually, they found what they were looking for: the mausoleum of Leonard Perna, a bar owner from nearby City of Orange, whose body had lain undisturbed for thirteen years. The men smashed through the plexiglass entrance, then heaved up the weighty marble slab covering Perna's coffin and remains. At this point, the nervous tomb robber – Franklin Sanabria (age 28) – panicked and fled the scene. His associate (who can't be named for legal reasons), more experienced in such matters, calmly pulled out Perna's remains, placed them in a large bag, and left the chill cemetery the way he had come in.

He was clearly a professional who recognised there was good money to be made in the bone trade. But it wasn't just about money. He was also a believer in the ancient, mystic power of Palo Mayombe – the West African religion that slaves took with them to Cuba in the nineteenth century and which, over the last few decades, was transported to the United States by Cuban immigrants. Franklin Sanabria was also a believer and his main motivation that night had been to get a leg up on the Palo ladder. He'd been told that if he went through with the tomb robbery the corpse could be used in a ritual to make him a Palero, or priest of Palo Mayombe.

Not surprisingly, when Leonard Perna's family discovered his remains had been stolen from the Holy Sepulchre crypt, which had been in the Perna family for 80 years, they were horrified. Rosanne Perna, the dead man's daughter, was quoted as saying that her family were in agony over the loss of their father's remains. 'My father is missing,' she said. 'My father cannot rest in peace. I have a grandmother who cries every time the subject comes up.' Perna's son, Michael, added that: 'Most members of my family are no longer planning to be buried. We will be cremated.' He also speculated that the Palo Mayombe robbers may have targeted his father because they thought he was related to a mobster named Michael Perna and thus a source of extra 'mojo' or magickal power. Michael Perna (the mobster) was part of the Lucchese family who operate out of northern New Jersey. They came to notoriety in November 1986 when the federal government brought 21 members of the Lucchese family, including Michael, to trial.[1] In 1988, however, all the defendants were found not guilty. It was a rare victory for organised crime and a huge embarrassment for the government.

The case was well known and made the Mafia mobsters heroes amongst the New Jersey criminal fraternity. Now, however, most of the leaders of the gang, including Michael Perna, are in prison and not likely to be released until 2016. The big irony was that Leonard Perna was not in any way related to the Perna Mafioso family. He was simply a bar owner who had died of stomach cancer in 1986. But maybe this didn't matter to the Palo bone stealers – the name itself may have been all they were after. The occult is not an exact science – it relies on creativity and ingenuity. Items are often used that represent attributes found in the everyday world. Sugar or honey, for example, may be used in a love charm to help 'sweeten' someone's affections. While steel filings in a binding or controlling spell could be included to 'strengthen' your hold over someone. So the fact that Leonard Perna had the same surname as the notorious Mafiosi family could have been the reason why his bones were stolen. The name was symbolic of power and this might have been the attribute the thieves were looking for – thus a genuine family connection would not have been important.

Whatever hidden power may have been in Leonard Perna's remains, Franklin Sanabria didn't benefit from any of it. Newark police lifted a fingerprint from the broken plexiglass in the crypt and picked him up. He admitted to breaking into the crypt with another man who was introducing him to Palo Mayombe. He also told them how he'd got scared and left the scene, leaving his associate to steal Leonard Perna's bones. Because of this, a grand jury decided against indicting Sanabria for theft, but charged him with burglarising the crypt. He pleaded guilty in February 2002 to third-degree burglary.

When his case came to trial, Sanabria was found guilty and Superior Court Judge Michael Petrolle sentenced him to four years probation. Sanabria was also given 200 hours of community service maintaining Rosemount Memorial Park in Newark and was ordered to pay $4,200 in restitution to repair the Perna crypt. Dean Maglione, then assistant Essex County prosecutor, explained that Sanabria's associate in the tomb robbery was in prison on other charges and was not likely to be prosecuted. He added that the remains had not been recovered and that the investigation was closed. This was not much consolation for the Perna family. Rosanne Perna reiterated that because her father's bones were missing he would not be able to rest in peace. She then criticised the Holy Sepulchre Cemetery, run by the Roman Catholic Archdiocese of Newark, for its failure to put up lighting in the cemetery, even though it had been plagued by vandalism. She said her family's crypt had been the target of vandals several times before. Holy Sepulchre officials referred questions about the Perna case and the issue of body thefts to the Archdiocese. But its spokesman, Jim Goodness, declined to comment.

*

The Perna family could be forgiven for feeling bitter. The case was closed and the likelihood of getting Leonard Perna's remains back looked remote. But, in fact, police had serious concerns about the growing number of tomb robberies occurring in northern New Jersey – which seemed to go hand in hand with the large Hispanic population (29.5 per cent) – and were doing what they could to stamp the practice out. On 7 October 2002, police raided a dilapidated tenement on Central Avenue in Newark. In the basement was a secret Palo Mayombe temple. Here police found a number of ten-gallon Palo cauldrons set up on altars and containing at least two sets of human remains, including two skulls. Later in the day, authorities dug up the rear yard of the building and found the remains of animals. Newark police detective Donald Stabile said the scene inside the worship room was ghastly. Animal parts were arranged on altars around the room. The basement 'had an odour that you keep with you – like your first DOA', he said.

Despite the sheer ugliness of the scene, there was some good news: Leonard Perna's remains had been found. A ring thought to be his, as well as a matchbook with his date of birth and date of death written on it, were discovered on the premises. The other set of bones belonged to a juvenile, which raised the prospect of an unreported grave robbery or a murder. The police arrested Eddie Figueroa (age 56), the owner of the building and a suspected high priest in the Palo Mayombe sect, along with his son, Eddie Figueroa Jr. (age 35). Both pleaded not guilty to possession of stolen property and desecration of human remains, at their arraignment on 8 October in Essex County Superior Court. Judge Alison Jones Brown set bail at $100,000 for the father and $150,000 for his son. Both came up with the money. The younger Figueroa admitted to being a Palero; but his father, a former maintenance worker with the Newark Housing

Authority, blamed others, unknown to him, for putting remains in the cauldrons without his knowledge.

The arrests were the work of a team that included members of the Newark Police Department, the Essex County Prosecutor's Office, the Federal Bureau of Investigation (FBI) and the County Medical Examiner's Office. Newark police chief Anthony Ambrose said that in one year alone there had been four thefts at local grave-yards, including Holy Sepulchre and Mount Pleasant Cemeteries.

Dean Maglione, also prosecuting on this case, said the two men faced a penalty of ten years on the charge of possession of stolen property and eighteen months on the charge of grave desecration. That could triple, he added, if the origin of the other bones was traced. As far as Maglione was concerned, the Figueroas and others like them are in it for the money and take advantage of credulous believers. 'They take the head and they put it in a cauldron,' he said. 'After that they put some other ingredients in there and they sell services, they sell ceremonies. People pay to sit in a room with a cauldron.'

## Commercial Magick

The truth is, people paying money to Palo Mayombe priests to work spells using their cauldrons is not as strange as Dean Maglione makes out. There's a big worldwide market for magickal services. And it doesn't matter how dark the practitioners might seem – they still get takers. If people don't get results from a 'white witch', they'll go to one describing themselves as a 'black witch', on the presumption that the dark forces are more powerful. So it's nothing to write home about that people are willing to pay to sit in a room with a Palo Mayombe cauldron. I can personally testify to the popularity of magickal services. After my first book, *Doktor Snake's Voodoo Spellbook*, came out in 2000, I got endless e-mails from people wanting me to do love or money spells for them. Some even wanted me to curse or hex people. I got these e-mails even though I stated very strongly on my Doktor Snake website[2] that I was a journalist and didn't do spells or occult work for people. Admittedly, I had the knowledge to act as a practitioner; I knew about all the potions, oils and powders used in Voodoo magic, as well as the more exotic ingredients like graveyard dirt and coffin nails. But it wasn't a career path I wanted to go down. Not only that, but I couldn't bring myself to callously rip people off.

In the end, I thought the best bet was to find a reputable purveyor of magickal services, who I could recommend. People were going to find someone to do spellworkings for them, anyway, I reasoned. So there was definitely a case for putting them on to someone who, at least, offered a fair deal. After a lot of looking around, I found a firm called the California Astrology Association (CAA)[3]. It had not only been in the business for 30 years but offered a one-year, 100 per cent money-back guarantee.

That looked ideal to me. So I directed all the requests I got to the CAA, pointing out that they should be aware that the efficacy of spells to return lost lovers and make you money (without having to work for it) hasn't exactly been proven by science, and that it might not be wise for them to raise their hopes too high. None seemed to heed my warning. They were off like they'd been fired from a high velocity rifle – so desperate were they to get lovers back or to generate some cash from the ether to get out of financial strife.

Then, after a week or so, I got people coming back to me saying they'd paid for spellworkings – many on more than one occasion – and they hadn't worked. Being Mr

Sensitive, I said: 'What did you expect?! It's your fault for being taken in.' I did add that the good thing was they could take advantage of the 100 per cent money-back guarantee, which unsurprisingly is a rare thing in the world of magickal and psychic services. I even went as far as checking into the guarantee offered by the CAA, as I was well aware that such promises can easily be worked around by the more cynical of merchants. But when I spoke to the CAA about it they insisted that if anyone was dissatisfied, all they had to do was return any goods or spell items they had bought, in good order, and their money would be returned to them.

Although this seemed perfectly above board, I eventually stopped recommending the CAA or anyone else offering psychic or magickal help because I felt it was feeding people's ignorance of what magick actually is. Even in its causal form, magick is most definitely not a cut-and-dried phenomenon where you perform a spell and the result comes to you on a plate. A love spell, for example, devised to attract a specific person may well seem to fail miserably. But the astute practitioner would be aware that spellworkings operate on the subconscious mind, which many magickians believe is the powerhouse of our being and knows what is best for us. Therefore a love spell aimed at a particular person might instead simply direct us to someone we haven't noticed before – someone who proves to be more appropriate.

People who look to commercial practitioners to help them overcome their problems in life, however, tend to be unaware of the subtleties of magick and so are forever disappointed when spells don't work in a direct cause-and-effect fashion. But instead of studying the subject in depth for themselves, and performing their own spellworkings, they invariably simply move from practitioner to practitioner in the hope that one day they will find one with the 'power' to solve their problems.

I didn't want to encourage this. As far as I'm concerned it should be DIY or nothing. Now I simply don't respond to e-mails asking for magickal help. Not that this will stop people flocking to self-proclaimed sorcerers and witches who claim to be able to bring back lost lovers, improve your fortunes, bring gambling luck, attract the opposite sex, break hexes and even solve mental and fertility issues. As early twentieth-century artist and mystic Austin Osman Spare said in his 1951 essay *Mind to Mind and How*: 'Consistent with other directions of abstract knowledge, the threshold of the occult is the market place for the charlatan. Coinage is sometimes different – lies have a strange longevity and fecundity – truth becomes blurred.'

## Loose Talk

Besides the Figueroas other Palo Mayombe groups had been active. On 17 December 2001, followers of the sect stole the bones of Richard Jenkinson (who died in 1930 at the age of 77) and his wife, Emily (who died in 1922 at the age of 67), from Mount Pleasant Cemetery on Broadway in Newark. And on 23 January 2002, they pilfered the remains of Joseph Rovi (buried in 1969) from Holy Sepulchre Cemetery, the same cemetery from which Leonard Perna's remains had been taken in 1999. The local newspaper, *The Star Ledger*, reported that Richard Jenkinson was once a prominent citizen in Newark. He owned a metal-goods manufacturing business, served on the boards of non-profit institutions, donated to the library and museum, and was a Republican candidate for mayor in 1900. Being a wealthy, public figure meant he was fair game for Palo Mayombe devotees, who would view such remains as ideal for spellworkings designed to attract money and power.

However, the police had a little unexpected help when it came to catching up with the tomb robber responsible for these thefts. Ramon Gonzalez came unstuck due to his talkative girlfriend, Ruth Santiago. She reportedly told anyone who'd listen how repulsed she'd been when she'd seen Ramon giving human remains to a priestess of Palo Mayombe called Miriam Mirabal. Word eventually reached an FBI agent and the authorities closed in. After his arrest in August 2002, Gonzalez, along with another self-confessed grave robber called Mario Delgado, pleaded guilty to the thefts. In a bid for leniency, both acknowledged that Miriam Mirabal had not only accepted the remains from them, but had instructed them to steal them. Mirabal (age 61), a Cuban immigrant from Irvington, West Newark, was arrested on 5 March 2003, by Essex County authorities. Inside her house, a turn-of-the-twentieth-century dwelling with a black Virgin Mary on the door, they found dolls, crosses, powders and potions – all items associated with the practice of Palo Mayombe magic. She was held on $500,000 bail after being arraigned on charges of directing the thefts of three bodies. Police said she acted both as a Palo Mayombe priestess and as an illicit entrepreneur who supplied bones to other priests for a fee.

Mirabal's trial began on 14 April 2004. Once again the prosecutor was Dean Maglione. He told the jury how Mirabal had directed a network of followers to pillage human remains for use in ceremonies to call down spirits of the dead. He went on to say that at least ten graves had been robbed from cemeteries in the Newark area before the cops busted the ring with a handful of key arrests. Mirabal's defence team protested that she had never been found with human remains; nor had she been identified by any witness at the scene of the robberies. But on 3 May, after only 90 minutes of deliberations, the Newark jury found her guilty of seven charges of conspiracy, theft and burglary. Mirabal, who 25 years previously had done time in a federal prison for drug smuggling, faced 5–50 years in state prison for her crimes.

Perhaps surprisingly, her trial, dubbed locally 'the bones case', was a low-key affair. But what it lacked in drama was made up for by its sheer strangeness. Amongst the legal pads, pencils and highlighters littering the table shared by the defence and prosecution lawyers was a clear plastic bag. Inside was a human skull. When prosecution lawyers made a salient point, they would thrust the skull high into the air for all the court to see. Also in the court-room was a cauldron, said by the same lawyers to have been used to boil the stolen bones.

On trial alongside Miriam Mirabal was Oscar Cruz, age 50, the owner of a Newark botanica (spiritual supplies store). He'd been charged in August 2002 after Newark police raided his store and found him in the basement with cauldrons containing the bones from five people. Two sets of the remains were later identified as those of Jacob Schmidt and Richard Jenkinson – the same one whose bones had been stolen from Mount Pleasant Cemetery in Newark by Ramon Gonzalez. Prosecutors said Cruz planned to use the body parts in a ritual to call down spirits and cast spells of misfortune on others. On 7 May 2004, Cruz was convicted of possessing stolen human remains and was sentenced to five years in state prison.

After the arrests of Mirabal, Cruz and their handful of associates, the cemetery break-ins ground to a halt. But Dean Maglione was openly sceptical that the arrests would put an end to it all. 'They'll never be smashed,' he said of the tomb-robbing ring. 'They're lying low. Where they're getting their remains from now, I don't know.'

Whether this was the case or not, there had been various reports of graveyard robberies going back a number of years. In 1997, for example, two men from Paterson, north of Newark, were prosecuted in Passaic County after breaking into a crypt at Cedar Lawn Cemetery and stealing a woman's skull. They were believed to have sold it to a Palo Mayombe group for $500, although the group itself was never identified. Then, in 1999, police from nearby Kearny charged a Palo Mayombe priest and several of his followers with stealing the 83-year-old remains of a 3-month-old boy from a crypt in Arlington Cemetery. Detective Tom Silkie, who handled the case, said a decapitated rooster was found inside the crypt with its head placed inside a small clay cup. After consulting with the FBI, New York City police and other authorities on religious cults, Silkie learned that Palo priests adopt a specific cemetery for their rituals and operate there exclusively. 'Cemeteries are the gateways of the spirit. Under ideal conditions, they'll strive for a recently deceased individual who led a violent life,' Silkie later said. 'If they're unable to track down a deceased violent criminal, they'll target the corpse of a white Anglo, because they believe the spirit of a white Anglo person is easier to control.'

If this is the case, you can't help but wonder why the remains of the 3-month-old boy were stolen. It doesn't fit in with the remit for bone thefts given by Silkie. You have to ask yourself whether the people arrested for the thefts were bona fide followers of Palo Mayombe or whether they were labelled this by investigators – which, as we shall see shortly, is a charge that has already been levelled at the cops.

Either way, Silkie went on to reveal that even before the theft of the remains of the 3-month-old boy, Arlington Cemetery staff reported a series of suspicious discoveries. They found machetes embedded in trees, symbols scrawled on the outside of the mausoleum, pots with nails, pennies, cow tongues on the ground and stuck to trees, and clothing buried just below the soil in front of graves. Silkie said police mounted a surveillance of the cemetery after the robbery and arrested Palo Mayombe priest and Cuban immigrant Alberto Lima after he was seen entering the cemetery. They also found a cauldron in his car. 'Palo priests typically use bones and skulls smuggled into the country from Latin America,' he said, 'and resort to thefts in this country less commonly.' But he added that there is a black market for such objects and that skulls can be sold for thousands of dollars. 'The rituals go on in cemeteries all the time,' he said. 'They are more common than the actual theft of bodies. But if police are not trained in the practice of Palo Mayombe, they won't even know what they are looking at.'

## Cops Turn Sorcerers' Apprentices

Bodysnatching is clearly illegal. But some of the practices of African-rooted religions, however macabre they may seem to the uninitiated, are perfectly legitimate – such as the sacrifice of animals. It's certainly helpful, therefore, if police dealing with ritual situations can tell the difference between what's legal and what's not. As Detective Tom Silkie has made clear, officers need to be educated in the practices of African-rooted religions. This need was strongly highlighted when Miami-Dade County police were called to a home in South Miami-Dade in April 2003. According to *The Miami Herald*, which reported the incident, the officers were confronted with people slicing up chunks of goat meat and plucking feathers from chickens. Blood spattered the feet of some of those in the house. The cops couldn't interpret what they were looking at. To them it was a frenzied blood bath. 'You're killers! You're all going to jail!' one officer yelled, which sent the elderly residents into a blind panic. The truth was, they weren't doing anything illegal. They were simply going about the legitimate practice of their religion, a central part of which is the sacrificing of animals.

The news report goes on to say that the cops didn't stop shouting and making threats until a call was made to both a local anthropologist and a detective with experience in alternative religions. The two experts explained to the officers on the scene that what they had encountered was a routine and legal Santeria ritual. The officers were told that Santeria was taken to the Caribbean with the African slaves and later to the US by Cuban immigrants, and that it is a blend of Christian and West African native faiths. It was also made clear that a 1993 Supreme Court ruling protects animal sacrifice by devotees of Santeria, so long as the goats and chickens are cut in a precise part of the neck, similar to the way kosher meat is prepared. The officers were also given the low-down on Palo Mayombe; how it originated in the Congo and how it is considered darker than Santeria because its worshippers believe they are empowered by the remains of the dead.

In this instance, it was Santeria that was being practised, not Palo Mayombe. But it wouldn't have made any difference. So long as nothing illegal was going on, the police had no legitimate right to arrest anyone. The initial harassment only occurred because the police lacked training in the practices of African-rooted religions. But it is easy to see how such practices as animal sacrifices, the casting of spells and the use of magickal powders and potions could seem alien to many police officers. It is not surprising that the cops calling on the house in Miami-Dade County freaked out. They might well have been brought up in the Christian or Jewish religion, and have had little experience of other, more exotic spiritual practices. Indeed, they could well have been brought up to view fortune telling and the casting of spells, which are found in Santeria and other African-rooted religions, as evil and the province of the Devil. So a reaction of disgust and horror would have been an instinctive, emotional response born of their cultural upbringing and religious milieu.

This needs to change, according to Jackie Ben, a long-time priestess of Santeria. She told David Ovalle from *The Miami Herald*: 'We really need more cultural sensitivity. Officers need to be educated in all these religions. Many of them tend to think that being a part of this religion means you are involved in criminal activity.' The City of Miami Police Department responded to Jackie Ben's call by providing officers with in-depth courses on Afro-Cuban Santeria, Palo Mayombe and Haitian Voodoo. These were – and still are – run by Dr Rafael Martinez, an acknowledged expert in Afro-Caribbean religions. During the classes, Martinez displays various artefacts on a table in a training room at Miami police headquarters. Typically there are large and small Voodoo dolls, machetes used in Palo Mayombe rituals (often still smelling of sacrificed chickens) and seashell-studded heads of Elegua, an important Santeria deity.

Jackie Ben has visited the classes to add her perspective. She believes officers must learn to respect the religions as they would Christianity or Judaism – irrespective of how unusual the practices and events they encounter might be. For example, they might come across followers in a possession trance – such as when Santeros (Santeria priests) have been taken over by Santeria deities, known as Orishas. These possession trances are by no means quiet affairs and are highly disconcerting for anyone who has never seen one before. They can be wild and uncontrolled. Normally dignified men can scream out and throw themselves on the floor, writhing and moaning in ecstasy. Or a young woman might light up a pipe and double over and lean on a walking cane, talking in the crackling voice of an old man. Others might laugh manically and gesticulate like a disjointed puppet. Some have been known to slug back whole bottles of strong liquor and smoke fat cigars, when in everyday life they touch neither.

If police officers with little knowledge of possession ceremonies did need to intervene, they could arguably be too heavy-handed, due to being thrown by the sheer strangeness of it all. To them it would look like something out of a horror movie, and they'd probably bark orders at worshippers, telling them to put their hands up against the wall or lie down on the floor – none of which would elicit the desired response. Martinez teaches officers that it is best not to directly question the possessed person. Instead, they should ask an elder priest to break the trance, or dismiss the Orisha. Otherwise, practitioners may be angry, resentful and outraged. 'Many times, officers are judging the rituals according to their perceptions, their upbringing as Christians,' Martinez explained in an interview with *The Miami Herald*. 'They immediately equate it to Devil worshipping.'

Possession to us in the West smacks of being taken over by demons. We naturally think of *The Exorcist* movie in which a previously innocent and good-natured young girl becomes possessed by Satan and indulges in all sorts of shocking behaviour, including masturbating with a crucifix, yelling obscenities and vomiting over the Catholic priest who comes to exorcise her. The movie shocked and terrified audiences. Within weeks of the first public screening, stories were circulating of people fainting, vomiting and having heart attacks. There were even reports of miscarriages. The story, which was only *very loosely* based on a true story of possession, cut deep into our deepest fears. Yet, interestingly, black audiences in Harlem were completely unfazed by it. In fact, they were reported to have enjoyed the film so much they made a party of it, drinking beer, passing joints and yelling along with the dialogue. They certainly took it in their stride – in stark contrast to some of the audiences. But why was this? Could it be that many of them had knowledge of or roots in African religions? If so, it would explain a lot. African religions, and their offshoots such as Voodoo and Santeria, see possession as a healthy and positive event. They don't see it as evil. As one prominent priestess told French writer Serge Bramly,[4] '[It's] a great honour to receive a god. I think that once the trance is over the mediums think only of their luck in having lent their bodies to the gods.' She also said that possession is seen as being of great benefit to the community: 'The mediums lend their bodies to the gods in order for them to become incarnate; so that they can be with us, speak to us, answer our questions, give us strength. It's a kind of exchange. We give life to the gods, and they in return agree to help us.'

Estimates suggest that Santeria in South Florida has up to 100,000 followers. According to Martinez, it is harder to put a precise number on the followers of Palo Mayombe and Voodoo in the region because these two religions are far more secretive. However, he does estimate that the number of those who practise Palo Mayombe is around 30,000 and it has grown exponentially with Santeria because many people follow both faiths. He also thinks that the number of practitioners of Haitian Voodoo has grown to the tens of thousands. Martinez makes clear that Santeria is an increasingly popular form of spirituality; not only has it outlived slavery, but it has spread among Cubans of all backgrounds. In South Florida communities, it has spread even further, he says, with many non-Hispanics and even some police officers becoming initiates.

## Ain't Never Gonna Stop . . .

With the large numbers of followers of African-rooted religions in South Florida – and in many other parts of the USA, including New Jersey, Los Angeles and Louisiana – it is essential that law enforcement personnel are educated in the ways of the more exotic spiritualities. They do need to put their own personal religious views and prejudices aside and recognise that the vast majority of devotees of Santeria and related paths are law-abiding citizens who contribute much to their local communities and to society at large. At the same time there is no escaping the terrible anguish caused to relatives of the dead when followers of Palo Mayombe raid tombs and take body parts for use in rituals. Worryingly, the macabre robberies seem to be spreading into more and more parts of the USA. Back in July 2003, for example, tomb raiders struck in Delaware – at the Wilmington and Brandywine Cemetery in Wilmington. True to type they targeted the crypt of a prominent citizen – in this case wealthy recluse Helen Rogers Bradford from New Castle County, who had been laid to rest 59 years previously at the age of 80. Her granite tomb was situated on a sloping knoll – a tranquil spot overlooking the Brandywine river, shaded by tall evergreens and surrounded by ancient boxwoods.

The grave robbers, however, shattered that peace when they squeezed through a narrow space above the mausoleum's arched, wrought-iron gate and lifted the 300-pound marble lid from the crypt. They took Bradford's skull, but left the woman's headless skeleton, which sat upright in the dark chamber, like a still from a horror movie. Her great niece, Holly Bradford Johnson, was horrified. 'What a thing to have happened after her life,' she said, echoing the fear many of us have that if our graves are desecrated it will somehow affect us in the great beyond. 'I'm appalled. It's so awful.'

Police believed Palo Mayombe devotees were responsible for the theft. As far as they were concerned the evidence pointed that way. Palo Mayombe followers, however, denied it, saying it could have been kids dabbling in Satanism. This claim was rejected by Dawn Perlmutter, an occult expert regularly consulted by East Coast police investigators and author of *Investigating Religious Terrorism and Ritualistic Crime* (CRC Press, 2003). 'Teenagers do lots of things in cemeteries, but they don't do this,' she told Delaware's *News Journal*. 'If it was kids in a mausoleum practising Satanism, there would be graffiti. This is completely different. This is definitely Palo Mayombe.'

Wilmington police sergeant, Robert Emory, who investigated the theft of a skull of a 29-year-old woman from Riverview Cemetery in November 2002, told the same newspaper that he didn't believe the thefts were isolated incidents. 'It's never going to stop,' he said ominously. Local detectives had no suspects for the grave robberies, but continued to investigate.

As we've seen, a lot of law enforcement professionals speak of the inevitability of Palo Mayombe grave robbing. They seem to see it as a curse that can never be broken. Why do they think this way? Could it be because Palo Mayombe is a religion and as with any religion it is nearly impossible to shake the faith of a true believer? We've all argued with Jehovah's Witnesses on our doorsteps. No amount of reasoning will shake their views – even though they believe things that fly in the face of basic science. Their *Watchtower* magazine is more like an apocalyptic graphic novel than a well-argued philosophic tract. You can't take it seriously. But millions of Jehovah's Witnesses do take it seriously, to the tune of shelling out a percentage of their income to the movement.

There is no shaking the faith. And it is the same with followers of Palo Mayombe. Telling them that there aren't any spirits and that you can't communicate to the dead is like trying to convince an anorexic that they are thin. It doesn't work. This was brought home to me when a Palo Mayombe believer wrote to me asking for help. He'd read my *Doktor Snake's Voodoo Spellbook*, and had decided I must be a powerful practitioner of the magickal arts. He was close to suicide because he believed he'd been cursed. Nothing was going right for him. His marriage had broken up; he was drinking and doing methamphetamine and other drugs. He'd tried everything to lift the hex, including rituals in cemeteries. I also got the impression he'd stolen bones from graveyards for use in rituals. None of it worked. So he came to me. Clearly he thought that my success in newspapers and with books was down to my magickal abilities and not to hard work. I took a rationalistic approach with him, telling him that the beliefs he held were not useful. They were getting in the way of him living his life and were making him contemplate killing himself. As far as I am concerned it doesn't matter whether spirits or magickal power exist or not. All that matters is how useful such notions are to your life. If they enhance it, fine. But if they don't, it's a question of dropping those beliefs. In my view, that holds true with any religion, not just Palo Mayombe. If you're a Catholic and it stops you being fulfilled in your life, you need to look at ways to deprogramme yourself. The same goes for other religions. If they're not useful, drop them. Belief should be seen as an engine; if it takes you somewhere good, pump it into your tank. If not, pump in a different belief.

Suffice to say, this line of reasoning didn't work with my Palo Mayombe correspondent. He didn't seem to take it in at all. He just wanted me to do a magickal working to rid him of the curse. He wanted me to go to a graveyard, select a dead person who was prominent in life and dig up their bones and do a ritual with them. To be fair, doing what he wanted may well have worked and lifted the curse – because, then, I would have been entering his belief system and would have been using psychological concepts he not only understood, but also considered real.

Richard Bandler, the flamboyant co-inventor of Neuro-Linguistic Programming (NLP) – a cutting-edge but somewhat controversial psychotherapy system – used to do this to good effect with psychiatric patients. 'We would take the basic premise that they weren't in touch with reality and see if we could simply change reality,' Bandler recalled in an interview with a new age magazine. 'If they heard voices out of the wall sockets then I put speakers in the wall sockets. If they saw a 60-foot Jesus, then I made a 60-foot Jesus.' Bandler also made use of fog machines, lasers, holograms, and even powerful rock and roll amplifiers, complete with reverb, to create the effects necessary for the patient to see their reality enacted literally. This strategy blew apart the patient's illusory reality, thus paving the way for the installation of a new, more useful model of the world. 'If somebody was talking to the Devil, who was making him do bad things,' Bandler said, 'we had the "Devil" come by and thank him for his co-operation, and say "I'm sorry, but I can't come by any more, there are other people out there I have to deal with".'

Bandler is right. Rationalising with someone who believes the Devil exists and talks to them is doomed to fail – just as my logical approach failed with my Palo Mayombe correspondent. When people believe something, there is no shaking it. All you can do is enter their reality and try and alter it so their belief system becomes more useful to their lives. With my Palo Mayombe correspondent, I'd have had to have done a spell to remove the curse. So long as he had enough faith in my powers, it might have been the answer.

As it was, I wasn't prepared to do that. I'd rather empower people away from religion and superstition than leave them enchained by a limiting belief system.

Keeping in mind the idea that beliefs are usually firmly entrenched, we can see how US law enforcement professionals could be proved right that Palo Mayombe-inspired grave robbing will not end – at least, not any time soon. Anyone who believes you can gain the assistance of the dead or spirits is going to find it near impossible to take on a more rationalistic belief system. It would only take a few things to go wrong in their life for them to think they were being punished by the spirits. They'd soon backtrack to their old beliefs and practices. They'd be 'hittin' the graveyard round midnight', as the old blues lyric goes. But anyone who has renounced a religion or belief system would be likely to fall back into their old ways if a run of bad luck led them to think they were being punished for turning their backs on it. Only the most exceptional people can offload the beliefs they've been brought up with.

As the old (reputedly Jesuit) maxim goes, 'Give me a child for the first seven years, and you may do what you like with him afterwards.'


## Death of a Palo Priest

Whatever your standpoint on religion, one thing is certain: devotees of Palo Mayombe, in common with everyone else on Earth, cannot cheat death. But they do have very specific ideas about how their spiritual and magickal belongings should be disposed of. This was illustrated in November 2004 when police were seeking to identify a human skull found near a bank of the Delaware river in Hopewell Township. A couple from Florida visiting people in the area spotted it in shallow water near Upper River

Road in Titusville and alerted the authorities. About 30 other apparently ritualistic objects were found with the skull, including animal skulls and bones. State police divers later snorkelled along the river's edge and found even more items of this sort.

After consulting with religious experts, police concluded that the skull might have been a ceremonial artefact used in cult rituals by a Palo Mayombe priest. 'In Palo Mayombe, when the priest or priestess dies, all their artefacts are disposed of in a river,' said police chief Michael Chipowsky. 'We think that's what this might have been.'

Before full forensic results came in, Captain George Meyers of the township police commented: 'At this point, we think the skull is very old. It could have been stolen from a grave, but [we have] no evidence to link it to any crime, recent or otherwise.' But he did note that there had been some sinister activity in the area. 'It was reported to us by area residents that a pick-up truck was seen on the road with a metal casket in the back. We have no leads from that at this point.'

Lisa Coryell, a reporter from the *New Jersey Times*, however, tracked down those who reported seeing the truck. In a news report on 24 November, she wrote:

> One resident who did not want to be identified said in the weeks before Halloween [that] he and other neighbours saw a black pickup truck travelling north of River Drive coming from the direction of the dumping site. In the pickup's bed was an old metal coffin, the man said. 'We all watched it go by' and [one neighbour] said, 'Boy they don't make coffins like that anymore,' the man added.

So what was going on? Out of the possible scenarios, police chief Michael Chipowsky said that the most serious charge facing the person who dumped the human skull and ritual items into the Delaware river was one of illegally disposing of a corpse. The other thing to bear in mind is the truck transporting what appeared to be a metal coffin could well have been completely unrelated and perfectly innocent. It could have been a red herring. All in all, the most likely explanation is that the possessions of a Palo Mayombe priest were being disposed of in a ritual manner.

But not everyone is convinced that Palo Mayombe was involved at all. Eoghan Ballard, from the University of Pennsylvania, spent many years studying Congo religions in the Americas as part of his doctorate in folklore and ethnography. He believes the religion is unjustly maligned. In a letter to the *Hopewell Valley News*, which closely covered the so-called 'Hopewell skull' case, he expressed deep scepticism that the skull was linked to Palo Mayombe. 'In all my research, both in the United States and in Cuba over the last decade,' he wrote, 'I have not yet heard of a Palo ritual that requires a skull to be left in or near a river.' He conceded that many branches of Palo Mayombe do use human remains, but argued that it is cultural differences that lead to such practices being perceived as a grotesque travesty of religion. 'While bones appear "grizzly" to many in this culture, the practise is not so different in intent from the relics kept in the Roman Catholic church,' he wrote. 'Both are for religious purposes, and magick is only a small part of the Congo religion – the main part is religious devotion. Most Paleros (priests) purchase the bones they use through legal sources and do not rob graves. There are multiple sources for human and animal bones and most are reasonably priced and easily accessible.' He was referring to spiritual supplies stores, or botanicas, which legally import human and animal bones from China and other countries in the Far East (see the section on the *Botanica Palo Mayombe* online store later in this chapter).

Ballard lays the blame for grave robbing and other illegal activities in cemeteries firmly on 'self-styled experimenters and teenagers seeking thrills'. He believes such people are inspired by 'legends and sensationalistic books written by commercial authors such as [Migene] Gonzalez-Wippler and [Raul] Carnizares (neither of whom are respected by followers of these traditions)'. The real followers of these traditions, Ballard insists, 'wish to stay out of the news and avoid problems [and] are by and large law abiding citizens'.

Ballard also cites another reason for Palo Mayombe being represented as a sinister brand of magic. 'Some of the information critical of Palo, that which speaks of grave robbing and negative magick and which characterises it as almost completely sorcery, come from sources which have long-standing political and cultural antagonisms and often hegemonic interests in Palo,' he wrote. '[For example] Santeros (priests in Santeria) are in competition with Palo and have built their image historically, in Cuba and in the US, by painting the Palero as evil in contrast to themselves whom they obviously present as deeply devout and spiritual. Other sources use startling images to either tell a good spooky story or to simply increase sales of their books.'

He went on to criticise the Hopewell police, who he said had, through no fault of their own, been aided by 'a few self-styled experts, who may have a few letters behind their names but little information other than that garnered from sources three or four times removed from practice'.

## 'Dem Bones, Dem Bones Gonna Walk Aroun' . . .'
(From 'Dry Bones', traditional gospel song)

In the districts where they are active, Palo Mayombists tend to be seen as sinister Devil worshippers – at least in the popular mind. Many would say, with good cause, after all, the religion has been associated with grave robbing. But Ballard may have a valid point when he lays the blame for the Hopewell skull case and other cemetery thefts on renegade practitioners. In his letter to the *Hopewell Valley News* he states that followers of Palo Mayombe don't actually *need* to steal bones from graveyards. They can obtain them from other perfectly legitimate outlets. This adds some weight to Ballard's contention that the body-snatchers were either rogue Palo Mayombe followers or kids looking for thrills – and not bone fide practitioners of Palo Mayombe. In his opinion, legitimate practitioners would always get their bones from legitimate sources and would not raid cemeteries.

One thing is for sure, it's a lot easier to obtain bones legally than it is to rob them – you can even order them from the Internet. Botanica Palo Mayombe[5] is one online store that sells human skulls and bones, along with the usual potions, powders, candles and other ritual items used in Palo Mayombe, Voodoo and Santeria. The website – which can be found at www.botanicapalomayombe.com – is not subtle. It indulges in the kind of Halloween kitsch that would scare the hell out of Scooby Doo and Shaggy, what with its night sky background, bats flying out of a full moon and a witch with a pointed hat stirring a cauldron. The store's 'spiritual' items, however, are decidedly not what you'd find in a blissed-out, new age or even traditional witchcraft store. For $24.95 you can get a bottle of Spanish Fly capsules. According to the blurb they are 'a hot sexy stimulator sure to bring erotic pleasure. Time-release capsules. The legendary sex exciter!' The label shows a man performing vigorous cunnilingus on a dark-haired Latina girl, so we can presume that whatever is in the Spanish Fly pills is doing its job. Alternatively, for men long in the tooth but young in the groin, there are the

Erection Plus Capsules ($24.95). 'Don't be down and out while she's begging for more,' runs the blurb. 'Get it up and keep it up, harder and longer. Fill her desire for long-lasting, hard driving action.' If you're into magick and spells, there's a whole range of ritual candles. The 7 Knob Red Ritual Candle ($4.95), for example, is used to bring love into your life and for dominating or binding a lover. Or there's the Black Female/Male Ritual Candles ($4.95 each), which are used for putting on hexes or for removing negative influences, people or couples from your life.

The Botanica Palo Mayombe is also a veritable super-market for human skulls and bones. Male and female skulls are on offer, as are femurs, fibulas and even whole shoulder and arm bones, including the hands. The website makes clear that the remains are sold lawfully:

> It is perfectly legal to sell human bones in the United States. Except for select antique specimens, all human bones for sale in the United States have been prepared overseas. Prior to 1985, the main supplier of human material for medical use was India. India ceased exporting bones in 1985 following changes in Indian law.

Botanica Palo Mayombe also stresses that there is no danger of anyone coming along claiming the bones belong to a long-lost relative:

> These remains are anonymous. Skulls and skele-tons can be sexed, but the vast majority of our stock consists of adult males. Individual post-cranial bones, with the exception of pelvic material, cannot be sexed accurately. Unless otherwise specified, prices are for A1 quality specimens. Having said that, not all bones are perfect. Since many of these

bones were prepped several years ago, they occasionally show signs of wear related to long-term
handling or storage. Bones that were previously held
in museum or academic collections may possess
catalog numbers. We will try and select the best-
quality bones available, but each bone is unique.

Amongst the many remains currently on offer – which
Botanica Palo Mayombe says come from overseas – is a
male skull, costing $500 and described as having 'Six teeth,
erupting third molar, mandibular abcess, minor damage
to nasal. Very nice color'. Also available for $500 is a
female skull with four-and-a-half teeth and 'damaged right
nasal [and] green staining on maxilla'. There's also a
complete foot from Haiti, priced at $190, with toes hung
on nylon or wire.

Botanica Palo Mayombe is careful to put a strong
disclaimer at the bottom of all its web pages. It says the
site is for adults only and that 'if you find the site objec-
tionable, you are not an adult, or the viewing and/or
purchasing of information, products, or services within
this site is not legal in your location, leave this site immediately, and do not return . . .'

Even though I'm used to the macabre – having played
in a band with a Voodoo man for some years – I was starting
to feel a little queasy looking over the bones on the Botanica
Palo Mayombe website. But I took a slug of Plymouth
gin and started to feel better. Then I looked up from my
laptop computer at the row of skulls, ritual dolls, ouija
boards and grotesque-looking roots I've got on my shelves
– all collected during my occasional travels to exotic parts
of the world. I realised that my study is even more sinister-
looking than the Botanica Palo Mayombe website. But it
seems completely normal and everyday to me. I can only
pray I never get raided by the cops . . .

## Shake, Rattle and Roll

I spent a lot of time trying to puzzle out who was right over the alleged Palo Mayombe grave robberies. Ballard makes a strong case against them being the work of genuine Palos and his views are based on close contact he had with various Palo Mayombe groups in Cuba and the US. So it has to be taken seriously. And the truth is it is very easy to tar everyone with the same brush, just because a small minority of rene-gade practitioners steal from graveyards. It doesn't mean all followers of Palo Mayombe are bad. One person who advises many US police departments on what is and what isn't a ritual crime is Dawn Perlmutter.[6] I decided I should contact her to get her take on the issue. So I called her while doing my True Crime Hour radio show, and asked if she would like to give some opinions on this messy business. She readily accepted. What follows is a transcript of the show that went out back in November 2005. It offers many insights.

## Programme Theme: Tomb Raiding in the USA

Future Radio; 10/11/2005; TRUE CRIME HOUR
Time: 6.00–7.00 p.m.

> *Track 1: Keith Richards, '999',*
> *from 'Main Offender' (1992)*

JIMMY LEE SHREEVE, host: Greetings! We've got a special guest on the show tonight, talking to us by phone all the way from the USA. We've got Dawn Perlmutter, an expert in ritualistic crime, who works with police departments in New Jersey and other parts of America when they are confronted with crimes they don't understand. Crimes that have magick and the occult as a motive.

Dawn didn't set out to pursue a career linked to law enforcement and gruesome crime. But in college she was intrigued by the symbols in ancient religious art, especially those relating to blood sacrifice. She noticed that they were entering modern life, but in distorted ways. She explored this theme in her doctoral thesis titled *Graven Images: Creative Acts of Idolatry*, which was also published as a book.

Later a New Jersey police officer asked her to help on a murder case, which he was puzzled by. Looking over the autopsy photos, she saw that the mutilation was similar to that found in ancient tribal blood rites – which was a big help to police. From there, she was invited to speak to various law enforcement groups. Now she works full time as a police consultant on ritual crimes.

Welcome, Dawn . . . are you out there?

PERLMUTTER: Yes, I am. Thank you for inviting me.

SHREEVE: So you're a ritual crime expert, could you tell listeners exactly what your job entails?

PERLMUTTER: Well, I essentially have an academic background, but I have segued into working full time with law enforcement on any kind of unusual ritualistic crime or religious violence. I train different departments all over the US – and that's basically it.

SHREEVE: During my research for *Blood Rites*, I found that your name kept cropping up, so I thought, 'I'm gonna have to talk to this person . . .'

PERLMUTTER: Anything with blood, my name crops up!

SHREEVE: (Laughs) Absolutely. But you got into this stuff by accident – is that right?

PERLMUTTER: Yes, it's not something I planned to do as a career. Basically I was similar to the main character in the *Da Vinci Code*.[7] Like I said, I had an academic background where I studied religious symbolism and image worship. And while working on my doctorate at NYU (New York University) I started interviewing avant-garde artists who were ritually mutilating themselves. They all described it as a religious experience. So that sort of segued me into writing about contemporary blood rituals. Then about twelve years ago, I had a local police officer come to me saying they had a case where someone was mutilated and could I help. And I said, what am I supposed to do? He said, just look at these pictures and I'm like, I don't know what I'm looking at. He said just look at them and tell us what you think. Maybe I got lucky, I don't know . . . but we just applied my knowledge of ancient rituals and I was able to help. I was then asked to speak to a law enforcement group and it all snowballed. Every time I would speak someone else would ask me to speak. Then when my handout became about 100 pages long, I figured it was time to publish it as a book. It worked out well because my theoretical research was always on sacred violence and the law enforcement work gave me actual cases and allowed me to prove theories that I had.

SHREEVE: One of the things that interests me is this business in New Jersey – the cemetery break-ins and grave robberies. People break into mausoleums and pull out the skulls or other remains and then take them off and use them in occult rituals. The bodysnatchers are allegedly involved in the Palo Mayombe cult. For listeners out there who may have no idea what Palo Mayombe is, it's kind of similar to Voodoo; it's got roots in the African Congo. Dawn, you've worked with police on some of these cases, haven't you?

PERLMUTTER: Yes, I've been involved on quite a lot of cases with Palo Mayombe. It's actually a combination of the African Congo tradition and Yoruba religion and like all the syncretic traditions it blends with Catholicism. I've had cases in New Jersey, Pennsylvania, Delaware, New York and Florida. They steal these skulls and bones and put them into what they call a nganga or prendo and do ritual work with it.

SHREEVE: A nganga is a cauldron, isn't it?

PERLMUTTER: Yes, it's an iron pot and it's very frightening – particularly when officers have never seen anything like it before. It'll often have quite a number of sacrificed animals in it, in different stages of decomposition. I often tell them in my training sessions that you will smell these crime scenes long before you see them.

SHREEVE: Yeah, one police officer I read about was quoted as saying, 'This is like your first DOA'. It smelled so bad. So for the listeners out there, these are cauldrons filled with – normally – animal bones?

PERLMUTTER: Yes and a human skull underneath all of it. Plus there are other objects, such as food offerings and religious items, such as crosses. If you're not familiar with it, it's very disturbing.

SHREEVE: Like something out of a horror film, I'd imagine, for the police?

PERLMUTTER: Well, usually there's more than one nganga. Plus it's in the midst of a lot of other types of symbols that are very frightening and they are usually in a dark area – so yes, it is like walking into a horror film.

SHREEVE: I guess they get used to it. I mean in the end you get used to most things and then it's just like another case. But you say there's a human skull in there too, does that worry them? Do they think, hang on, has there been a homicide here?

PERLMUTTER: Well, in the cases that I've worked on they have never included a murder. Although the Matamoros,[8] Mexico case did involve actual murders – like 28 of them for his cauldrons. All of the cases I have worked on involved cemetery desecrations ... taking the bodies out of there and that is a crime. As is animal sacrifice, if it's not done properly and doesn't meet health guidelines [that is, it must be done in a humane manner, similar to the kosher or halal slaughter of animals, and meet health and safety rules].

SHREEVE: From a human point of view, it must be very upsetting for the relatives of the deceased, whose bones have been stolen. I've read that people say things like, 'None of our family are going to be buried in a crypt ever again. We are going to be cremated.'

PERLMUTTER: Yes, very upsetting to the relatives of victims. Ironically, high priests in Palo Mayombe, known as Paleros, who've had their cauldrons for a very long time, ritually dispose of them when they retire. When we find them, they are very upset that we've disturbed their sacred ground. But, then, what comes around goes around. It's like they already disturbed someone's resting place to get this thing going . . .

SHREEVE: That's ironic isn't it? I remember one case near the Delaware river – Hopewell Township. There was some stuff found which must have belonged to a high priest of Palo Mayombe.

PERLMUTTER: Yes I worked on that case. That was a very old cauldron too. It had coins from 1920; objects that were very old and they will keep these cauldrons for their entire lives. It was a very old skull too.

SHREEVE: So you think it could have been a high priest of Palo Mayombe that died?

PERLMUTTER: I think so.

SHREEVE: He might have been working way back into the 1920s and 1930s?

PERLMUTTER: Exactly. This is a very old tradition, which has come to the US with different groups of people who have emigrated. It's like any other religion; it's passed down from generation to generation.

SHREEVE: How do you advise the police to deal with devotees of Palo Mayombe?

PERLMUTTER: What I usually advise is for police officers to gain a rapport with the leaders of a community or the people who are in the botanicas, the religious supply stores used by those into Palo Mayombe. To encourage them not to leave these dead animals around and just advise them that grave robbing is an illegal practice. I think they understand it's illegal, but they don't quite grasp that it's also sacrilege – to the people who are buried. It's just more important to them to do this required ritual.

SHREEVE: They don't have the sensitivity. Okay. Let's play a track and if you can hang on the line I've got a whole list of questions.

*Track 2: R.L. Burnside,*
*'Wish I Was in Heaven Sitting Down' from*
*'Wish I Was in Heaven Sitting Down' (2000)*

SHREEVE: Welcome back. You're listening to True Crime Hour on Future Radio, and we're talking to Dawn Perlmutter from the USA, a ritual crime expert. Are you still out there, Dawn?

PERLMUTTER: Yes, I'm here.

SHREEVE: Great. We're talking about how graveyards are reportedly robbed by practitioners of the Palo Mayombe cult. They use the bones for magickal rituals. Now, what I've discovered is that some academics and doctorate students, in particular, are defending Palo Mayombe. They say practitioners of Palo Mayombe are predominantly law-abiding and the only ones that do grave robbing are self-styled practitioners who aren't genuine Palo Mayombe devotees. They say that the grave robbing is the work of teenage Satanists, looking for kicks. How do you respond to that?

PERLMUTTER: Well that's just inaccurate. I was in academia for a long time as a professor and I just know that those who defend these religious movements are really protecting religious freedom, which is all well and good, but the theology of Palo Mayombe is inconsistent with that. The rituals are centred around the spirits of the dead. In other words, the religion doesn't work unless you have somebody's body to do this with. So, theologically, it's simply incorrect to say that they don't rob graves. I mean it doesn't mean that teenage Satanists and other types of things are not going on in cemeteries – all kinds of things are going on in cemeteries. But it's pretty obvious when it's Palo. There are very specific crime scene indicators that are indicative of that.

SHREEVE: Why do you think the academics miss this?

PERLMUTTER: I think with academics a lot of it's naivety – just not wanting to believe that a novel tradition would be doing that. And unfortunately practitioners are not going to show them that side of themselves when they are being interviewed for a research paper or something.

SHREEVE: Does dealing with these types of crimes make you cynical about religion?

PERLMUTTER: Oh no, it hasn't made me cynical at all. Kind of the opposite. Having studied all types of religions, I see how they evolve and how they assimilate different traditions and see how much they have in common. The dark side I see is obviously very disturbing, but I think that it's kind of a primal instinct and, if anything, I think that other types of traditions help us to keep a lid on that. So it depends on the tradition. Certain traditions embrace the dark side while others help suppress those aspects. I think there is a need for spirituality and I think it's going to come out one way or another.

SHREEVE: Despite the negative things you work with, you are still positive about religion . . .

PERLMUTTER: Well, there's a balance out there. I can't say I'm not shocked by a lot of it, but I think that, as I said, it's part of human nature. We have to aspire to something to keep ourselves in check.

SHREEVE: Okay, one more question before we play another track. You say Palo Mayombe practitioners do spells and sometimes put hexes on people. For example, they'll make a doll from clay or cloth to represent an enemy and then will stick pins in it, while intoning dark incantations. Do you think such practices work?

PERLMUTTER: Well, I get asked that all the time. I can tell you that people who practise Santeria and related syncretic traditions are terrified and believe it works. I have seen people manifest physical symptoms, they were so convinced it was working. It's all part of magickal thinking. As to whether their spells work, well, if they did, I don't think I'd be here right now – because I've testified against too many of them.

SHREEVE: Ah, yes, I wondered about that . . .

PERLMUTTER: It's like when a few negative things happen, which are like coincidence, I sometimes think to myself is it really worth it? It's not good to start thinking like that . . . if you start thinking like that you can't do what I'm doing. So, no, I don't believe that Palo Mayombe works. I don't like having all that negative energy thrown at me, but I think if it had worked then something would have happened to me now.

SHREEVE: My opinion is that the unconscious mind is very powerful. So when someone believes they've been cursed they will manifest symptoms – the subconscious makes this occur. Interestingly, I recently came across an American narcotics agent, who was forever dealing with people into Palo Mayombe and similar traditions. He was being cursed all the time. So he set up his own magickal altar to protect himself. He decided to play the same game.

PERLMUTTER: Yes, I must admit, I collect books on psychic protection. Anytime I see one I'm like, 'I think I'll file that.' But I haven't gone as far as to set up an altar.

SHREEVE: You've kept your strength of mind.

PERLMUTTER: Yes, you have to stay grounded. That's one of the things I advise when I'm training police officers who are working on these cases, to try to avoid falling into magick thinking because it will really hinder their investigation.

SHREEVE: It could be someone's downfall . . . On that note let's play another track and if you can stay on the line I'll ask you a few more questions.

*Track 3: John Campbell,*
*'Wiseblood' from 'Howlin' Mercy' (1993)*

SHREEVE: Let's move on to the subject of Satanists, who have been blamed for grave robberies by some academics. What interests me about this is that rock stars like Marilyn Manson are forever getting blamed for influencing Satanist killers, who are usually teenagers. When the cops find Manson CDs in a killer's house, they tend to immediately blame him. What do you think of this?

PERLMUTTER: Well, that's a difficult question. I'm certainly not for censorship. After all, there are millions of people who listen to Marilyn Manson. But I have assisted on cases where teenagers have said they were influenced by him. So I guess the position with Marilyn Manson is I don't think he's innocent in all this. I mean you send out certain messages and people are going to interpret them in different ways. So should he be held accountable? I don't know how far you go, but I think it would be nice if he just thought about it a little bit. Especially since there've been so many murders and suicides that he's been pulled into.

SHREEVE: I see him as a great artist, highly articulate and intelligent. But you think he's missing this point?

PERLMUTTER: I would just like to look in his eyes and have a conversation with him. There was a video that we were both on called *Pact with the Devil* about three Italian teenage girls who murdered a nun, saying Manson influenced them. At the end of it his response was 'If you don't raise your kids, I will.' And that just about says it all.

SHREEVE: Okay, good points. Lastly, what are you up to now? Do you have any new books coming out?

PERLMUTTER: Well, there are all kinds of things I'm working on. I do have a future book, which will be published by CRC Press. It's called *Color Atlas of Blood Rituals and Occult Crime* (August 2007). It will contain around 600 colour photos of blood rituals in almost every spiritual tradition.

SHREEVE: Right, well, I look forward to seeing that. It's been fascinating talking to you and I'm sure listeners out there have enjoyed it too. So thank you very much for coming on.

PERLMUTTER: Thank you for inviting me.

SHREEVE: It was a pleasure. Anyone wanting to find out more about Dawn Perlmutter's work should visit www.ritualviolence.com. Okay, time for a final track.

*Track 4: Buddy Miller, 'Worry Too Much', from 'Universal United House Of Prayer' (2004)*

## Ancestor Power

'When there is no more room in Hell, the dead will walk the Earth.'

From the movie *Dawn of the Dead* (1978),
George Romero.

'I have to be honest with you, I'm running demented and deranged and out of control,' I said to Mick Marshall, an old friend I hadn't seen in years. He'd just got in touch again, and it turned out he was now living in the next county to me. So we met up one lunchtime, just before Christmas 2005, and spent the whole day and evening drinking in the only pub worth visiting in Norwich – the Walnut Tree Shades. It not only plays good blues and country music, but is adorned with Americana kitsch – vintage Wild Turkey and Jack Daniels signs, along with ads for Black Cat cigarettes. It's a pub for the crazed and eccentric; ordinary and average citizens are barred (but there are plenty of tacky, plastic joints for them to go to). It's a place where people feel comfortable to drop in on their own to read a book and have a glass of beer. In fact, while we were there, a woman of about thirty-five sat down with her young kid and read a book to him, while she had a pint of lager. Some might say, 'Good God! that's outrageous; how can she take a young child into a drinking establishment?' My answer would be: maybe it was the only place she felt truly at home, and, certainly from where I was sitting, she was doing a great job of paying attention to her kid and helping him learn to read. Mick – who has a full, blond beard and the craggy, world-worn looks of Kris Kristofferson – wanted to marry her. But I said: 'Beware lone sirens lest they lure you into stormy waters and tear your ageing body asunder – and, besides, there's no time for that. I need to talk to you about grave robbing.'

'Ah, you want us to get into the bodysnatching game?'

'Not quite,' I replied. 'But we won't rule it out if we fall on hard times. For now though, I wanted to get your opinion on how crazy, or not, these Palo Mayombe practitioners are, who allegedly rob people's remains from cemeteries in the US for use in magickal rituals – you remember, I told you all about them on the phone?'

The reason I was talking to Mick about this was I was sure there was another piece to the puzzle, something else that needed to be said – hence my desperate and deranged state. I needed to get this chapter finished, but I couldn't see how; I couldn't see an ending. And by now I'd had enough of acknowledged experts and their opinions – after all, the only reason they are 'acknowledged' is because the establishment says they are and gives them a piece of paper to 'prove it'. Mick, on the other hand, is one of those rare people who, at just over 50 years of age, has 25 doctorates from the University of Life – he'd have more, only there isn't room for all the plaques on his wall. No. I needed street wisdom and down-to-earth talk, along with something uncontrolled – a wild card. That was the only way I was going to make sense of the tomb-raiding deal, and finally finish this section of the book.

Mick lit up another cigarette, laying waste to his already haggard appearance and increasingly compromised health. His feverish chain-smoking was close to inhuman. It had already filled the pub with unnatural levels of tobacco smoke, making it nearly impossible to even see the bar, and giving me the eerie feeling that I'd entered the swirling mists of limbo. Mick looked thoughtful for a moment, then said: 'You can understand this ancestor worship stuff. The fact is, there is more to heaven and earth – something the police on both sides of the Atlantic don't understand, unless, that is, it revolves around biblical themes.' He swigged the final dregs of his neat bourbon, then added: 'But robbing graves indiscriminately is a pretty crappy thing to do. After all, how would they like it if their grandmothers were lifted and stuck in cauldrons?'

Mick went on to say that the idea of ancestor worship might seem alien to most of us in the West. But it didn't to him. And he told me the following story to illustrate why:

When I was working as an orderly in a psychiatric hospital in Cambridgeshire, pretty much everyone who'd worked there for some time accepted that weird things were going on. When I started I thought it was a load of crap. People said, 'You'll see,' and I thought, 'Yeah, yeah . . . ,' and just got on with the job. One part of the building went back to Victorian times and wasn't in use anymore for patients. We were using it for storage, towels and stuff. But quite a few of the staff had reported the room turning unnaturally cold; some claimed to have seen and heard things. I'd also felt it suddenly go freezing in there. I couldn't find any reason for this, especially considering that the hospital's boilers were blasting out heat. It made no sense, but I didn't worry about it.

Then one time I'd loaded up a trolley full of towels. I checked over the shelves where I'd got them from to make sure I'd got them all. And I had. So I turned away. Then just as I was about to wheel the trolley out, I happened to look round again and noticed a towel was on the shelf. And yet it couldn't have been. I looked closer and it was covered in blood. What's more, the whole room had turned deathly cold. I went up to the office to find out if there had been any incidents with patients that had led to injury, but none had occurred for ages. No one could explain the blood on the towel. So we just put it in the trash. Because similar things had happened to other members of staff, we filed it in our minds as just another weird and unexplainable happening.

But another incident really gave me the freaks. I was wheeling another trolley down to the same room, which had two doors, both spring-closing, safety doors. I was unloading towels and the room went arctic again. I wasn't too concerned, as I'd pretty much got used to it, but I was half expecting something to happen. But it didn't. I emptied the trolley of towels, then made to leave. But I couldn't get the door to open. It was locked tight. I presumed someone was mucking about, but I hadn't seen anyone about at all on my way down; it was usually pretty deserted. Anyway, I tried the other door. But that wouldn't open either. I yanked at both of them and couldn't budge them. So I shouted, 'Come on, stop fucking about, it ain't funny anymore!' But there was just an eerie silence and this icy cold. By then I started to think this was a ghost or spirit, someone from the great beyond trying to get a message across – and doing it in more and more extreme ways because no one was listening. So I said, 'Whatever it is you want, just tell us, we'll help you. Just let me out of here – open the fucking door.' Moments later it warmed up and I tried the door and it opened. I was glad to get out of there.

When Mick finished his story, he fixed me with a direct gaze and said: 'I'll tell you, Jimmy Lee, you can be as sceptical as you like, but when these kind of things happen, you're forced to think again. When it comes to Palo Mayombe and Voodoo devotees, or anyone like that, we shouldn't be condemning them for ancestor worship. We should be *learning* from them.' If we did that, he said, our knowledge of the world and the nature of things would expand. 'I for one am certain,' Mick concluded, 'that in some circumstances the dead continue to walk this earth. And it's not air- fairy theory, it's from personal experience – and it's very likely the same for the people into Palo Mayombe.'

# Gimme Some Head . . .

> 'The harvest is past, the summer is ended, and we are not saved.'
>
> Jeremiah 8:20

Two months later, I was in a fevered, crazed, werewolf state, and was howling at the moon every night. I had just days before the deadline for this book, and I hadn't slept for weeks. In what presumably must have been a waking dream, fuelled by paranoia and inhuman amounts of caffeine, my editor at Random House, Tim Andrews, was screaming down the phone: 'You've already had three extensions for this book. We need it now. And in fact, if I don't see the files in my e-mail box by next week, we will be sending out a hitman to finish you off, you worthless piece of carrion!' A similar thing happened a few days later. This time my agent Andrew Lownie appeared in a swirling blue mist and was equally despairing: 'I knew I shouldn't have taken you on my books. In fact, I should have called the pest control people when I had the chance and had you shot down like vermin . . .' Even though these visions were not real – or at least I *think* they weren't – I understood their position. But I knew there was one final story that needed to be added to this ugly tale, a story that would show that tomb raiding and use of body parts will not go away. Something to show that the terrible clash of cultures can only come to a head – unless we all start talking and listening to each other. After all, it's no good targeting the weird in demented witch-hunts, because one day the weird will rise up and take you by the throat and make you listen.

The story came in at the eleventh hour. Mick called

me around midnight on Saturday 11 February 2006. 'Jimmy Lee, have you seen the news?'

'No,' I said. 'I haven't had time. I'm fucking deranged here trying to get this book finished – Random House are going to literally have me assassinated if I don't deliver the manuscript by next week. What's more, I haven't got time to talk to motherfucker scumrats like you. Precious time is being eaten up as we speak . . .'

'You *should* check the news,' he said, ignoring my diatribe. 'You'll find some Voodoo woman tried to carry a decomposing head through Miami airport.'

'My God,' I said. 'You've done it. You've found the story, you've brought it home to roost.' I cranked up Google News and there at the top of the list was the Voodoo head story, reported in the *South Florida Sun-Sentinel*. On Thursday, 9 February, went the report, federal agents at Fort Lauderdale-Hollywood International Airport pulled in Myrlene Sevère (age 30), a resident of Miramar, Florida, who was returning from a visit to her home country of Haiti. Customs officials searched her carry bag and were horrified to find a skull, with teeth and hair still attached. She told investigators that she purchased the skull from a man in Haiti to use in religious ceremonies (she was a practitioner of Voodoo), and hoped it would ward off evil spirits and bring her luck. Sevère was arrested and charged with intentionally smuggling a human head into the United States and not having the proper paperwork, as well as bringing hazardous material on an aircraft. Each count carries a five-year maximum sentence, which means Sevère could spend up to fifteen years in a federal slammer if convicted.

The skull was taken to the Broward County medical examiner who determined that it had once belonged to a black male, roughly 40 years old or younger. The *Miami Herald* also picked up on the story and got in touch with Chief Medical Examiner Dr Jushua Perper. He told reporters: 'Our conclusion, at this time, is that this is a skull that has been buried and taken out for a Voodoo kind of ritual . . . The people who practise this particular type of worship . . . go to the graves of their relatives and they believe they can ask for permission [from] the spirits of their relatives to take the skull out of the grave.'

Perper said he had never seen a case like this in Broward County. But in Miami-Dade it's a different story – the medical examiner there even has a 'Bone Room'. '[They are] usually skulls brought in for some religious purpose,' Larry Cameron, the office's director of operations, told the *South Florida Sun-Sentinel*. 'We may get eight or ten skulls a year and almost every case comes from Miami International Airport.' The skulls end up in the Bone Room, which is where all the skeletal remains found in the county are stored, until claimed by relatives.

The *Miami Herald* contacted Clotaire Bazile, a Little Haiti Voodoo priest, who said it's not uncommon for a skull to be used as part of a Voodoo ritual designed to help someone who believes he or she has been possessed. For instance, he explained, one treatment calls for the skull to be washed in Haitian moonshine, along with a special plant. The person is later given a bath with the concoction. 'It's not for anything bad, it's to help the person,' he made clear.

Some of Sévère's neighbours were not surprised that she'd been pulled in by the cops. Guerlain Desrouleaux, age 47, originally from Haiti, told *Miami Herald* reporters that he had seen chickens, a goat and a fire in front of Sévère's home. 'She does Voodoo for a lot of people,' he said. Another neighbour told the *Sun-Sentinel* that Sévère's arrest only feeds the stereotypes about Haitians and Voodoo. 'Not all Haitians do that,' he said.

Rafael Martinez, the anthropologist and expert in Afro-Caribbean religions, quoted earlier, also weighed in. He said it was common for practitioners to put a human skull on an altar in the home dedicated to spirits of the dead, collectively known as Gede. The spirits contained in that skull are thought to have a powerful, positive influence on one's life. In Palo Mayombe, he added, human bones are often put into a ceremonial pot or nganda, for similar purposes. 'The belief is that the spirits of those people will help you in life, will do things for you,' he said. He went on to stress that the use of skulls and bones can be seen in almost all world religions. He cited Catholicism as an example, where many relics are purported to be the human remains of saints. 'People need to have an open mind about these things. We keep in our living rooms the ashes of our loved ones and that doesn't come across as unusual,' he said. 'We need to recognise these are all very valid religions. Very different, but very valid.'

Clearly, as with in any religion, there are some good, morally upstanding devotees and some bad eggs. Some Catholic priests molest children and some Christian fanatics torture and kill kids to drive the Devil out of them. Likewise, some Palo Mayombe and Voodoo practitioners rob graves and even murder and torture innocent victims, as happened at Matamoros. But the body of evidence shows that these are aberrations. The fact is the weird and unusual practices found in minority religions scare the hell out of average citizens with cushioned lifestyles and closed minds. In the past, they've had little exposure to different cultures. But now those cultures are jumping up and making themselves heard. We can either condemn them or find out what they're about and gain an understanding of them. I think the latter is the way forward and offers the best chance of not just making a better world, but of bringing rogue practitioners (of whatever religion) to book.

*

I slammed my laptop shut. It was 4.00 a.m. I had no will left to write. So I called Mick back. 'Hey Mick,' I said. 'Thanks for putting me on to the Voodoo head story. You saved my life.'

'Well, there are very few of us who would say no to some Voodoo head,' he replied. 'Sometimes it is the only thing that can preserve our sanity.'

During my research into tomb raiding, I tried to imagine myself carrying a rotting head home in my rucksack. But I couldn't. I also tried to imagine myself breaking into a graveyard and purloining someone's remains. Again I really don't think I could do that. Apart from the strong possibility of landing in trouble with the law, it's just too gruesome and macabre. But if I truly believed it would help me become a millionaire I might be tempted. Wouldn't most of us? Especially if we could say goodbye to work and we could live in a great place – maybe a mansion out in the countryside. And all it would take would be a spot of grave robbing, a seance to contact the dead, and petitioning the spirits.

But as I don't believe such things are possible, being tempted is not an issue (of course, not believing could be a limitation on my part and the reason why I'm not currently a millionaire). But what I'm trying to illustrate is that the lure of easy money by enslaving the dead to petition the gods is very powerful and compelling – especially if your cultural belief system backs up the legitimacy of this idea.

But, obviously, such practices are unsavoury and disrespectful to the dead and their surviving relatives, and therefore need to be stopped. In my opinion, the best way to put a stop on tomb raiding by Palo Mayombists and other ancestor worshippers is not to make them conform, but to gradually encourage them to break the rules and dogmas of their religion – many of which (in common with those of all religions) are limiting. The first dogma to break is the literal belief in gods and the spirits of the dead. This needs to go because followers of Palo Mayombe live in superstitious dread that if they offend the gods or ancestors in some way, they will be punished. Therefore it makes sense to defy these entities, to usurp their power and take control – and thus walk into freedom, having broken the bonds of blind faith and superstition.

Being totally irreligious, I would recommend this policy to all followers of religion. Rather than worship the unseen, we should take responsibility for our destinies and become gods ourselves. Why not?

# Chapter 7: Last Rites: Split Brains and Sacrifice

A Strange Experience at the Metropole...
Bicameral Man ... The Bicameral Mind and Ritual
Slaying ... Autonomy

'O God, if there be a God, save my soul, if I have
a soul!'
Anonymous, prayer of a common soldier before
the battle of Blenheim, 1704.

## A Strange Experience at the Metropole ...

During the planning and writing of this book I naturally
immersed myself in books and articles on human sacrifice. Not surprisingly, it made for gory and shocking
reading – with case after case of people having their
throats torn out or limbs hacked off by blood-crazed
fanatics looking for favours from divine or diabolic entities. But nowhere along the line did I find a convincing
theory that explained exactly *why* people believe that sacrificing a fellow creature – be it animal or man – will bring
worldly rewards. Most of the academic books on the

subject – which *should* have provided answers – fell down miserably in this respect. Maybe it was because the authors found the idea of ritual killing so shocking and beyond belief that they simply couldn't tackle the reasons for it head-on. And you can't blame them. Either that, or it was because they were commenting from the sheltered world of academia and weren't getting their hands dirty enough.

Being a journalist I'm used to getting my hands *very* dirty. For good or ill, I have long walked an unsteady, and often totally uncontrolled, path through the gutter of humanity. Because I operate on the raw edge and have a penchant for pushing things way too far, I sometimes land in hot water. But one situation that went seriously out of control led to me having an experience that put me on the road to finding a good model to explain the motivations behind the practice of blood sacrifice. It enabled me to bring together a number of disciplines – from hypnotherapy and split-brain research to theories on the evolution of consciousness – and come up with possible answers not only to why it is people are driven to sacrifice, but why they believe in invisible entities that can offer them rewards in exchange for blood.

Obviously I'm not a scientific researcher. So whatever I put forward is intended to stimulate debate – it is meant to be a catalyst, and not the last word. The unusual experience I had, for example, serves to illustrate the way we humans seem to have two inner selves – often called the conscious and unconscious. In the modern world, it is mainly the conscious mind that is dominant, whereas in the ancient past the unconscious, more visionary mind, would have been more to the fore. But in certain circumstances today the unconscious still springs up and seizes control. I would suggest that this is what is happening in those who commit ritual human sacrifice. They are responding to the dictates and directions of their unconscious minds.

But before we look at this idea in detail, let's look at the experience I had, which highlights how we seem to be a 'two-brained' species:

It was back in 1992. I was covering an anti-drugs conference, held at London's Metropole Hotel, for the now-defunct magazine *Outlook*.[1] The magazine's resident illustrator, known as 'Suntan', and I were doing a report on the conference; he'd do the pics and I'd do the scribble. The conference had an illustrious guest speaker – the late Princess Diana. It was the closest I've ever got to royalty. But I can't say I was impressed: she spouted interminably about the dangers of drugs, and looked and sounded like she'd been hitting the anti-depressants too hard. Not to be outdone by royalty, Suntan had the bright idea that he should attend the conference under the influence of magick mushrooms. He took about a hundred in the belief that it would help with his artwork. 'Are you totally *insane*?' I said when we took our seats in the auditorium. But he just grinned maniacally, saying his 'altered state would provide the proper stimulus for us to get to the root of the story'.

It didn't work out that way. Suntan went completely deranged and tried to kill me. But not before screaming his undying love for another one of the speakers – the then Tory MP Virginia Bottomley. I spent most of the day trying to keep him under control. At one point I had to bundle him to a quiet area on the mezzanine to avoid getting thrown out of the conference. It was there he suddenly turned on me. His eyes were glazed and wired, and I was certain he didn't know me any more – there was no sign of recognition on his face. He was literally 'out of his mind'. What's more, his face was contorted into an expression of sheer rage and hate – all of which was directed at me. Then, without warning, he grabbed me and slammed me over the railings, muttering under his breath, 'I'll kill you, you ugly fucker!' With seemingly super-human strength, he was trying to push me over the balcony – which was a twenty-foot drop. I struggled against Suntan's weight, but it was all I could do to stop myself from going over, and falling to my doom (even if I survived the drop I knew I wouldn't have a life left).

I tried to reason with Suntan, saying: 'It's me, Jimmy Lee . . . you're strung out on mushrooms . . . they've addled your brain.'

None of it worked. But then I remembered the cutting-edge hypnosis material I'd learnt from the books of the late Milton Erickson – one of the world's most respected and influential hypnotherapists – who could put people into a trance at the drop of a baseball cap. He'd talked about how you can speak directly to people's unconscious minds – to their 'right brains'. According to Erickson, you just say something like: 'Talking now . . . to your un-conscious mind . . . to the deeper levels of your being.' Erickson said that, by doing this, you are doing the unexpected and breaking the social norm. This puts people into a state of confusion and allows you to bypass their conscious minds.

All this sounded a bit ridiculous to me. I mean, you just don't say to someone at a bus stop: 'Excuse me, I am bypassing your conscious mind and addressing your unconscious mind directly. Talking now to your unconscious – can you hear me? Would you like to have a conversation?' It was crazy. But as I was hanging off the balcony at the drugs conference – and facing my certain doom – I was prepared to try anything.

So I spoke directly to Suntan's unconscious (or as best I could considering my throat was being squeezed): 'Suntan, talking directly to your deep mind, your unconscious . . . to the side of you that thinks in pictures and hears the voice of intuition and inspiration . . . speaking to the deeper levels.' Amazingly, his grip started to ease. I presumed I'd simply managed to confuse him. But then I tried an experiment: 'Still talking to your deep mind . . . I can see you are feeling a little weary . . . would you like to let go of me, and slowly sit yourself down on the chair over there to relax . . . you will feel far better and the strains of the day will fade away . . .' Incredibly, he responded to the indirect suggestion. Within moments he was sitting on an armchair, overlooking the balcony. I sat on the chair next to him, then told him to raise his right hand in the air. He did – and also lowered it, when I told him to. I immediately recognised that I'd put Suntan into a state of deep trance.

Fortunately, no one had witnessed the struggle on the balcony, as most people were in the auditorium listening to the various speakers. But they'd soon be coming out. And someone was bound to notice that Suntan was in a strange state. So I decided to try another experiment. I said to him: 'Still speaking to your unconscious . . . would you remove the effects of the magick mushrooms . . . it would he in your interests to be in a normal state of mind until you get home . . .' I repeated these type of suggestions over and over again for about five minutes, then said: 'I'm going to count down from five to one, when I reach one, you will wake up feeling alert and full of energy ... five, four, three, two, one ... wake up.' It worked. His eyes turned from glazed to bright, and he was wide awake and alert, but a little confused as to what had gone on. There seemed to be no sign that he was still under the influence of magick mushrooms.

The reason I related this story is that it provides a very clear illustration of how our minds are made up of two aspects – the conscious and unconscious. I was able to speak directly to Suntan's deeper, unconscious self, and it responded to my communication (luckily for me). Obviously, saying that our minds have two separate parts is an over-simplification of a very complex subject. But hypnotherapists (as well as occultists and magickians) have found that such a cut and dried model is useful for practical purposes; by using it they can put subjects in and out of trance and help them overcome the problems in their lives. This model of the mind has a basis in science – in 'split brain' research.

Over the last few decades, scientists have come to the conclusion that although the two halves of the cerebral cortex (which constitutes the top 80 per cent of the brain in man), are mirror images of each other, they serve very different functions. The left hemisphere (or left brain) controls the right half of the body in most people and is more adept at verbal reasoning, logical thinking, and deciphering abstract symbols such as numbers and words. The right hemisphere (or right brain), on the other hand, controls the left half of the body and is more skilled at non-verbal, intuitive thought. It is also thought to be the seat of creativity. What's more, it's been found that the left hemisphere processes information in small, analytical steps, while the right hemisphere looks at an entire situation all at once and responds accordingly – sometimes by providing an 'intuitive flash'.

There had been speculation for a hundred years or so that the two hemispheres of the brain held independent functions. But it wasn't until the 1940s that compelling evidence was found to back up this notion. The breakthrough came as a result of the development of a radical surgical procedure to treat severe and incurable epilepsy. The procedure involved severing the corpus callosum – the thick, pencil-shaped band of some 50 million nerve fibres that connects the right and left hemispheres of the brain, and makes possible the transference of information from one hemisphere to the other. Before the development of this procedure, epileptic patients with incurable seizures – who did not respond to medication – died from the extensive brain damage resulting from the seizure crossing from one brain hemisphere to the other. Surgeons found that, by cutting the corpus callosum, they could restrict seizures to a single hemisphere, thus saving both lives and brain cells.

Not only was the surgery successful in treating severe cases of epilepsy but, much to the astonishment (and relief) of surgeons and patients alike, it also appeared to produce no noticeable change in personality, temperament or intellectual abilities. Subtle neurological changes, however, had occurred – changes that only became fully apparent some twenty years later, when split-brain patients were given a more thorough set of evaluative tests.

These specially designed tests were conducted at the California Institute of Technology under the guidance of psychobiologist Roger Sperry (1913–1994), who later won a Nobel Prize in physiology and medicine for his split-brain research. The tests provided startling evidence that severing the corpus callosum had, in fact, isolated the distinct functions of the brain's two hemispheres.

Sperry and one of his students, Michael Gazzaniga, began their tests on a 48-year-old man nicknamed 'WJ', who had undergone a corpus-callosum-severing operation to cure his epilepsy. The scientists found that when a simple written instruction, such as 'move your hand', was flashed to WJ's left visual field (which projects only to the right hemisphere of the brain) WJ would not respond. Although his right brain had received the message, it could not instruct the hand to move.

In another experiment, WJ was given a set of red and white blocks to arrange in a picture design. His right hand, controlled by the left side of the brain, was unable to perform the task; but his left hand could do it quite easily. 'The claim that we based on those findings,' Gazzaniga later recalled, 'was that the left hemisphere is dominant for language processes and the right hemisphere is dominant for visual-constructed tasks.'

Through the study of WJ and other split-brain patients, Sperry and Gazzaniga confirmed the remarkable independence of the two brain halves. The hemispheres were even found to be capable of working simultaneously on different tasks. Using a split-screen monitor, the doctors flashed the word 'clap' to a patient's right brain and the world 'laugh' to her left brain. She immediately laughed and clapped. But when asked, the woman said the only command she had seen on the screen was the one to laugh. Her right brain could not verbalise the command it had seen (to clap) but could carry it out, even while the left brain was obeying its command to laugh.

Findings like this have led to speculation that, within each individual, there may exist two separate selves, or personalities – one residing in the brain's left hemisphere, the other in the right. In fact, Gazzaniga concluded that each hemisphere has its own memories, values and emotions. At times, he says, they may not agree with each other. For example, when Gazzaniga asked the right hemisphere of a young split-brain patient called Paul what he wanted to be when he grew up, the answer came back 'an automobile racer'. But when he asked the same question of Paul's left hemisphere, the answer was 'a draftsman'. Paul was also, periodically, given a multiple choice test in which he was asked to rate some of his interests on a one-to-five scale, from 'like very much', to 'dislike very much'. The test was administered separately to his left and right brains. One day, the answers from the two brains were diametrically opposed to each other. Whatever one hemisphere liked, the other disliked. Paul himself was in a very bad temper that day, verbally abusive and argumentative. A month later, on a day when he was in a calm and relaxed mood, he took the test again. This time his two hemispheres rated all the items on the test the same. Gazzaniga concluded that the human brain is constantly involved in this type of warring, and that dissonance between the two hemispheres may be the explanation for the anxiety and tension many people suffer.[2]

Paul's case also highlighted another intriguing aspect of split-brain research. His left brain would sometimes use its superior language skills to rationalise the puzzling actions performed by the right hemisphere. In one test, a picture of a chicken's claw was shown to Paul's left brain while a picture of a snow scene was shown simultaneously to his right. After that he was asked to look at a series of other pictures and choose a shot that corresponded to the one he'd just seen. With his right hand, Paul chose a picture of a chicken, and with his left hand he selected a picture of a snow shovel. Paul explained his choices by remarking: 'The chicken claw goes with the chicken, and you need a shovel to clean out the chicken's shed.' This, of course, was Paul's left hemisphere talking. His right hemisphere could not speak for itself and explain why it had chosen the snow shovel, so his left hemisphere – which had no knowledge of the snow-scene picture – constructed the most plausible explanation it could.

Judging by the above findings, it's not a great leap to suggest that split-brain research could provide a plausible explanation for why people see or hear non-human entities. Their minds could be interpreting common experiences in a distorted way, because the two hemispheres of their brains are in conflict. The two sides rebel against each other; all hell breaks loose, and the right brain or unconscious taps its wells of primal memory and makes 'gods and demons', or God himself, appear, giving out words of wisdom – or not, as the case may be. The conscious mind would then rationalise these visions using a 'magickal universe' model – i.e. gods and demons exist – and would act on the directions and commands given by these apparently real creatures. Obviously, such a response requires that the person is predisposed towards believing in magickal and religious notions. Although, in a sceptic this response could, of course, turn them into a believer – providing them with a St Paul-on-the-road-to Damascus-type experience.

## Bicameral Man

I recently came across the work of Julian Jaynes (1920–1997) – a professor of psychology at Princeton University, New Jersey – that could further explain man's reverence for otherworldly beings. Jaynes was fascinated by the development of human consciousness. He put together a startling theory about it, which he recorded in his controversial 1976 book, *The Origins of Consciousness in the Breakdown of the Bicameral Mind.* Jaynes argued that each hemisphere of the brain in prehistoric people worked on a separate track and that the thinking of the right brain was heard as 'voices'. He said these auditory hallucinations, which were taken to be the voices of the ancestral dead, and later the gods, had an aura of enormous authority; and if they gave instructions to the left hemisphere – the waking, daily consciousness – it would obey. Jaynes called this condition the 'bicameral mind'. These voices, he said, were not necessarily heard as if 'in the head'; they could have seemed to emanate from a point in the environment such as a tree, standing stone or waterfall (hence the belief that spirits haunted such places). Jaynes also maintained that such hallucinations are still experienced today during various forms of artistic creativity (such as automatic or 'channelled' writing), religious frenzy, hypnotic states or in unmedicated cases of schizophrenia.

But auditory hallucinations can also be experienced at times of stress. In fact, Jaynes claimed to have experienced a vivid auditory hallucination of his own. It occurred during his late twenties, at a time when he was living alone in Boston and struggling to work out the ideas that later became his theory of the bicameral, or divided, mind. 'One afternoon, I lay down in intellectual despair on a couch,' he wrote. 'Suddenly, out of absolute quiet, there came a firm, distinct loud voice from my upper right which said, "Include the knower in the known!" It lugged me to my feet absurdly exclaiming, "Hello?" looking for whoever was in the room. The voice had an exact location. No one was there!'

One of Jaynes' most striking ideas concerned the events described in Homer's *Iliad*. Jaynes believed the ancient Greeks quite literally heard the voices of their gods. Like schizophrenics, they had only a tenuous grasp on the thinking 'I', which most of us take for granted today. So when the voices spoke to them in commanding tones, they obeyed – completely understandable; after all, would you say no to the booming voice of Zeus, especially if it sounded like it was located outside your mind? It's a controversial theory. But it goes a long way towards explaining the way the ancient Greeks and other pagans – and monotheistic peoples, for that matter – thought their gods were involved in initiating and partially controlling their actions.

## The Bicameral Mind and Ritual Slaying

The idea that ancient cultures perceived their gods as a literal reality, their voices appearing to come from 'outside' the human mind, would explain why it was many societies performed human sacrifice – sometimes on a mass scale. The gods demanded that ancient peoples offered up sacrifices to them. And they expected to be obeyed, even when they asked for the blood of people's children. There was no choice in the matter. All the evidence pointed to these deities being not only real, but all-powerful. If you didn't obey them – if you rebelled – they would likely have wreaked terrible revenge, maybe wiped everyone out. The all-powerful nature of the gods is presumably why victims seemed to go to their deaths willingly. They were resigned to their fate – how could they hope to win in a fight against the gods?

Of course, why these 'voices' demanded such a bloody practice as human sacrifice is still something of a mystery. It begs the frightening question: is man a naturally murderous species? Does a desire to kill lurk deep in our unconscious minds? And when we were in the bicameral mind state, did our unconscious processes create blood-thirsty gods to satisfy this need?

And what about today? Could it be that those who perform ritual sacrifice in contemporary times still have the vestiges of the bicameral mind? I think so. In case after case in this book, we've seen how ritual slayers claim to have committed their brutal murders and mutilations at the behest of an invisible entity or deity. Of course, some murderers will always use the excuse of 'the voices made me do it', in a bid to gain leniency from the courts. But this does not account for all cases of ritualistic killing.

Jaynes' bicameral mind theories certainly provide a model by which we can come to understand how an individual can take a knife to a child and cut them up while they're still alive. It also explains how they can drink a victim's blood, and even get charged up when subjecting someone to an excruciatingly painful and unimaginably terrifying death. Some sacrificial slayers have been known to go into almost Dionysian states of ecstasy; presumably they become one with their gods, who really do seem to talk to them and direct their lives – and, even more crucially, promise earthly rewards in exchange for blood and horror.

Clearly, I would have given a lot to speak to Julian Jaynes, whose work I have enormous respect for, to get his take on my views about why people sacrifice. But sadly he's departed this life. So I opted for the next best thing and spoke to Marcel Kuijsten, who is based in California, and runs a highly respected society devoted to Jaynes' work and ideas.[3] What follows is a transcript of the conversation we had:

SHREEVE: Would you agree that you can apply Jaynes' thinking to the subject of human sacrifice?

KUIJSTEN: I think you can definitely apply Jaynes' theory to human sacrifice. But I wonder to what extent modern human sacrifice and human sacrifice in ancient cultures bear similarities? Of course, even in modern societies, there are cases of people carrying out murder based on hallucinatory commands. There have been a couple of recent cases of schizophrenic mothers killing their children at the command of their voices. Authors like Levy-Bruhl discuss the important role of hallucinations in primitive societies. It would be interesting to know to what degree actual auditory, verbal hallucinatory commands are present in those carrying out human sacrifices. In other words, to what degree is modern human sacrifice part of culture and customs, and to what degree is it in response to the direct hallucinatory commands in an individual?

SHREEVE: People who perform ritual killings are clearly believers in the power of the dark side of magic. They are convinced that spirits and other entities exist. Would you say their unconscious minds are providing them with evidence that their gods exist and that their magick works? Could it be that the more ancient, right-brain type of mind is stronger in some people today than in others? And are believers in magic, Christianity, paganism, and Islam more likely to have a dominant right brain/unconscious mind?

KUIJSTEN: This is a difficult question to address and obviously there is a lot of potential for controversy here. Personally I believe that there are differences in levels of consciousness vs. more 'bicameral-like' thinking, both in different cultures and different individuals, the same way there are differences in intelligence. However, I haven't seen anywhere where

Jaynes directly addressed this issue. But I think one can make a case that certain cultures (Arabic, for example), followers of Islam, Christian fundamentalists, etc. tend more toward bicameral-like thinking. This is not to say that they are bicameral in the strict sense, just that they exhibit stronger vestiges of the bicameral mind: more literal-mindedness, strict adherence to religious law over internal decision making, etc. Those that develop their consciousness more look to their own internal dialogue to guide their actions, whereas someone in a more bicameral mode of thinking (using the term very loosely) would look to outside authorities, such as religious doctrine, political or religious leaders, or cultural customs to guide their behaviour.

SHREEVE: What would be the ideal mind state for future humans? We've gone from a dominant unconscious mind to a dominant conscious mind, but what is the ideal balance? And how does it fit with religion and spirituality? Is there any room for spirituality? And – when it comes to human sacrifice and other forms of religious violence – would a balance remove this inclination?

KUIJSTEN: Another tough question! I think that in general we are moving away from bicameral tendencies and toward an expanded role of consciousness in decision making. I think, as this process takes place, we're seeing a diminished role of religion in society as well as magick and superstition etc. Obviously we have a long, long way to go. Whether a place remains for religion and spirituality as consciousness expands is difficult to say. It does seem to be a basic human need for most people, although

I would imagine eventually religion and ritual will no longer dominate people's daily lives as it still does in some societies. I've thought about the consequences a bit in the past and I think there will certainly be both positive and negative consequences. While there could be less international conflict based on religion, I think many people (especially those that have a less fully developed consciousness) may feel lost or hopeless without the prominent role of religion in their lives, as it often serves as a form of social control.

At that point, Marcel handed me a quote from his forthcoming book, *Reflections on the Dawn of Consciousness: Julian Jaynes's Bicameral Mind Theory Revisited*, which relates to this topic:

> Jaynes maintained that we are still deep in the midst of this transition from bicamerality to consciousness; we are continuing the process of expanding the role of our internal dialogue and introspection in the decision-making process that was started some 3,000 years ago. Vestiges of the bicameral mind – our longing for absolute guidance and external control – make us susceptible to charismatic leaders, cults, trends, and persuasive rhetoric that relies on slogans to bypass logic. The tendency within us to avoid conscious thought by seeking out authoritative sources to guide our actions has led to political movements such as Marxism-Leninism and Nazi Germany, cult massacres such as Jonestown and Heaven's Gate, and fundamentalist religions worldwide. By focusing on our inner dialogue, reflecting on past events, and contemplating possible future outcomes, we expand the role of consciousness in

decision-making, enhance our ability to engage in critical thinking, and move further away from the commanding guidance of authoritative voices and non-thinking, stimulus–response behaviour.

## Autonomy

Marcel is right. As we move into the future, it looks more and more likely that the critical-thinking mind will gain yet greater dominance over the bicameral mind state. If this does prove to be the case, we would see ritual killing – and the belief in invisible entities that goes with it – relegated to history (not to mention putting an end to religion-motivated wars). No more blood would be spilt in the name of beings that don't exist. But none of this will come to us on a plate; it is up to us to make it happen. Gaining control of our minds, for example, should be a number one priority, along with accepting that there is nothing outside, and that man is the only god. To save us from ourselves, we need to gain mental autonomy, and no longer be controlled by gods and spirits, or God and the Devil. We need to create an unwavering 'I', or ego-self, that is not beholden to unseen beings. Yet at the same time we need to be able to access, at will, the creative waters of the unconscious mind (the world of magick) – which spawned the gods and spirits – but *not* be controlled by it.

# Postscript: Final Notes from the Ritual Killing Ground

*May 2005*: London. Scotland Yard detectives investigating the killing of Adam, whose torso was found on the banks of the Thames in 2001, announced that they had discovered that, at the time Adam was killed, 300 African boys had gone missing from London schools in one three-month period alone. The questions were: (1) Were the boys sacrificial victims, whose bodies had been more effectively disposed of than Adam's? (2) Had they simply returned to Africa? (3) Had they moved on because their families were on the run from immigration officials?

*June 2005*: London. A confidential Metropolitan Police report was leaked to Radio 4's *Today* programme. The 86-page document, a product of a ten-month investigation, suggested that children were being trafficked from Africa and sacrificed in the UK. It also gave examples of children being murdered because their parents and carers believed them to be possessed by evil spirits. The report was commissioned by the police following the death of

Victoria Climbié (the 8-year-old girl brought to Britain from the Ivory Coast who had the 'Devil' beaten out of her by her great-aunt) and also because of concerns over other so-called 'faith crimes'.

One section of the report stated:

> People who are desperate will seek out witchcraft experts to cast spells for them . . . For a spell to be powerful it required a sacrifice involving a male child unblemished by circumcision . . . Boy children are being trafficked into the UK for this purpose . . . Specific details were not forthcoming as the belief was that they would be 'dead meat' if we tell you any more.

London's *Evening Standard* picked up the story, with a headline screaming: 'Children sacrificed in London churches, say police'. It later turned out that the media were focusing on the more sensational aspects of the report, and it was said that these particular aspects were, in reality, speculation and hearsay. The black community were understandably outraged by the reportage. 'Some of the coverage reminds me of the racist 19th century anthropological literature,' said black academic Dr Robert Beckford, the author of *Jesus is Dread: Black Theology and Black Culture in Britain* (1998). While John Azah, chair of the British Federation of Race Equality Councils (BFOREC), added that the undertone to the reports was 'scratch an African and under the skin he is just a superstitious primitive and open to the most terrible kinds of barbarism.'

*February 2006*: Buland Shahar, Northern India. In a gruesome case of human sacrifice, a woman and two of her sons were arrested for the murder of a 7-year-old boy called Akash. The boy had gone out to play but didn't return. His family and other villagers promptly mounted a search, but this proved fruitless. Later a neighbour, called Subhadra, told the dead boy's father that someone had left Akash's body at her home. No one believed her and a confession was beaten out of her. It turned out that Subhadra had been having nightmares and one of her sons had 'abnormalities', as she put it. So she consulted a tantrik (psychic/sorcerer) for help. He told her that the only effective cure would be to offer a sacrifice.

That was enough for Subhadra and two of her sons, who promptly kidnapped Akash and viciously murdered him. Prem Vati, the victim's mother, said: 'My son was brutally killed. His nose, ear and neck was cut.' Villagers said that Subhadra's brother was known to be a tantrik and that he had been jailed the previous year for involvement in a human sacrifice case. 'They must have offered [Akash] as a human sacrifice under the guidance of her brother,' said a neighbour. Subhadra and her two sons are now in jail. But police continue to search for her husband, brother and two other sons, all of whom are on the run.

BBC reporters visited the jail where Subhadra and her sons were being held. The prison warden told them of over 200 cases of child sacrifice in the region over the last seven years.

April 2006. News comes in that South Africa's Occult Related Crimes Unit has quietly been disbanded. According to a police spokeman, the unit, which once numbered fifty-two officers, was closed because the number of reported crimes was too low to justify its existence. The unit's founder, Colonel Kobus Jonker, however, described the closure as 'unbelievable', stating that in 2000 alone the unit had dealt with 300 ritualistic and muti-related crimes and that the number of 'definitely increasing'.

Anthony Minnaar, a professor of criminal justice studies at the University of South Africa, had similar concerns: 'Because it is often done in secret and the bodies disposed of down a mineshaft or similar, the incidence is much higher than is reported.' Some of the 800 to 900 children reported missing in South Africa every year are likely to have been murdered for muti, he added.

The killing continues . . .

# Notes

## 1 A Voodoo Orgy Of Madness

1. See 'The groundbreaking hunt for Adam's killers', *Toronto Star* (Canada), 2 August 2003.

2. Find out more about Dr Richard Hoskins' work at: www.religion-in-crime.com/.

3. Some scholars say the term 'Juju' is not correct. I use it throughout this book partly because it is a convenient catch-all term for traditional African religion and partly because many shamans and priests still use it themselves.

4. For more details see Chapter 2 of this book, 'Professional Human Sacrificers'.

5. My book on Voodoo was written under the pen name 'Doktor Snake'. See: *Doktor Snake's Voodoo Spellbook: Spells, Curses and Folk Magick For All Your Needs* (St Martin's Press, 2000). Or check out two free chapters posted at www.jimmyleeshreeve.com.

6. The term 'root doctor' is most commonly used in the southern States of America to describe a herbalist and sorcerer working in the Hoodoo tradition, which is the folk magick relative of Voodoo. I use the term here because Earl Marlowe often described himself as a root doctor,

which he saw as a convenient way of distancing himself from religion. He saw himself more as a magickian than one of the faithful. Labady struck me as the same.

7. See 'Voodoo Britain', *The Daily Mail* (*Femail* section), 7 November 2002; byline: Sarah Obanye.

8. Muti is the Zulu word for medicine. A muti murder allegedly occurs when an individual dies as a result of their body parts being harvested for use in traditional medicine. The body parts are then mixed with other ingredients such as herbs or plant roots to make the muti.

9. 'Obeah' is a religion from Guyana in Africa. Its practices range from preparing magickal potions to advising solutions for family disputes. Obeah activities are illegal, and can result in prosecution, but there is widespread belief in the effectiveness of Obeah in nearly all segments of Guyanese society.

10. *Blue Roots: African-American Folk Magick of the Gullah People*, by Roger Pinckney (Lewellyn 1998).

11. Robert Anton Wilson is the co-author, with Robert Shea, of the underground classic *The Illuminatus! Trilogy* (1975), which won the 1986 Prometheus Hall of Fame Award. His other writings include *Schrödinger's Cat Trilogy*, called 'the most scientific of all science fiction novels' by *New Scientist*, and several non-fiction works of futurist psychology and 'guerrilla ontology' (as Wilson calls it), such as *Prometheus Rising* and *The New Inquisition*. See: www.rawilson.com.

12. *A Shadow in the City: Confessions of an Undercover Drug Warrior*, by Charles Bowden, Harcourt 2005.

13. William S. Burroughs, 1914–1997, novelist and cult figure whose ground-breaking novel *Naked Lunch*, first published in Paris in 1959, was both praised as a work of genius and denounced as incomprehensible ravings and pornography. His life was as extreme as the experimental fiction he pioneered, involving alcohol, heroin, homosex-

uality, a celebrated obscenity trial in Boston and, in 1951, his accidental killing of his wife while shooting a glass off the top of her head. In his last years, he became a recurring popular culture icon, with cameos in movies and even a Nike advert.

14. Allen Ginsberg, 1926–1997, was an American Beat generation poet, best known for *Howl* (1956), a long poem about consumer society's negative human values.

15. Adam Kuper is professor of anthropology at Brunel University, a Fellow of the British Academy, and a member of the Academia Europaea. His books include: *Anthropology and Anthropologists: The Modern British School* (Routledge, 1996) and *Culture: The Anthropologists' Account* (Harvard University Press 1999). Read his criticism of the Adam case in full at: http://mail.sarai.net/pipermail/reader-list/2005-April/005440.html. Find out more about Adam Kuper at: www.brunel.ac.uk/about/acad/sssl/ssslstaff/anth_staff/adamkuper.

16. See 'Possession and the law', *Financial Times*, 30 July 2004. Byline: Sarah Duguid.

17. The gothic music Internet forum, *DarkLight: Nocturnal Entertainment*, can be found at: http://darklight.co.za.

18. The South African Police Service's website can be found at: www.saps.gov.za.

19. *The Satanic Bible* by Anton LaVey was first published in 1969 and does not present some 'horned goat' Hollywood conception of Satan. Instead, LaVey's Satan is more a symbol than a literal reality. And LaVey's philosophy is about accepting and celebrating our humanity for what it is, without the need to keep striving for something greater and better.

20. A more detailed discussion of Satanism can be found in Chapter 4 of this book, Satan Loves You.

21. Kerr Cuhulain has been a police officer (under his real name Charles Ennis) for the past 20 years, and a Wiccan for 30. In fact, he was the first Wiccan police officer to go public about his beliefs 28 years ago. Cuhulain has served on the SWAT team, Gang Crime Unit, and hostage negotiation team. He travels throughout North America as a popular speaker at writers' conferences and pagan festivals, and he has been the subject of many books, articles and media interviews. He is the author of *The Law Enforcement Guide to Wicca*. Horned Owl, 1997. An interview with Cuhulain can be found at: www.twpt.com/cuhulain.htm.

22. The Subculture Alternatives Freedom Foundation (SAFF) maintains a large archive of cases detailing how alternative and minority religions have been persecuted and defamed by the activities of Christian fundamentalist groups. See: www.saff.ukhq.co.uk.

23. Victoria Climbié (1991–2000) was born in Abobo near Abidjan, and aged 7 was sent by her parents to Europe with her great-aunt Marie Thérèse Kouao, to get a good education. In London, Kouao met bus driver Carl Manning, and she and Victoria moved into his flat in Tottenham in July 1999. Here, Victoria was abused by both Kouao and Manning. She was admitted to casualty on 24 February 2000, unconscious and suffering from hypothermia; she died the next day. The Home Office pathologist noted 128 separate injuries and scars on her body. Marie Thérèse Kouao and Carl Manning were charged with child cruelty and murder. During police interviews, both claimed that Victoria was possessed. To 'drive the Devil out of her' they beat her and burnt her with cigarettes and scalding water. They also fed her scraps of food like a dog and forced her to sleep naked in a bath with only a bin liner to cover her. Kouao and Manning's trial ran from November 2000 to 12 January 2001. Both

were found guilty, and sentenced to life imprisonment.

24. Tony Rhodes of SAFF gave me two links to a large body of evidence detailing incidents of Christian fundamentalists committing child murder and cruelty. See: www.saff.ukhq.co.uk/everyman1.htm and www.saff.ukhq.co.uk/sickvics.htm.

25. Find out more about my friend Dr Crazywolf at www.wolfshaman.com.

26. Midewiwin is pronounced 'Mi-day-win' and means 'grand medicine society'.

27. See: *9.11 Revealed: Challenging the Facts Behind the War on Terror* (Robinson, 2005) by Ian Henshall and Rowland Morgan.

## 2 Hearts of Darkness

1. Stephen Ellis is a researcher at the Afrika Studie Centrum in the Netherlands. A historian by training, he is a former editor of the newsletter *Africa Confidential* and was director of the Africa Program at the International Crisis Group between 2003 and 2004. He is co-editor of the journal *African Affairs*. Ellis is the author of *The Mask of Anarchy: The Destruction of Liberia and the Religious Dimension of an African Civil War* (New York University Press, 1999).

2. Fred van der Kraaij was born in 1946 in Den Bosch, the Netherlands. He obtained a Ph.D. in economics from the University of Tilburg. His dissertation on the role of foreign investments in the development of Liberia 1900–1977 was published as *The Open Door Policy of Liberia – An Economic History of Modern Liberia* (Bremen, 1983). He has written extensively on West Africa where he lived for over sixteen years. His website offers a huge repository of in-depth and useful information on Liberia. See: www.liberiapastandpresent.org.

3. *National Geographic*, 'Who Rules the Forest?' by Paul Salopek. September 2005.

4. See 'Traditional Healing in a Modern Epidemic' by Laura Engle at www.thebody.com/bp/oct98/uganda.html.

5. See: Prometra, www.prometra.org.

6. See: The African Union, www.africa-union.org.

7. Credo Mutwa (1921–) is author of the insightful *Zulu Shaman: Dreams, Prophecies, and Mysteries* (Destiny Books, 2003).

## 3 Professional Human Sacrificers

1. 'Máximo Coa' is a pseudonym, the only one used in Patrick Tierney's 1989 book, *The Highest Altar: The Story of Human Sacrifice*, which is now out of print.

2. For more on the initiatory sickness of shamans, see Mircea Eliade's *Shamanism: Archaic Techniques of Ecstasy* (New Edition: Princeton University Press, 2004).

3. Teacher Ray Vogensen's report on *The Book of Saint Cyprian* can be found at the following website: www.portcult.com/SAINT_CYPRIAN.01.htm.

4. The editors of the various versions of *The Book of Saint Cyprian* include Joaquim Sabugosa, N.A. Molina and Pierre Dumont. All claim their edition provides the 'true' wisdom of Saint Cyprian.

5. The day of Saint Cyprian's martyrdom, 26 September, became his feast day.

6. *El Mágico Prodigioso* (The Wonder-Working Magickian) was written by acclaimed Spanish dramatist Pedro Calderón de la Barca in 1637.

7. See *Doktor Snake's Voodoo Spellbook* (St Martin's Press, 2000). Or visit www.jimmyleeshreeve.com to read two free chapters.

8. Evan Hadingham's *Lines to the Mountain Gods of Peru* (1987) was published by Random House.

9. This case is chronicled in *Conjuring Up Philip* (Pocket Books, 1976) by Iris Owen and Margaret Sparrow, both members of the Toronto Society for Psychical Research.

10. Hilary Evans is author of a whole string of books on the paranormal and unexplained, including *Seeing Ghosts: Experiences of the Paranormal* ( John Murray, 2002) and *Visions, Apparitions, Alien Visitors* (Aquarian, 1984).

11. Isaiah Oke's *Blood Secrets: The True Story of Demon Worship and Ceremonial Murder* (as told to Joe Wright) was published in 1989 by Prometheus Books. It's now out of print.

12. A pseudonym. My actor friend asked me not to cite his real name just in case the person described in his anecdote reads this book and is not happy.

13. See Chapter 2, Hearts Of Darkness.


*4 Satan Loves You . . .*

1. Books by innovative Satanist Anton LaVey include *The Satanic Bible* (1969); *The Complete Witch, or, What to do When Virtue Fails* (1971); *The Satanic Rituals* (1972); *The Devil's Notebook* (1992); and *Satan Speaks!* (1998), which has a foreword by multi-talented rock star Marilyn Manson.

2. Austin Osman Spare's books include *The Book of Pleasure: (Self-love) the Psychology of Ecstasy* (I-H-O Books, 2005); *Anathema of Zos: The Sermon to the Hypocrites, an Automatic Writing* (I-H-O Books, 2001); and *The Book of Automatic Drawing* (I-H-O Books, 2001). All highly recommended.

3. Dave Lee's books include *Chaotopia!: Sorcery and Ecstasy in the Fifth Aeon* (Mandrake of Oxford, 2006) and *Magickal Incenses and the Wealth Magick Workbook* (date unknown). He's been a central figure in a magickal

organisation known as the Illuminates of Thanateros for many years. For more details about Dave, see: www.illuminates.org/dave_lee/.

4. Peter Carroll's books include *Liber Null and Psychonaut* (Red Wheel/Weiser, 1987); *Liber Kaos: The Psychonomicon* (Red Wheel/Weiser, 1992); and *Psybermagick: Advanced Ideas in Chaos Magick* (New Falcon, 1997).

5. Future Radio goes out in Norfolk on 105.1 FM. See: www.futurefmradio.co.uk.

6. See *The Book of the Law* (Red Wheel/Weiser, 2004), which Aleister Crowley claimed was dictated to him, through his wife, by a praeter human intelligence in 1904.

## 5 Death Dealers

1. See Migene González-Wippler's *Santeria: The Religion* (Llewellyn Publications 1994).

2. Jack Sargeant's essay 'Blood and Sand' can be found in *Death Cults* (Virgin, 2002).

3. Lyn Clarkson, from the Coventry Writers' Group, researched the necromancer tale in the Coventry Archives collection for a short story she was writing. This can be found at: www.cwn.org.uk/arts/coventry-writers-group/the-necromancers.htm.

4. By far the best edition of *The Book of One Thousand and One Nights* was translated by Sir Richard Burton. You can read it at the following website: www.wollamshram.ca/1001/index.htm.

## 6 Tomb Raiders

1. For a full account of the Lucchese family vs. the US Government case read Robert Rudolph's *The Boys from New Jersey* (Rutgers University Press, 1995).

2. The website associated with *Doktor Snake's Voodoo*

*Spellbook* (St Martin's Press, 2000) can be found at: www.doktorsnake.com.

3. The California Astrology Association provides psychic and magickal services, as well as selling a range of spell-kits and Voodoo dolls. See: www.calastrology.com.

4. See Serge Bramly's *Macumba* (City Lights, 1994).

5. Check out Botanica Palo Mayombe, which legitimately supplies human bones and skulls, at: www.botanicapalo mayombe.com. Buy a skull for your mantelpiece . . .

6. Details about ritual crime expert Dawn Perlmutter's work can be found at: www.ritualviolence.com.

7. Dawn Perlmutter is referring to Robert Langdon, the professor in *The Da Vinci Code* by Dan Brown (Corgi Books, 2004).

8. Charismatic cult leader Aldolfo De Jesus Constanzo enslaved a circle of followers in Matamoros, on the US-Mexican border, during the 1980s with his malevolent magnetism and blend of magick and mass murder. Seemingly ordinary men and women killed for him again and again. By the time police found the violated corpse of US student Mark Kilroy in 1989, Constanzo's occult and Palo Mayombe obsession had claimed at least 24 victims. For the full story, see the 'Death Dealers' section of this book.


*7 Last Rites: Split Brains And Sacrifice*

1. *Outlook* magazine ran from 1987 to the mid-1990s. Its publisher and editor-in-chief was Ian Henshall, who sprang to global notice in 2005 with his book *9/11 Revealed: Challenging the Facts behind the War on Terror* (co-authored with Rowland Morgan).

2. When it comes to this kind of split-brain research, it should be kept in mind that the experiments were done on people whose brains were malfunctioning in the first

place. The results, arguably, could have proved different if they had been performed on people whose brains were operating normally – but, obviously, no healthy person was going to volunteer to have their corpus callosum severed in the interests of science.

3. The Julian Jaynes Society can be found at www.julian jaynes.org. It's run by Marcel Kuijsten. His book, *Reflections on the Dawn of Consciousness: Julian Jaynes's Bicameral Mind Theory Revisited*, is expected to be out soon. It's a collection of essays by scholars from various fields such as psychology, philosophy anthropology and linguistics.

# Acknowledgements

## People

Thanks must go to crime author Carol Anne Davis (www.carolannedavis.co.uk), and to ritual violence expert Dawn Perlmutter (www.ritualviolence.com), for agreeing to be interviewed as part of this book. Both added great insight and depth – well done! A big cheers is due to my friend Ian Henshall, author of *9/11 Revealed* (www.911revealed.co.uk), who added much with his unique analysis of the Adam case. I'd also like to thank Commander Andy Baker, Detective Inspector Will O'Reilly and Kate Campbell of Scotland Yard (www.met.police.uk) for granting me an interview and discussing the Adam case with me (but it should be noted that Scotland Yard in no way endorses this book).

I'm greatly indebted to Tony Rhodes, Christopher Bray and John Freedom of SAFF – the Subculture Alternatives Freedom Foundation (www.saff.ukhq.co.uk). All three went out of their way to help me and brought the much-needed sceptical side to the Adam case, which, up until now, has not been discussed in the media. When it comes to so-called 'occult crime' all media organisations should have SAFF on their list of contacts.

Thanks are also due to Adam Kuper, professor of anthropology at Brunel University, for introducing me to the aspects that lay unreported in the Adam case.

Thanks are equally due to Dr Fred P.M. Van Der Kraaij (www.liberiapastandpresent.org), a leading expert on Liberia, whose thoughts on ritual killing in West Africa helped me immensely. A big handshake of appreciation must go to Tony Naylor and David Christian of Oxfordshire publisher and book distributor Mandrake Press (www.mandrake-press.com). They kindly dropped everything to talk to me when I called in search of stories and anecdotes.

Thanks to John Brauns at www.ex-premie.org for the informative chats about gurus and cults.

Cheers also to prize-winning American author Charles Bowden (*A Shadow in the City: Confessions of an Undercover Drug Warrior*), for his thoughts on human sacrifice and how it has been used by drug traffickers in Mexico. I'm seriously indebted to Marcel Kuijsten of the Julian Jaynes Society (www.julianjaynes.org) for the interview he gave and for his thoughts on the nature and development of human consciousness.

Thanks also go to my friend Canadian shaman Dr Crazywolf (www.wolfshaman.com) for adding an unexpected element to the Adam case. Plus I must thank my old pal, the movie actor Robert Goodman, for his truly wonderful thoughts and insights into the nature of magick (an English gentleman indeed). Appreciation is also due to Martin Bradsworth, who reminded me that when the moon is full it is my duty to howl.

I must not forget my uncle, Bernard Billings, who unearthed a necromancer in our family tree. And a big hi-5 to my friend Kenny Heimbuch (http://livesafely.org), a renaissance man from Canada who was always there when I needed assistance with software and website coding.

Plus I must thank Tim Andrews, my editor at Random House, whose comments and advice made all the difference to this book, and who understood that while the king of gonzo is dead there are still those that keep the faith. Equal thanks must also go to my agent Andrew Lownie (www.andrewlownie.co.uk), who I see as the John Buchan of our times. In other words, a fine fellow.

Lastly, a huge thanks to my wife Nicky for her help in getting this book into readable shape – it would have been demented and deranged without you! And a big thanks to my daughters, Audra and Imogen, for helping me ride the wild horses through this green and pleasant land.

## Software

Apart from the Windows operating system, this book is a Microsoft-free title. The software applications used in its creation were either free or low-priced. All were high quality and beat Bill Gates' offerings hands down. They included:

* FireFox web browser and Thunderbird e-mail application, both open source (i.e. freeware). See www.mozilla.com.
* PolyEdit – the 'Swiss Army Knife' of word processors. Also great for web page coding. Made in the

Russian Federation. See: www.polyedit.com.

* EasyBlogs – desktop blog and content management system. Powers my website. See: www.easy blogs.com.
* Insight – text editor and personal information manager. Very useful for storing research files and snippets. See: www.dataomega.com.
* UltraPlayer – best desktop MP3 music player around. Freeware. See: www.ultraplayer.com.

## Rock 'n' Roll

Music played during the writing of this book included the Americana crew Buddy Miller, the Bottle Rockets and Lynyrd Skynyrd. The late and sadly missed blues crew John Cambpell, R. L. Burnside and Howlin' Wolf. And the out-and-out rock crew Monster Magnet and Marilyn Manson. Burn the highway and kick out the jams!

## Fuel

Special thanks are also due to Mountgay rum and Plymouth gin, the necessary requirements to even contemplate writing a book.

## Cats

Lastly, my biggest debt is to BW and Fluff, my cats who actually wrote this book for me while I absconded to the Bahamas for six months on the advance money . . . (Christ only knows how I'm going to deal with interviews – I haven't got a clue what this book is about).

# Further Reading

Bird, Stephanie Rose. *Sticks, Stones, Roots and Bones.* Llewellyn Publications, 2004.

Bowden, Charles. *A Shadow in the City: Confessions of an Undercover Drug Warrior.* Harcourt Inc. 2005.

Carroll, Peter. *Liber Null and Psychonaut.* Red Wheel/Weiser, 1987; *Liber Kaos: The Psychonomicon.* Red Wheel/Weiser, 1992; *Psybermagick: Advanced Ideas in Chaos Magick.* New Falcon, 1997.

Chesnutt, Charles W. (retold by Ray Anthony Shephard). *Conjure Tales.* E.P.Dutton and Co, 1973.

Claremont, Lewis de. *Legends of Incense, Herb and Oil Magic.* Dorene Publishing, 1966.

Crowley, Aleister. *The Book of the Law.* Red Wheel/Weiser, 2004.

Davies, Nigel. *Human Sacrifice in History and Today.* Dorset Press, 1988.

Davis, Carol Anne. *Couples Who Kill.* Allison & Busby, 2005.

Dunning, John. *Occult Murders.* Senate Press, 1997.

Finn, Julio. *The Musical Heritage of Black Men and Women in the Americas.* Interlink Books, 1992.

González-Wippler, Migene. *Santeria: The Religion.* Llewellyn Publications, 1994.

Green, Miranda Aldous. *Dying for the Gods.* Tempus Publishing, 2002.

Guenter, Abe. *Jungle Pilot in Liberia.* Regular Baptist, 1992.

Haddon, Alfred C. *Magick and Fetishism.* Constable and Company, 1921.

Haskins, Jim. *Voodoo and Hoodoo: Their Tradition and Craft as Revealed by Actual Practitioners.* Scarborough House, 1990.

Hoskins, Dr Richard. *Sacrifice: Who Killed Adam?* Little Brown, yet to be released.

Humes, Edward. *Buried Secrets: A True Story of Serial Murder, Black Magic, and Drug-Running on the U.S. Border.* Dutton, 1991.

Hurston, Zora Neale. *Mules and Men.* Harper Perennial, 1990.

Hyatt, Harry M. *Hoodoo – Conjuration – Witchcraft – Rootwork.* Self-published, 1978.

Junge, Werner. *African Jungle Doctor: Ten Years in Liberia.* Harrap, 1952.

Lampe, H.U. *Famous Voodoo Rituals and Spells.* Marlar Publishing Co., 1982.

Lee, Dave. *Chaotopia!: Sorcery and Ecstasy in the Fifth Aeon.* Mandrake of Oxford, 2006.

London, Sondra. *True Vampires: Blood-Sucking Killers Past and Present*. Feral House, 2004.

Lewis, Brenda Ralph. *Ritual Sacrifice: A Concise History*. Sutton Publishing, 2001.

Murray, Colin and Sanders, Peter. *Medicine Murder in Colonial Lesotho: The Anatomy of Moral Crisis*. Edinburgh University Press, 2005.

Mutwa, Vujamazulu Credo (edited by Stephen Larsen). *Zulu Shaman: Dreams, Prophecies and Mysteries*. Destiny Books, 2003.

O'Brien, David M. *Animal Sacrifice and Religious Freedom: Church of the Lukumi Babalu Aye v. City of Hialeah*. University Press of Kansas, 2004.

Oke, Isaiah (as told to Joe Wright). *Blood Secrets: The True Story of Demon Worship and Ceremonial Murder*. Berkley Books, 1991.

Pelton, Robert W. *Voodoo Charms and Talismans*. Original Publications, 1997.

Pelton, Robert W. *The Complete Book of Voodoo*. Original Publications, 2002.

Sickafus, James E. *Papa Jim's Spellbook*. Papa Jim, 1997.

Snake, Doktor. *Doktor Snake's Voodoo Spellbook: Spells, Curses and Folk Magick for all your Needs*. St Martin's Press, 2000.

Spare, Austin Osman. *The Book of Pleasure: (Self-love) the Psychology of Ecstasy*. I-H-O Books, 2005; *Anathema of Zos: The Sermon to the Hypocrites, an Automatic Writing*. I-H-O Books, 2001; *The Book of Automatic Drawing*. I-H-O Books, 2001.

Tallant, Robert. *Voodoo in New Orleans.* Pelican Publishing Company, 1990.

Tallant, Robert. *The Voodoo Queen.* Pelican Publishing Company, 2000.

Tierney, Patrick. *The Highest Altar: The Story of Human Sacrifice.* Bloomsbury, 1989.

Vernon-Jackson, Hugh. *African Folk Tales.* Dover Publications, Inc., 1999.

# About Veves

In Voodoo practice, veves are intricate symbols of the Loas (gods), and are used in rituals. Each Loa has his or her own complex veve, which is traced on the ground with powdered eggshell or cornmeal prior to a ritual. A veve is believed to be more powerful if it is drawn with the correct details – the better the detail, the better its power to invoke the Loa.

## About Loas

Loas are similar to saints or angels in Western religions. They are thought to be messengers between the Creator and humanity. Unlike saints or angels, however, they are not simply prayed to, they are also served. They are not easily categorised into archetypal forms, being distinct beings with their own personal likes and dislikes, sacred rhythms, songs, dances, ritual symbols, and special modes of service.

Below are just a few examples of veves and a little about the Loas they symbolise:

**Maman Brigitte** – the Loa of cemeteries, money, and death. She is usually depicted as a white woman and may be related to the Celtic goddess Brigit; having arrived in Haiti in the hearts of deported Scottish and Irish indentured servants. The first woman's grave in a cemetery in Haiti is dedicated to her.

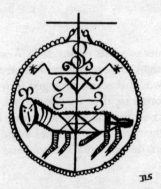

**Simbi** – the water snake Loa. One of the three cosmic serpents of Voodoo. Also seen as the sun's messenger, with the power to confer the ability needed to accomplish difficult tasks.

**Ogoun** – god of war, fire, politics, iron, and thunderbolts. He is the guardian of the forge, and the patron of civilisation and technology. He is responsible for tools of progress such as farming implements and surgeon's knives. He is also often associated with locomotives, and because of this offerings are often made to him at railroad tracks. Ogoun is thought to be especially fond of rum and tobacco.

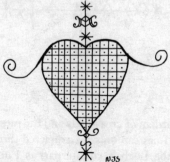

**Erzulie** – goddess of love and **Ogoun's** spouse, the embodiment of femininity and love. Similar to the goddess Venus.

**Baron Samedi** – Loa of the dead. Also seen as the protector of children, god of sexuality, eroticism and libido. Often pictured as a grinning skeleton in a top hat he is one of the most recognised of the loas outside of Voodoo.

**Legba** – guardian of crossroads and the messenger of the gods. Other Loas can only be contacted through him. In Palo Mayombe Legba's counterpart is Lucero, a devil-like trickster.

**Damballah** and **Ayida** (the Rainbow Snake) his companion – **Damballah** is the most important god of Voodoo religion in the Caribbean. He is a snake-god and lives in the trees near springs. He is also a fertility god and the father of all the Loas.

**Marassa** – the divine twins. They are symbols of the elemental forces of the universe,.and come from ancient African beliefs. The veve, symbol of the Marassa, has three figures, and symbolises the mystery of duality – unity, harmony, balance.

Source
http://altreligion.about.com/library/weekly/blvodoun.h
tm